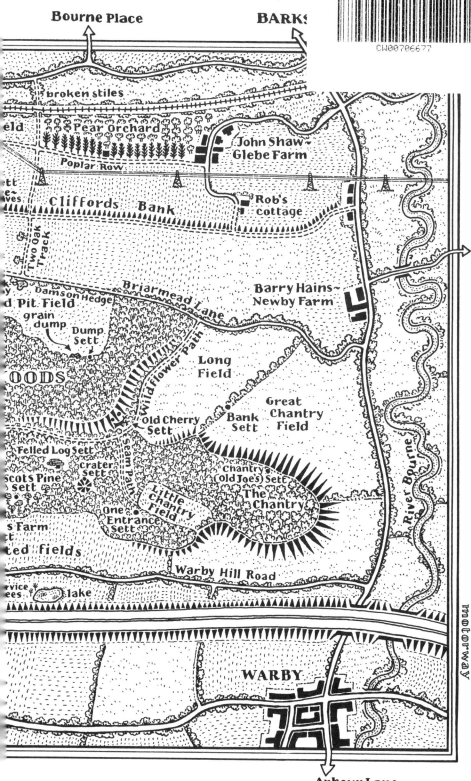

Bourne Place

BARKS

SLEY

CROSSHAMPTON

broken stiles

Pear Orchard

John Shaw~
Glebe Farm

Poplar Row

Cliffords Bank

Rob's
cottage

Two Oak Track

Damson Hedge

Pit Field

grain
dump

Dump
Sett

Briarmead Lane

Barry Hains~
Newby Farm

Long
Field

Great
Chantry
Field

OODS

Wildflower Path

Old Cherry
Sett

Bank
Sett

Felled Log Sett

Steam Path

Crater
Sett

Chantry
(Old Joe's) Sett

Scots Pine
sett

Little
Chantry
Field

The
Chantry

One
Entrance
Sett

Farm

River Bourne

ed fields

Warby Hill Road

vice
ees

lake

motorway

WARBY

Arbour Lane

OUT OF THE DARKNESS

The Revelations of a Badger Watcher

Chris Ferris

Illustrated by Andy Martin

UNWIN HYMAN
London   Sydney

First published in Great Britain by Unwin Hyman,
an imprint of Unwin Hyman Limited, 1988.

UNWIN HYMAN LIMITED
Broadwick House, 15/17 Broadwick Street,
London W1V 1FP

Allen & Unwin Australia Pty Ltd
8 Napier Street, North Sydney, NSW 2060, Australia

Allen & Unwin New Zealand Pty Ltd
with the Port Nicholson Press
60 Cambridge Terrace, Wellington, New Zealand

British Library Cataloguing in Publication Data

Ferris, Chris
  Out of the darkness
1. Badgers – Biography
I. Title
599.74′447   QL795.B2

ISBN 0–04–440126–4

Set in 10 on 12½ point Joanna by
Nene Phototypesetters Ltd, Northampton
and printed in Great Britain by
Mackays of Chatham Ltd, Kent

To my son and daughter,
my greatest friends.

Anyone wishing to start a Badger Group in their area,
or requiring advice on badgers, can write to:

The Chairman, John Taylor
National Federation of Badger Groups (NFBG)
16 Ashdown Gardens
Sanderstead
South Croydon
Surrey CR2 9DR

Family Tree

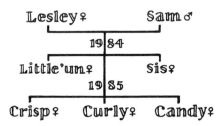

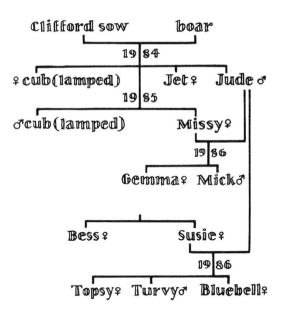

Chapter 1

One night in March 1985 I stood watching the young badger sow Lesley with her three tiny cubs at the Old Cherry Sett. Already the cubs were altering and losing their purblind, helpless look. At eight weeks they were still too young to play – but they explored their small world within the trench dug eighteen months previously by the terriermen, who had taken three badgers away. Strangely, the sow had used that part of the sett in which to bear her young and their 'nursery' entrance opened straight out into the shallow trench which was almost a 'play-pen' for the young animals. The crumbly clods of earth and dead leaves were softly nosed by the tiny creatures. A beetle was accidentally trodden on by one cub who, feeling it move beneath its paw, retreated timorously to the safety of the nursery entrance.

The Old Cherry Sett in Ashcroft Woods where they lived was a hillridge which was honeycombed for perhaps 200 metres with the entrances dug by generations of these badgers. Many such entrances were by now disused and hidden by brambles and bluebell greenery which carpeted the ground beneath the trees. Other holes were taken over by rabbits. But with that spell of mild, damp weather, the badger's instinct to dig, coupled with the mother's need to have alternate accommodation for her young in case of danger, had caused Lesley to re-open disused entrances both there and at another, unoccupied sett – the Bank Sett. One of the fascinations of the surrounding farmland for me is the steep banks between some of its fields. The sheerest contains

Bank Sett which is situated between Great Chantry Field and Long Field. Unfortunately, the huge heaps of sandy earth or 'spoil heaps' caused by the mother's digging, were terribly obvious to human eyes.

My study area comprises this wood, the smaller Prossers Wood, three farms and a rough area of derelict orchard and scree slope known as High Ridge. Within these 800 acres there were fourteen badgers including Lesley's three cubs. She and her mate Sam, the dominant boar, produced two cubs the previous year which as yearlings had gone independent. I named them Little'un and Sis. Little'un, the former runt who used to hide her head against my anorak whenever she was frightened was now one-and-a-half times as big as Sis and felt like a sturdy battering-ram when she decided to use me in a game of charge. She was living at the Chantry Sett and her sister at the tiny One Entrance Sett at the wood edge. There were two other yearlings, Bess and Susie, living on the bank of Colts Farm where the farmer, Pete Williams, his wife and three children kept a close eye on them.

On the other side of Ashcroft Woods are the other farms of my area, Newby and Glebe, and between them runs a boundary bank called Cliffords Bank, part of which contains an ancient badger sett. The old Clifford sow denned here with her two very young cubs and Jet, her beautiful and unusual yearling. The pelage of a badger's back and flanks is made up of a short, thick, felt-like underfur and long guard hairs which give the animal its characteristic greyish look, though the hairs themselves aren't all grey. They start light at the base with a band of darker colour further along, then are light again to the tip. Jet's guard hairs were unusually dark and her blackness stood out startlingly at night; an all-black animal is only truly hidden in the deep, dark shadows of a moonlight night. Jet had a white mask with black stripes, like her yearling brother, Jude, and the other badgers here. Jude, as a young male and therefore unwelcome near his mother's newborn cubs, had gone to live alone in the wood at the Crater Sett. He joined the other yearlings, Little'un, Sis and Jet, during his nightly foraging for food and I ruefully dubbed this mischievous band, the Four Musketeers.

The whole area contained only two pairs of foxes, though both vixens had cubs. Relatively few of these foxes reach maturity and fewer still survive more than three years. They are either illegally dugout, snared, shot or lamped by poachers, as a pelt in prime condition fetches a good price. Josh my oldest dog fox was the great exception.

Thus my five-year study of *Vulpes vulpes* here was not carried out in a typical situation. Foxes are said to be promiscuous and perhaps in some areas, they are, but certainly not here though their relationships tend to be understandably curious. Josh and his vixen were father and mother of Tagless and his vixen who were born of the same litter. Tagless was later shot, and his vixen mated in due time with Sandy, one of their grown cubs. I doubt if this would occur in normal circumstances.

Being out all night and every night has become a way of life. I can sleep for only an hour or two at a time because of back pain and over the years have found I need little rest. I like to have a 'head-count' of badgers at least three times a week, but my fresh scent is always somewhere in this area as I travel several miles nightly. During my fox study, I covered a minimum of 14 miles (often double this distance) within these 800 acres each night, as a fox crosses and re-crosses its territory.

Over the years, different badgers have regularly musked me, that is, set their scent on me – usually on my boots. These animals live in a world of scent and the musk from the gland beneath their short tails tells each badger who the other is, as well as proclaiming possession of territory. Their eyesight is poor, but their senses of hearing and smell are acute and they follow scent trails through woods and across farmland, musking at intervals along the route. All badgers of one social group or family regularly musk each other, even small cubs musk one another as well as objects in their near vicinity. Like the habit of bringing in bedding backwards, this is an inherent trait not taught by the parent and both practices are apparent from as early as eight weeks, when young cubs normally first appear above ground. To be musked by one badger of a social group is to be accepted by all its members. In this way, I have been with them whilst they foraged, groomed, played, mated and occasionally, fought.

I would dearly love to see them underground, though, as the noises I have sometimes heard during the day suggest, sleeping is only one of their many sett activities! Undoubtedly they must often groom, both individually and mutually, below ground; and most certainly they sometimes mate within the sett where tunnels join and open out into a large area, but mostly cubs and adults will play, racing though the chambers, back and forth along the labyrinth below one's feet. All badgers play and I often get caught up in their games.

Badgers are creatures of habit and season which makes them an easy prey for knowledgeable poachers. In late summer they will forage under hedgerows and orchard trees in their quest for dropped fruit. In June and September they glean hay from the meadows for bedding. Where the plough has been during the day, they will be found the following night taking beetles, larvae and roots from the upturned earth. One of the farmers here regularly sees lurchers and terriers apparently being exercised on his land by day and knows full well that the owners are checking out these fields and setts, but with public footpaths nearby, there is nothing he can do about it.

That March we all took stock of the situation. The three local farmers who helped me so much were wondering what the year had in store. A few years ago, we merely had terriermen to contend with; they came with their dogs and equipment for foxes and badgers, or with ferrets and terriers to go rabbiting.

Sporting equipment for the enterprising terrierman had become highly sophisticated, ranging from the folding spade or shovel, to the terrier-finder for the dog trapped underground – a transmitting collar with a minimum working range of 15 feet which sends signals to the receiver held by the terrierman. Since its introduction, this has been widely used for locating exactly where the terrier is trapped, so saving hours of digging, and it has rescued many dogs. It has also been widely mis-used for locating exactly where a barking terrier is confronting a badger.

As local vigilance makes it harder to dig out badgers in peace, these determined terriermen are turning up as lampers on farm and common land where the badgers forage at night.

Lamping was originally the sport of hunting game, using a light with specially bred dogs called lurchers running along its beam to kill and, in the case of rabbit, retrieve to hand. Dogs may be run from coursing leads or off slip, that is, let off a quick-release lead incorporating the collar which opens at the lurcherman's touch.

Any lamper who has 'been on the beam' for long will almost certainly have encountered a badger, though that is not to say that he wished to do so. Asking lamper friends what they would do if their dog confronted a badger had had an interesting response. To switch off the beam and recall the lurcher (fervently praying that it comes); is the commonest. But once the blood is up even the most obedient dog can be reluctant to leave its quarry and many lurchers can hunt without a light by following the scent, so that switching off the beam would make no difference.

Lurchers or longdogs are bred usually from greyhound stock for speed, with collie, terrier or other breeds for intelligence, stamina or strength, depending on what quarry you mainly pursue. Lurchers are often beautiful dogs and the best are valuable as they are excellent gaze (that is, sight) hounds as well as scent hounds. The first time I ever saw lurchers was 25 years ago at a ploughing match when such dogs were something of a rarity. In the intervening years I have watched many lampers and have been taught the techniques at first-hand as well as from books. The lurcher will always be my favourite dog but whereas the lurcher of the past was a gentle animal towards man as many still are, the longdogs that are appearing with poachers now are often of a different breed. They are still reared for their speed, but also for their 'game' qualities, that is, their fierce or brave nature, as well as for their size of jaw and strength of shoulder.

Lamping equipment, once a motorbike lamp and battery, has been developed into a handheld or gun-mounted spotlight that can, if necessary, shine out for half-a-mile, catching many animals in its beam. Red filters may be bought as well as cages, decoy calls and whistles and a wide range of nets.

Thanks to the innovation of the gun-mounted beam, lurchers may be dispensed with; it just depends on the quarry and whether you mind retrieving. Also, if you are illegally on the land as a poacher then man and dog may become separated; to avoid this, many dogs are trained to return to the vehicle. Gun-lamping outfits come complete with mountings for shotguns, side, up/over or single barrel, also rifles or air rifles.

Do-It-Yourself taxidermy is increasingly popular with catalogues listing items from brain and eye hooks, scalpels and blades, embaming fluid, preserving techniques to a choice of eyes. I wonder, rather uncharitably, how many DIY taxidermists 'sweeping along country lanes in search of corpses', as one article puts it, may not help a few along? It is illegal to have a badger or any part of it in your possession if it has been obtained unlawfully. But a badger road casualty (unless you were speeding) can, and often is, the subject of lawful taxidermy. And mounted badgers heads are much in demand.

Poaching, whether for deer, fish or pheasant, has reached pandemic proportions. Because it usually occurs at night it is difficult to detect. I was worried that badgers were also being taken at night, yet few people were aware of this widespread problem.

In many country places, dogs have been bred for generations for badger-digging and no mere Act of Parliament is going to stop a man doing what his father and grandfather did before him. Nowadays there's more of a financial incentive too, plus the excitement of avoiding being caught. Betting on organised badger-baiting and dogfighting is increasingly popular, so badgers and badger cubs are much in demand. With baiting, dogs are encouraged to attack and fight a badger which is often maimed or tethered to give the dogs a more equal chance. As one dog tires or is injured, it is removed from the shallow trench or pit where the fight is taking place, and others are put in to continue till the badger is killed. Dogfighting is big business and the training of such dogs (often

American pit bull terriers, sometimes cross-bred with English bull terriers), is expensive. Badgers or stolen dogs may be used in the training, whilst badger cubs are popular to encourage half-grown dogs to fight. A young dog can be put off fighting for life by a tough opponent, but a cub is ideal and may be put first to one, then another dog before it is eventually killed. Thus there is a ready market for a badger whether it be young or old, whether you want it for a 'bit of fun' with your terriers, to sell, or for taxidermy.

Our local RSPCA Inspector, Steve Hammond, helped me wherever he could, especially if I had to work on a Saturday morning, when he would take over from me here even if it happened to be his day off. Weekends are popular times for the terriermen and their dogs to dig out badgers.

March was rushing by. In the woods the bluebell greenery was advanced with primroses, daffodils, lesser celandine and wood sorrel all in bloom. The weather see-sawed between snow flurries and hail on the one hand and still, mild weather on the other. Lesley's cubs appeared in the trench again; she would nurse them above ground, lying on her side to do so and washing them carefully afterwards. Once as I sat above her watching on the old trunk of the fallen cherry tree, my legs stretched out in front of me, she appeared from the nursery pit and climbed up purring. I stayed with her between my legs as we watched a big rabbit feeding just below us. She always loved stretching out on her back in this position and groomed herself leaning against my chest. I pointed with my finger to some milk drying on a bald patch by a nipple and she nosed it. Then, drawing up her snout to bring her mouth into contact with the teat she sampled her own milk. I stroked the sleek, black fur of her legs, then her smooth neck, whereupon she righted herself and on hindlegs, front paws on my shoulder, began to groom my hair. My hair tends to come in for a lot of badger attention; fortunately it is short.

The Old Cherry Sett was my focal point as it housed Lesley and her three cubs (as well as Sam much further along), but equally important were the other badgers there. A sett might be only 10 minutes walk away from another, but that took 20 minutes there and back, plus a little more to make certain no one was hiding, to get on with the job the moment I left. From my own experience I know it takes just 20 minutes (well organised and with dogs), to locate and dig a badger out. There were four woodland setts occupied and however well I checked for vehicles before dawn, a van might come in after I had checked. There were several secluded parking places round the perimeter of this area as well as inside the wood itself. So I could not adequately guard the occupied sett on Clifford's Bank. It was too far off and I couldn't see it clearly from the wood edge. The local police patrolled the lane when they could but obviously they often had more pressing work to do than keeping an eye on badgers. Nevertheless, with farmers, constables and Steve helping, we hadn't had anymore badgers taken by diggers – only lampers.

One morning going home, I met Barry Hains driving down Briarmead Lane. He farms this side of Clifford's Bank, whilst his neighbour John Shaw has the farm beyond. Over the years Barry has helped me immensely, not least in keeping an eye on strange vehicles during daylight hours. That morning I gave him the new van number of a terrierman who had recently troubled us and discussed the recent lamping. With so few foxes now on his land, he was overrun with rabbits. He wouldn't mind lampers in theory (quite an effective way of dealing with the problem), if only one could trust them to stick to rabbits. He asked me about Lesley's cubs. She was our special badger, daughter of Old Joe and in spite of everything had survived to have her second litter of cubs – a tribute to the farmers, their men, Steve and the police interest here. I mentioned that Inspector Hogarth had discussed the continuing badger problem with me a few days previously. I had a lot of respect for this police chief. He was a very busy man who always found time and was never impatient. I told Barry how the Four Musketeers had found a tap left running in his neighbour's yard and had a marvellous time splashing one another – and me – and making a tremendous noise.

March ended as it had begun – by fits and starts. One night was so mild and balmy that all the badgers seemed to be digging out at least one or two of their entrances. Lesley went one better. After working hard for three hours of darkness and backing out at intervals, half dragging, half pushing the soft dirt to the surface, she finally went below just before daylight. But at 7.15 a.m. I came round to the Old Cherry Sett in time to see her grey rump at the main entrance as its owner sent yet more sandy earth flying backwards. She heard my movement and dived inside just as I said 'Les!' in horror at her action in full light. A moment later and her head appeared framed in the hole. Then a dirt-covered snout was thrust into my face as I bent forward. I scolded her harshly (normally I speak very quietly), and tapped her muzzle. She got the message and hastily went below!

As always at this time of year many bluebell bulbs had been dug up round the sett by the badgers. Some are eaten or partly nibbled, but often it is merely the result of their quest for grubs in the dampness. I noticed that the Council men had cut back and coppiced along the path below Lesley's sett. They had also removed the twigs and debris brought down by the great cherry tree's fall last June. The trunk itself had shifted after heavy rainfall earlier that month and had moved the earth of the spoil heap where it lay. The Council men had improved the general look of the place though it was fortunate for me that they hadn't done it earlier. I was waylaid and attacked by two men just here but saved from being really hurt when I slipped into a hole Sam had dug. There I was safe, hidden unseen amongst the twiggyness, in semi-darkness. I owed a lot to that badger. Now Sam's hole had disappeared with the settling of the great weight from above.

On the last night of March there was a starry sky and a deep, deep frost. The grass on the fields and the leaves in the woods crackled underfoot, making silent movement impossible. Everywhere the ponds and soakaways were full and frozen.

Dawn was silent; the only birds I had heard were the tawnies calling to one another, the male owl sounding the boundaries of his territory. I love such mornings, with everything in the grip of deep frost. The rising sun crept into the wood touching the trunks with a golden glow and glittering on their white coverings. Yet 15 minutes later it was snowing, the wind sending great gusts of snow across the open fields. As I walked home through Pete's farm, it began to hail, the stones bouncing off the frozen track, stinging my face and eyes. Then, as suddenly as it had sprung up, the wind and hail were gone. I met Pete's children by the farmhouse, waiting to go to school. Rebecca's bright little face beamed a smile as she asked 'How are the cubs,' and 'How many?'

There was no work for me to go to as it was the Easter vacation at the college where I worked. Normally I would dash home well before that time, change out of my very scruffy clothes which inevitably smelt of badger-musk, and get ready for work. Ever since my badgers were dug out and taken in the early morning of autumn 1983, I stayed as late as possible after dawn to prevent it happening again. There is no guarantee of course, that they wouldn't be taken during the day, but it is far less likely as people are generally about, walking their dogs or driving along Briarmead Lane. Certainly, badger-diggers favour dawn, especially if the weather is bad as it discourages even the illicit shooters. Badgers like an eastern-facing slope or bank in which to live and I've noticed that such entrances are rarely frozen, unlike the surrounding land, even in a deep frost. So they can still be dug out easily with a spade.

The first day and night of April were showery with high, almost gale-force winds and the moon nearly full. The next night was gentler however, and I was determined to tidy up the rubbish thrown down the bank from the Motorway on Colts Farm before it ended up in the lake below. There's a bin in Pete's yard and I was quietly carrying two arm-loads across the field when I found I had a badger escort – the Four Musketeers had picked up my scent trail and found me again. These yearlings were endearing rascals, but rather a nuisance, especially when I tripped over one. Ever since the water episode in Glebe farmyard, they seemed to have a 'who-can-find-her-first' contest.

This is a market-garden farm and some fields had long strips of plastic sheeting covering the spring-onions and young lettuce to bring them on earlier. One such piece had been torn away in the strong wind. I heard sounds of violent flapping, then growling, as I returned from the dustbin and discovered the Four Musketeers quarreling over this length like overgrown puppies. Sis was trying to drag it away, but her sister and Jet were standing on it. Jude came to her aid, and getting a good purchase with his powerful jaws, pulled with her. Something had to give. When the two sows stepped off their end, it did!

Later that night I found Lesley still digging at the Old Cherry Sett. Though the fields were exposed and wind-swept, on the sett slope it was warm and pleasant. She had dug out an entirely new entrance that night, under the bole of a rotting, once-coppiced chestnut and a good way past the other used entrances. Then she went inside and emerged three minutes later opposite the great tree itself. I wondered how many apparent rabbit holes were, in fact, old badger entrances that had sunken with age and lack of use. As an experiment I dug out three 'rabbit' holes and found two of them to be badger entrances. Then I felt a nudge and turned round to find Sam just behind me watching with great interest!

Sis suddenly appeared and nosed her mother as she emerged, pushing earth behind her as she came. Next the young sow investigated my trowelwork – clearly substandard. Then the daughter went much further along and dug out an old entrance I had not seen in use for twenty years – in the morning she chose to den there too! By then this Old Cherry Sett had fifteen badger entrances in use (excluding my efforts).

Good Friday was a mild night of the full moon with clear skies. At 2 a.m. I was by the Old Barn ruins with the yearlings when Jude mated long-duration with Little'un. Perhaps an hour later, I came across Sam and Sis on the field just above the Cherry Sett. By their attitudes and their grooming, I'm sure they too had just mated, but I didn't actually witness it. The presence of a boar probably stimulates ovulation. Badgers often indulge in rutting behaviour when penetration isn't deep and coupling brief. But long-duration, which may be anything from 15 minutes plus, generally leads to fertilisation and only occurs when the sow is in oestrus.

These animals may mate at almost any time of the year but give birth at one season only. Here cubs had been born from the end of January till the beginning of March, though the parents may have mated at any time the previous year. Delayed implantation is the cause of this and once the fertilised egg is implanted in the wall of the uterus it takes a mere seven weeks plus a day or two till birth. What triggers off implantation isn't known for certain, though possibilities have been suggested such as the slowing down of the badger's metabolism during the winter period.

Another fascinating badger subject is just how closely these animals are related over a wide area. I had promised Steve Hammond of the RSPCA that I would try to record setts round my home town and the outlying villages that Easter vacation, on a large-scale ordnance survey map. I found many setts dug out with spades and empty of their owners. As the days went by, with more setts entered on the map, I thought about this subject a great deal. Someone who knows far more about badgers than I, once asked me if I'd ever observed strange, mature boars coming into my area and mating with the sows there, unchallenged and unmolested by the resident, dominant boar, only to disappear as suddenly as they had come. I hadn't. But Old Joe had sometimes disappeared, for a few nights or, more occasionally, for much longer, and I did wonder if he had been trespassing. This raised the question of why other badger clans accept such intrusions; boars with sows are extremely territorial and will normally attack strangers. Certainly badgers are related, if only slightly, over a very wide area. Could it be that they have a memory for scent as we have for faces? Is there a 'family likeness' in scent? It would explain a lot.

Easter Sunday was a damp, mild night with a waning moon. I found several toads on Briarmead Lane making for the soakaway there. The great toad migration had begun. So for the next few days and nights many of these amphibians would congregate here to mate in the deep water and spawn, then gradually disperse again. When the migration is in full swing with hundreds on the move and many already in amplexius, that is the smaller male 'riding' on his chosen mate, it is a curious sight.

After midnight the rain began in earnest and I went in search of my badgers. The Four Musketeers must have been of the same mind for Little'un found me first. My plastic anorak attracted her interest (it makes a slight noise when I move). She grasped part of a sleeve, ripping it before I could stop her. I left them worming in the rain, in the dip below Cliffords Bank, and went in search of the old sow, knowing she would not be far away from her young cubs housed in the sett of the Bank. Sure enough, there she was, near the pylon parallel with the Poplar Row. She was very friendly, greeting me with an excited purr and snuffling my gloved hands before backing on to and musking my boots. This was only the second time she had musked me since the birth of her cubs though I had watched her at a short distance. Gently stroking her head I wondered just how old she was. She had an 'old' look, the once-black stripes of her face very flecked with grey and her eyes rheumy, but stress can age animals just as it does humans, and I suspect, from the condition she was in when she came to my area, that stress more than anything accounted for her appearance. The whole family had come here together though the boar was later taken by lampers. Jet and Jude had been their young cubs. I would have loved to stay around this night to watch her with her new cubs, but felt it wasn't right to do so.

Standing by her in the rain with the wind rising, I thought I saw figures. Moments later, a beam cut a path across the rape field to our right. On the instant, another shone along Poplar Row. We were caught in a right angle and could only move upfield to avoid the lights; luckily this was towards the sett in Cliffords Bank. I remember hoping that the yearlings I had left worming would move fast and not linger. My frightened sow ran for home and I paced with her, anxious to see her safely underground and also to locate the youngsters. Then yet another beam appeared from our left, completing the triangle and cutting us off from the sett. I turned with my back to it as the light swept over us and the sow at my side gave a great snort. I crouched down, pushing her squat body under mine with my arms round her, conscious that my greatest danger might be from the badger herself, for animals in fear may snap at those nearest and a badger's bit is severe. I glanced up briefly, before the other lights dazzled us, to see four longdogs looking at me uncertainly. (If terriers had been used too, I would almost certainly have been set upon). I had great difficulty keeping my sow beneath me and was surprised at her fury (she sounded more like a boar), till I recalled she had her cubs nearby.

Then something hit my back with force, leaving me breathless, followed by a blow on my shoulder. I realised that flints, long-broken by the plough were being thrown at me, together with a lot of verbal abuse.

Two spotlights were switched off, leaving the third shining on us crouching there, as the men came together beyond the beam to talk. Stroking the dazzled badger with one hand, while holding her with the other, I kept my head averted, listening. I had heard two of the voices before on these fields. One of them shouted that next time I'd get hurt if they found me there, then the beam was switched off and the men went their separate ways. I think four went towards the farmyard and two towards Briarmead and we were left with two lurchers guarding us, the others having gone with their owners. I guessed that they were going to get safely to their respective vehicles and whistle up the dogs. The sow beneath me moved restlessly, no longer dazzled and less fearful now that the men had gone, she wanted to return to her cubs. The dogs crept closer at her movements and I found myself looking into the watchful eye of a big lurcher all scarred about the face and head. I spoke softly to it and its companion too brought its head nearer. Lurchers at their best are beautiful dogs and this one certainly was.

Time passed, and the fitful rain stopped, the strong winds blew jagged clouds across the sky. Close to the earth like that, I could smell its freshness; the wet grass and vegetation growing on the nearby Bank and the musky badger scent. The dogs' heads turned suddenly, listening. One quick glance at us and they were off like coursing greyhounds, down field towards the farm. I let the sow go and she disappeared into the sett. To my surprise I heard trilling sounds as I moved closer – I hadn't realised all this had happened so near the nursery entrance.

There was no point in contacting the police. The nearest phone was in the farmyard and it was far too late for them to catch anyone. The only things I could honestly say were that at least three lampers wore balaclava-style headgear hiding their features and that by their voices, two were the lampers of last September and November. On the first occasion they attempted to take one of my vixens and on the second, they netted Lesley; but I had taken their photo as they weren't masked, and in their anxiety to secure the camera, they let her go.

At home hours later, I found the musky badger scent was still clinging to my anorak and it remained so for some days; I have noticed this particularly with plastic garments.

A couple of days later, Barry Hains' car drew alongside me as I was walking home. Pointing to the field ahead he asked me if I knew 'What the hell's been going on over there?' A vehicle's wheels had come off the track and churned deep into the growing crop. I explained about the lampers two nights earlier. Looking at the tyre marks with me, Barry concluded that a heavy vehicle, probably a landrover must have been temporarily stuck in the mud. We both felt it probably brought the lampers with the third beam into the area. The tracks came off the path where the grass verge stopped, which pointed to a driver approaching without headlights, otherwise he couldn't have failed to see the way.

Barry told me of a sheep farmer friend who discovered lampers terrifying his sheep and newborn lambs. The farmer and his shepherd went out to remonstrate and were badly beaten up. One of the poachers almost bit off the end of the farmer's nose. 'These men are less than animals themselves,' added Barry bitterly. 'The lampers said that as their fun was being spoilt, they would get all their friends to swamp the land with lamping, take everything and fix the sheep. They will too, these people pass information like a bush telegraph. I know how you feel about the badgers, but I'd let them get on with it. You were lucky not to get badly beaten up or worse. If you'd been a man you wouldn't be here today.'

Now there were fourteen badgers, including the cubs, and I would not let one of them be taken without a struggle. Eighteen months ago the diggers had taken every badger in these 800 acres except for Lesley. She was a cub then and I had vowed to protect her.

The following night I took my two wild service saplings with me and planted them in prepared ground. They were nearly 4 foot high, with their leaf-buds unfurling and I was proud of those sturdy young trees. Of all the trees I had planted over the years – hornbeam, oak, beech, lime, yew, gean, willow, spindle, to name but a few, those meant the most to me.

Saturday night was showery, with a strong wind but excellent visibility. I came out of the wood just after midnight to find a van I knew only too well tucked out of sight at the foot of the scree slope we call High Ridge. The gate on to the road below was apparently closed but the padlock, broken some weeks ago, hadn't been replaced. Like the wooden stiles of the railway crossing on the farmland above, they were smashed with monotonous regularity, so each new padlock never lasts long. With the stiles gone it is easy to bring lurchers and equipment straight on to the land, just as the unlocked gate gives a quick escape route off it. Tonight's van was owned by a digger turned lamper who would take anything, ranging from pheasant, quail, rabbit, hare or fox, with a badger as an extra bonus. I had no idea where the badgers were just then for I had been foxcub-watching in the wood, so I ran quickly up the scree slope. Almost immediately I saw two men with their beam and dogs on the field below Cliffords Bank. Last year I had been told that the police could only touch them for taking a badger, so it would be pointless going down to phone at the farm unless they actually had one in their possession or let their dogs harry one. My problem was that if they did take a badger and I then contacted our police with the van number, the patrol had to catch them with the animal in their possession. All I could do was watch, wait and if they dazzled a badger in their light, try and stop them taking it.

It seemed a lifetime that I watched them lamping and I kept my distance lest the lurchers should scent me. They caught three rabbits, retrieving them to hand, but fortunately there was no sign of the badgers. Both men wore balaclava masks, probably because they knew about my camera. One man held a net and bearing in mind that it was getting late in the year for fox pelts they were probably on the lookout for badgers. I checked the wet fields carefully, one eye on the lampers and concerned about the Clifford Bank sow, though she could of course, have already been below ground in the sett with her cubs. She found me, however. I was standing near Rob's cottage worriedly looking upfield towards the beam, when something touched my trouser leg. Kneeling down, I put my arm round her, rubbing behind her ears. It seemed an eternity that we stayed there, both quietly watching. The speed at which a lurcher can turn is amazing. Neither hare nor fox are a match for such a greyhound-cross-longdog. What must be going on in the sow's brain I wondered. One human she trusts, all others she fears. I had noticed before that unless the badgers could scent men or dogs, they appeared merely to watch and in some instances, to continue foraging at least till the beam got nearer. The danger in this, with a spotlight that could illuminate a 1,000 foot area and dogs with such speed, was that a badger would be caught in the beam, dazzled and at bay before it knew what had hit it.

Just then my sow turned her head towards me and whined softly. The beam was off, the men were walking along in our direction. I decided to get her safely home by taking her on to Briarmead, through the wood and so by a roundabout route, back on to Cliffords Bank from the field above, if she would come. She refused at first, but as the men drew nearer, my urgency coupled with her fear made us run together.

By now the wind and rain had ceased with stars appearing between fluffs of cloud and no moon. I saw her safely into the sett and stayed sitting on its bank watching the beam as they worked the far fields and listening to the sounds of mother and cubs just below me. The elmbush had grown up greatly here and all was in tiny leaf. I wasn't bothered by my wet and muddy state for I felt an inner warmth at the tiny muffled barks and occasional whimper of the family just below. I was determined to stay until the men had left. They would possibly pass this way on their return to High Ridge and their van. Animals get over a fright quickly and

14

the Clifford sow could be out foraging again before dawn.

A streak of light appeared in the sky ahead and a lark began singing from the corn below. They are always the first to sing on the open land. Then a stoat, stalking an unsuspecting rabbit, saw its prey thump and dash for cover as the men returned, now unmasked. Their dogs were on slip and I was glad of this for it had occurred to me they might roam about and find me hidden amongst the elmbrush. As it was, one lurcher strained in my direction, scenting upwards as they approached and its owner remarked, 'Bet there're cubs in there – hold it.' He lit a cigarette and they stood talking. 'Young brockies fetch quite a bit. What d'you think?'

'What about the cottage down there – bit risky.'

'They don't see a light at night. Wouldn't need one to dig early morning. Give it a go?'

'No. They'll spot us on the bank.'

'Depends how early they get up. Couldn't do it on our own though. I'll walk round here this afternoon and take a look. Think about it.' Then they moved on, still talking, towards High Ridge.

I sat a while longer in the quiet of first light, making a mental note to warn John Shaw at the farm and Rob at the cottage. Just then I saw the sow standing on the top of the bank looking out over the lower field. I just stayed enjoying the sight of her. Then she scented the air, snout raised like a little statue, till I called softly. Down she came, purring loudly, winding her way through the brush, and musked my boots. I never intended to become friendly with her, it just happened through the badger-hunting business. I'm so glad she wasn't taken.

Over the years I have developed good night vision, but undoubtedly there are those special nights when one's surroundings have an extra clarity. One beautifully warm, mild night in mid-April, with no wind or moon and perfect visibility, I watched Lesley's ten-week old cubs at play. Favourite games that night were rolling down the sett slope until they ended up at the prone trunk of the great tree. Then up they would run and tucking their heads between their front legs, roll down yet again. Chase was popular as well as tag when one would nip another's tail or rump, then rush off with the 'tagged' one in hot pursuit. All young animals tire suddenly and badgers are no exception. It was so mild that they hadn't gone below to sleep, but had curled up together against the old trunk, one almost hidden and one with its head cushioned on another's back. Their mother, who had been foraging below on Long Field, came up to me as I sat above her family on the great cherry, my back against a small branch and head pillowed on my arm. She settled herself between my legs, began to groom, then changed her mind and went to sleep. A night to remember – the odd squeak of a mouse somewhere amongst the wood anemones; a tawny calling in the distance and the ghostly white cherry blossom seeming to float just above.

Two nights earlier, Sandy's vixen had led her cubs to a new den at the far end of this Cherry Sett. Her five youngsters followed her, single file (no pausing or playing *en route*), along the path by the Old Barn ruins, across the top of Briarmead and round the field edge where she met me. I knelt and spoke softly as she approached, whilst her pups huddled together behind her nervously. Then I watched as they continued across the top of the sand pit and so down to the slope of their new home. Since that night, both badger and fox cubs had been aware of one another, but hadn't to my knowledge, made contact. The young fox cubs at six weeks were nearly weaned and both parents were fetching-back for them. Once I saw the vixen regurgitate as a youngster licked and pulled at her mouth. Partly digested food, often something small like a vole, will be vomited back for a cub to eat. The licking round the parent's mouth stimulates this, though sometimes the adult regurgitates voluntarily. Badgers do this too, though less frequently, perhaps bacause their cubs go from milk to worms, which are soft enough for them to cope with unaided.

Watching Lesley's cubs that night had made me wonder if John Shaw and his daughter had been as fortunate with those of the Clifford sow on his land. He had asked me the best time and place to sit and watch them. I told him about the lampers' possible plan to dig out the badgers there. I mentioned that Cliffords Bank was too far away for me to guard in the early morning as well as the woodland setts and he had promised to warn Rob at the cottage. John has sounded very concerned, so I felt I could safely leave the old sow and her cubs to this farmer and his foreman and concentrate on those here. The lamping problem remained.

By the third week of April the smell of 'incense' hung heavily on the night air as I crossed the fields to my study area, so I knew the balsam poplars' leaves were unfurling. Several times that month I had been met by my old dogfox Josh, waiting in the bracken of the field edge. Josh had periods of doing things like no other fox I had known. One winter he had decided to dawnwatch with me and followed me round from sett to parking place for weeks, then just as suddenly stopped. No other fox had decoyed for me when danger threatened. A vixen will draw attention to herself and away from her cubs to save them from dog or man, and a fox will do likewise for its mate. But Josh had done it for me in the past and sometimes I wondered just how he viewed me, for he had saved me from my own kind. We might have little contact for weeks except to see one another at a distance. Yet now he was waiting for me again, part of a rabbit in his jaws, so I guessed he was taking it to his cubs or vixen. Sure enough, on the farmland above High Ridge she came trotting along the field edge from the den and I held back as they met. She stood there, brush waving as he came down the slope. He dropped his burden and stood nose to nose with her, whilst both made soft noises in their throats. Then she grasped the rabbit, turned and trotted back along the path with her mate following. I watched from a distance as their pups surged round them with excitement, then quietly slipped away.

That night I found that Lesley's three cubs and Sandy's five pups of the Old Cherry Sett had finally got acquainted and I don't know when I've enjoyed a nightwatch more. Twice the young badger sisters had stolen along the trail that wound through the bluebells, drawn by the noisy games of their new neighbours. And twice they had been discovered, the little foxes ceasing their play to creep uneasily back to their den. Then it had been the fox cubs' turn to steal along the sett path and gaze at the burly young badgers vandalising the bluebells. One badger was standing on the chestnut bough seat with a flower in her mouth, daring the others to topple her. There were gruff little barks, whickers and the odd yelp as someone was nipped too hard, then the 'king' fell backwards off the 'castle' into the flowers and the next was up top. The foxcubs loved this too, but they hadn't made friends with the badgers that night. Yet when I arrived after leaving Josh and the family on Newby farmland, the eight little hoodlums were playing together on the old cherry trunk.

When they had gone to earth, a streak of light lay like a scarf to the east, in the breathless silence of that magical moment when time stands suspended between night and day.

Ten minutes later I came upon two men at the Crater Sett where Jude was denning. One was standing, the other kneeling and holding a terrier at the entrances under the holly. They turned as I ran down into the hollow just behind them. One was armed. I had seen both the young man and the thickset man in his forties many times, but not together. Just then sounds of barking came from below ground and another sound. That dog had met its match. I saw the scarred black terrier the younger man was holding had a trasmitting collar and wondered frantically about the other setts, as such men tend to poach in groups. What was happening to Lesley and her cubs? I told them to get the dog out, though doubting that they could. Then the problem solved itself, as a jack russell backed out, shaking its head, its ear and neck torn and bleeding. The older man pushed his shotgun into my face and threatened to shoot, but fear for Lesley and her family made me angry and I told him contemptuously to grow up. I was looking at the sett as they left but decided Jude was probably all right and looked round just in time to see the older man bringing the shotgun down on to my head. I jumped back and warded off the gun with my left arm, feeling it jar as it took the blow. Then the men left. I hurried to the Cherry Sett but nobody was there.

A squirrel, passing in the branches overhead, sent a flurry of white blossom floating gently groundwards. I stared at the trampled bluebells where the cubs had been playing. I had no way of contacting the police and could only guard the animals here on a day-to-day basis. With a terrible sense of inadequacy, I wondered how long it would be before all my badgers were taken. It only needed someone like that morning's man, to lose his temper and fire, then anyone could help themselves to the badgers here.

I later found that my forearm had a hairline fracture. That evening a young constable, Philip, was sent to see me and while we talked I found that off-duty he walked his dog in Ashcroft Woods and had come to know the setts there well. He asked me at which sett the trouble had occurred and as soon as I described it, he immediately knew the one. I told him that it would be he and others like him who would catch the diggers, as I could do nothing about the daytime. I was glad he had come, for he had done me more good than he could have possibly known. Philip was interested and he cared.

One night towards the end of that month, I came upon Lesley, Sam and their cubs on the old cherry's trunk, exploring the fissures of its deeply twisted bark. The mother was ahead of the others, tearing with her long front claws at a rotten limb. On such a damp, mild night, snails and slugs are active and the latter often move into trees to feed on algae growing in the bark. The cubs were still too young at twelve weeks to cope with these, however. One discovered a slug, turned it over with a paw and discarded it. Lesley was beginning to wean them and an hour later I saw mother and cubs at the edge of Long Field. Her mate and the two sows Bess and Susie from the bank of Colts Farm were worming under a spray between the motorway and Madden Lane. Pete had started irrigating these fields in March; market gardening was in full swing now and would continue well into the autumn. Lesley would undoubtedly have been foraging there too, but a sow keeps close to home with cubs so young.

At first light I saw a weasel reconnoitring, that is rearing up on hindlegs to look about. It was amongst the growing barley of Briarmead Lane and would disappear briefly in the green blades, only to bob up again a short while after. Once more it disappeared and when a skylark flew up with a frightened cry, I memorised the spot, and moved as softly as possible over to it. The weasel had located the nest and was lapping a broken egg, one of four in the grassy nest that fitted cuplike into a slight hollow between the rows. Just then something startled the weasel which darted back to the cover of the bank. Josh was approaching. It would sound good to say that he was coming to see me, but I'd a sneaking suspicion it was what I was watching – as so often it's edible!

It was a breathtaking dawn from the wood edge. The place seemed filled with the scent of bluebells; the ground, a blue-green sea. The fallen cherry straddled the slope, old, gnarled and ugly now as it settled ever more deeply into the earth of the sett. Yet part of it lived on as five small branches were a haze of green young leaves and frothy blossom.

Long fingers of sunlight touched the chestnut trunks and Sandy's russet fur as he stalked a squirrel on the sett slope. He had been sitting on top of an enormous spoil heap when he raised his head higher and stared intently ahead. Silently the dogfox moved to the right, skirting a log, all the while keeping a trunk or shrub between himself and his prey. When the squirrel stopped feeding to look and listen, the predator froze. When the squirrel commenced feeding, stealthily the hunter moved in. Then he tensed and shot through the air, coming down on his victim and killing it with one bite.

One mild night in May, with a full moon behind the clouds and excellent visibility, I watched a pair of lampers far down field on Glebe Farm. I was not unduly worried for I had spoken to them the previous November and saw them from time to time. They hadn't the equipment to lamp badgers and though I'd rather not have had any lampers around, these were quite civil, reasonable men, father and son, so I just kept out of their way.

The Clifford badger's two cubs had come to know me, though Lesley's three had not. Ever since the night that the old sow and I had been lamped, she had gone out of her way to meet and greet me. Her cubs, a boar and a sow, were twelve weeks old now and the young male already had a broader head and fluffy cheeks whilst his sister's head and neck were narrower and sleeker.

The badgers were feeding on young rabbits that night, the adult was using her fine sense of smell coupled with acute hearing to locate a nursery stop. (Nests of voles and mice are also discovered in this way.) The cubs nosed the blind and naked rabbits, chewed one, then dropped it. Then their mother, who had moved on, returned and ate them. Moments later she regurgitated for her cubs, who snuffled over the undigested rabbits, then began to eat. The sow moved along the grassy verge of the path, snout to ground, and dug swiftly down again.

Then two things happened simultaneously. A distant light touched us and something shot into the sow, catapulting her into the air. Next moment the dog reached us, grabbed up the nearest cub and shook it. I held the lurcher's neck, shouting 'drop it!' and the screaming cub was released into my hand. I sat down, one hand on the cub in my lap, the other still grasping the lurcher. I would never have thought such a tiny animal could make such a terrible noise, like a human child in pain. I felt shattered by the sheer volume of noise and the suddeness of the whole thing. The older man came up, took the dog from me and gave it to his son to hold. Then he came and sat by me. He was as upset as I was, I examined the now silent animal and found it hardly marked at all, but almost certainly it was internally injured. He asked if I wanted their names and address but I shook my head. It was as much an accident as running- over a badger on the road. I asked him not to lamp here again as he was after all trespassing. He gave his word and returned to his son. They stood a few minutes talking together, then the young man came up and apologised. I showed him the cub, now moving about and nosing my anorak. He told me he'd seen badgers before, but never a cub. Did I know how old it was? If ever a badger came within their beam, they switched if off and recalled the lurcher. He repeated that he was sorry, then shook my hand and left. These past months I'd been hit on the head by lampers, knocked down and kicked, shot at – and finally, had my hand shaken. It's an odd world.

As I set the boar cub on its feet it began to whimper. The mother appeared, nosed it then licked it, whilst its sister stood watching close by. Then all three went to earth in the bank. Perhaps the cub was merely frightened, but a dog shakes to kill by breaking the spine.

Chapter 2

Sadly, the following night the badger cub died on my lap. I had come early the previous evening as I was concerned over the lamping situation and worried about the injured animal. But there were no lampers, probably because the full moon chose to ride out of the ragged clouds and remain shining over the countryside for the rest of the night. Such a moon is not ideal for lamping as animals tend to keep close to the hedgerows when it is bright and don't venture so far into open ground. I could tell immediately that the cub was very sick; it was crouched, shivering, its coat wet with sweat. I took off my pullover, made a 'bed' of it on my lap, and watched the young animal settle into it. The Clifford sow nosed it a little, then went with her remaining offspring towards the field of oilseed rape shimmering under the moon. I knew why they went there. Sometime after the snow in February, a vehicle was bogged down on that field leaving deep ruts in the soaked earth. The golden rape had grown and was flowering. The ruts remained and still contained water.

It was much later, quietly sitting there, that I realised the cub was dead. A skylark began singing in the field below. Soon it would be first light and sure enough, two figures were returning to the sett. I wondered what the sow's reaction would be. Would she stay with it awhile or go to earth? The moment her nose touched the small body, she knew it was dead. She stood there looking at me for so long that I spoke softly to her and touched her head. She came slightly above me on the sett slope and grasped the cub in her powerful jaws. Carrying the cub, she disappeared backwards into the darkness of the tunnel.

21

It is thought that badgers wall up their dead in disused parts of the sett. This is difficult to prove, though it might explain why old badger bones are sometimes found on spoil heaps when disused entrances are re-opened and dug out. I have such bones and skulls myself. On the other hand I have found the bodies of cubs a few days old, in bracken or a hedgerow near a sett.

The water level of Pete's lake was as low as my spirits as I walked home that morning. One of his tractor drivers caught up with me, asking how my arm was, and we stayed talking. I happened to mention Philip and discovered the man had already seen the young constable looking at the setts and had queried who he was. I had to smile, but at least it showed the men here were alert.

On the 14th May we had heavy rain, the first for many weeks, and everything seemed to have suddenly grown. Perhaps the crops had become high enough to make lamping unprofitable in my area. Heaths, pasture, the marshes and downs would still be lamped, but here the oilseed rape was high and the wheat and barley growing fast enough to hide fleeing animals.

Steve Hammond came that afternoon to collect the sett maps and to tell me he would soon be leaving. He had long wanted to devote more time to following up cases of cruelty and investigating them; his new job at RSPCA headquarters, Horsham, would give him the opportunity. I was very pleased for his sake but selfishly, I'd miss him. Talking to Steve was helpful and he had proved a good friend in the sixteen months I had known him.

We discussed the badger problem. I told him that I wanted to alert other people to the problem of badger lamping and that what was happening here must be happening elsewhere. Steve told me that a few reports of badger lamping had come into headquarters, but the chance of detecting poachers was very small and it would only be people out on the land at night like myself who would be aware of the situation. That diggers were now turning up as lampers was disturbing but, like the increase in organised dogfighting, it was a sign of the times. Months earlier, a burglar who was also a keen dogfighting man had moved into our neighbourhood and was living in considerable style at a place called Crawfords. Recently he had joined forces with Don Francis, a long-standing resident who included holding badgers for collection and terrier breeding among his many and varied occupations. Crawfords was an old, old mansion with thick walls, cellars, a priest's hole, plenty of garage space and other interesting features and several times I had wandered round that way. The old, scarred guard dog running lose in

22

the grounds might have been a problem, but under that massive head and ugly face I found the gentle veteran was susceptible to affection and kindness. What had started on my part as a blatant attempt to befriend, had ended up as something special to us both. 'Uglybug' seemed instinctively to know that our meetings must be a secret, though the marks he carried of old beatings may have had a lot to do with that.

Two nights later I was met by Sam as I came along the field edge of Madden Lane. He snuffled my hand very playfully when I stroked him, but there were no gloves in May! This badger had a weakness for my gloves and had gone to earth with one on several occasions.

My forearm was not yet healed, so I dared not let him play too roughly, but enjoyed his company none the less. I found he was aware of the mallard on the Main Pond and realised he could easily reach the hen's nest if he located it. I hastily diverted his attention by taking a handkerchief out of my pocket and flicking it at him. He made to grab it, so by playing with him and keeping all the while on the move, we came to Briarmead and so out of the woods and down the land. Now I expected him to have a weakness for handkerchieves! It was Sam whose dung pits lined Sand Pit Field and the lane edge here. Searching for grubs under the hedgerow, he left snuffle holes, one of which he later converted into a dung pit. Dung perhaps seems a curious subject, but is the quickest way of telling what the animal was eating if you weren't around at the time. Watching badgers I've found that their dung is sometimes deposited on the open ground, however, and the pits they dig can be used solely for urine, which contradicts the belief that badgers always deposit their dung in pits.

By 3.40 a.m. that morning I thought Sam had gone to earth, but in a while I heard him snorting and digging somewhere below me. Then the cubs returned with Lesley and I forgot all about him. She scampered along the trunk to where I sat amongst the Old Cherry's branches, and purring, first musked my jeans, then reached up on hind legs to nuzzle my face. After which, of course, my hair was groomed. Her three cubs came to watch us from a distance. I made no attempt to approach them. Forty minutes later, when his family had gone to earth, Sam was still digging. It was nearly 5 a.m. and well light when finally he dragged to the surface the cause of his efforts – an odd flint, shaped rather like the letter L and very heavy. I later found it weighed slightly over two kilos. Its shape looked man-made and I wondered how it had got there.

At 1 a.m. the following morning I found the badgers *en masse* (a gathering of badgers is called a colony or cete), all worming under a rotating cable-drawn spray on Pete's land. Thirteen animals including the four cubs – a sight to remember. I stood revelling in the scene and felt my efforts in protecting them, rewarded a thousand fold.

When the badgers worm under the irrigation, the lettuces on the fields are not damaged. As I watched I realised why. Every fifth row is left unplanted for the sprinkler-head trolley to pass along. Water runs down this row and the badger moves slowly along, worming as it goes. A few rows away another badger will be doing likewise. They never crowd each other and each respects the other's foraging area.

Within an hour, the cubs had had their fill of worms and were a short distance away, playing at the wood edge. Little'un and Sis, (Lesley's yearling sows) had joined in. I had noticed before how good such 'aunty' badgers were with the young cubs, playing, grooming and generally keeping an eye on them, whilst the mother was still foraging. Even Jude had joined in the game. The cubs weren't completely weaned yet and as one aunty washed herself, she had her belly carefully examined by a cub obviously searching for non-existent milk. With cubs as big as this, fourteen weeks old, their mothers generally lie on their backs to nurse them.

By 23rd May the yearling sows Bess and Susie from the bank on Colts Farm had moved into the Old Cherry Sett. As young females, they had little difficulty in being accepted into the family group and I suspect they were distantly related. Badgers are sociable creatures, there was plenty of room at this sett and an abundance of food in the area. The nights were dull, warm and misty and many hours of darkness were spent by the badgers in digging out and collecting bluebell greenery for their bedding. Lesley's cubs joined in with great enthusiasm and clearly enjoyed getting in the adult's way. They carried in their own small bits, dropping most of it en route! Each animal moved backwards to an entrance with a bundle tucked against the chest and beneath the chin. Their forefeet were partially engaged in holding, which gave them a shuffling, ungainly gait though they moved with surprising speed and an unerring sense of direction.

Sam had a habit of gently chewing the toe of my boot when I was sitting down. Like Lesley's trick of grasping my wrist, it was a bid for attention when I happened to be pre-occupied with something or someone else. Walking through the floodwater on lower Briarmead, I found my boot let in water at the top of the toe.

A few nights later I discovered Bess was missing. She hadn't returned to the farm bank and was unlikely to have moved as she and her sister had seemed very settled at the Cherry Sett. I spent much of that night searching the farmland as I feared she might have been shot. At 6.15 a.m. I had to go home for work, feeling rather uneasy.

As I went to my area on the last Sunday of May, waves of warm air surged passed me and flashes of distant lightning showed in the west. The fields that I crossed contained many rabbits and I caught three very young ones in my cupped hands, then gently put them back where I found them. Just before dawn the storm suddenly struck – a rush of wind foretelling the rain, then the deluge itself. I had been in the company of Sandy's vixen a short time before, and would have walked about the wood quite happily enjoying the storm, but she, contrary creature, wouldn't leave my side, though clearly she was fearful of the crashing thunder overhead. So I finally sat down under a holly tree, vixen between my knees, my arms and head covering her, and there we stayed. She huddled within my body-space while I, chin on knees watched the creamy-white holly flowers lit by the violent flashes overhead. It was then I heard a mistle-thrush (aptly named the storm cock) singing above us. An hour or so later it was just light rain, so together we went down the slope to the Wildflower Path, the vixen quite dry and playful now. Briarmead was a rush of floodwater bringing silt and vegetation down from its banks. I played with my vixen on the high bank overlooking the lane and wondered why she had acted so strangely in the storm. Now she jumped up, brush waving, tongue lolling, just as Sandy appeared carrying a young rabbit. At that moment, something small and alive was swept along on the water below, touched the bank and gained a hold there – a hedgehog. The vixen pounced and bit into its face; a tightening of jaws, a crunch and it was dead. She ate it there on the bank of the lane, leaving only the skin and spines. Then fox and vixen disappeared into the wood, the latter now carrying the rabbit and heading in the direction of the den.

Half an hour more and the sun was pushing the clouds aside. Turning slightly I saw my back was steaming in its warmth. The ash trees, always last in leaf, were covered in tiny leaves that sparkled with raindrops. The lane's banks were clothed in white upon green – hedge parsley, May blossom and stitchwort. I still hadn't found the missing badger, but I hadn't had much chance to search that night.

On Bank Holiday Monday I found her dead and decomposing, not far from the Crater Sett in Ashcroft Woods. The warmth and rain, helped by maggots and beetles, had advanced decomposition with part of the skull and rib cage exposed. When I last saw her she had been healthy and active, so I felt her end had been violent. I later found shot in her fully decomposed remains, so she must have been hit as she emerged to forage one evening.

The following nights were mild and damp – fine badger foraging weather. I met the Clifford sow and her remaining cub and was made such a fuss of that I remained in their company till well after first light. It's amazing how many grubs, caterpillars, beetles and larvae are accounted for by a single badger in one night. The cub foraged quite successfully and was a bouncy little character, full of high spirits, yet gentle. I played with her before I left, whilst her mother dug out another entrance in Cliffords Bank.

As I walked towards Briarmead the skylarks were filling the air with song, but distinctly came a wispy call from the barley on my left. Quiet yet clear amongst the other birds, it came again, then again. The quail – how I had waited to hear that call. They were late, but they had come at last.

The month ended cold and frosty with the hedgerows fragrant with the cloying scent of May blossom. I had left the Clifford sow and cub at 3.45 a.m. when they had gone to earth. At this time of year, mid-May to mid-June, badgers make their earliest returns to the sett. (This varies between individuals and depends on the ease or difficulty with which they find food). These last few mornings with clear skies, it had been just light at 3.10 a.m. so they went to earth in good light. Yearling badgers, like human teenagers, may keep late hours, nevertheless, they return comparatively early. Badger-hunters also know this, so 4 a.m. onwards was the vital time to guard the woodland setts.

When I left sow and cub I returned to High Ridge; standing out in the open, high above the slope, I heard the scree rattling and rolling under-foot as someone came up. I hid behind a clump of birches as a man appeared walking briskly with two dogs, a terrier and a greyhound-lurcher. The dogs would have stayed to catch the rabbits that stampeded away on all sides, for there were plenty on the Ridge. But the man spoke sharply as he hurried along and they came to heel. I followed, at a distance, as there is virtually no cover on the plateau. By the time I reached the first corner of Cliffords Bank, they had disappeared. As I walked uneasily along the path above the bank, I realised that the leafy elmbrush hid me. There was a 'chink' as something struck a stone. It came again, followed by other sounds and the truth hit me. Someone a short distance down the bank was using a spade. The brush and bramble were almost impenetrable, so I ran back and down on to the lower field and along the bottom of the bank, passing noisily through the long, wet wheat. I came up the slope of the field in time to see three men – one of them the man from High Ridge with the dogs – running down field through the corn on one of the 'lanes' made recently by the spraying tractor. I ducked under the elmbrush and clambered on to

Cliffords Bank. Five entrances to the sett had already been filled in by the men, the spade-marks clear where the earth above the holes had been dug. The summer foliage concealed anyone on the bank from the outside, let alone from Rob's cottage, two fields distant. Something about one of the running figures had struck a chord in my memory, could they have been the April lampers? What had been said that morning 'Young brockies fetch quite a bit . . . couldn't do it on our own though'. As I stood there in the closeness of the hedgebush, I heard an urgent barking in the distance – Rob's dog at the cottage, hearing them pass.

Our old cat died early that June. Her favourite food had been a dried dog food and I had nearly one pound left. I decided to give it to the badgers rather than throw it away, though feeding either foxes or badgers goes rather against my principles.

It was a beautiful clear, starry sky with the moon near the full, a light wind and very mild. I found the Clifford sow and cub at the back of High Ridge amongst the heather and close-cropped grass where there were many snuffle holes made by the badgers in their search for grubs and larvae. The penny bun (*Boletus edulis*) grows abundantly here, also parasol mushrooms (*Lepiota procera*), but in the main, it was young rabbits they were both digging out and eating and the cub, now weaned at sixteen weeks, could tackle most things unaided. I dumped the moistened dog food down in front of the young animal, curious to see what she would make of it. Very excited, she snuffled over the heap and began to eat. Her mother came up and warned her off, growling, then gobbled it up herself. Her cub snuffled about indignantly on the empty turf, then ran up to the parent and licked around her muzzle; the sow hastily turned away, but her offspring would not be put off, whining and pulling at her mouth. I had a strong desire to laugh as the dog food reappeared on the grass and the cub set to with a will. The mother stood some moments watching, then slowly began to eat also. Who said you can't have your cake and eat it too?

Later, looking down over the valley, I watched the moon from the Chantry headland. The winding river and its lakes shone under the white light and circles of trees in the water meadows sent long shadows across the fields.

Suddenly there was a rustle, a soft whickering and a moist snout touched my hand. Little'un musked me, then went behind me into the Chantry and I could hear the sounds of lapping as she drank the water trapped between gnarled, exposed beech roots. Moments later she returned and together we walked down the side of Great Chantry towards the Bank Sett, following the field edge and keeping in the shadow of the beeches, Little'un foraging as we went. Three sturdy cubs shot out of the concealing cover of the bank, one knocking into my legs, the others bumping into the sow. Little'un grunted at the suddeness of the 'attack' but took it good naturedly. Next moment we were involved in a game; a riot of swirling badger bodies under the moon; a fleeting glimpse of striped heads or a light tail amongst the mad movement. The game ended as abruptly as it began and mutual grooming followed. Lesley herself appeared from the bank, musked my boots, then stood on hind legs against me, reaching upwards. Seeing their mother engrossed, the cubs came snuffling at my feet and musked me also. This was the first time Lesley's cubs had made physical contact with me.

It was cold and raining hard the night I discovered one of the cubs had an injury to her hind leg. Something sharp had cut into part of the pad and the young animal was limping badly. I decided to go home for some hydrogen peroxide to clean it with and be back before they went to earth. On the way back, I spoke to a WPC parked off the motorway who I was beginning to know quite well.

It was growing light by the time I returned, so I went straight to the Old Cherry Sett and sat on the great tree itself. Rolling the cub on to its back between my legs, I cleaned dirt and blood from the pad, assisted by the pouring rain. Lesley and Susie (curiosity seemed to have overcome the latter's usual caution towards me), approached to watch, their bodies shiny and dark-looking in the wet. I removed four fine slivers of glass embedded in the paw, and set the cub on her feet again. Her injury I assumed had been caused by a broken bottle in the woods.

The next night it was still raining as I checked the cub's paw, but decided there was no need to worry now as she was cleaning it well herself. I had been given some recording equipment from BBC Bristol to make a background tape for material already recorded at home, about my badgers. The equipment was quite heavy, unwieldy and valuable, so I was a little apprehensive. The moment I was ready to start, Sam appeared as if from nowhere – the one badger I had been hoping to avoid. I shooed him away and began recording on top of Cliffords Bank. A few minutes later, Sam returned and jumped up at me. I pushed him away, not realising that he had become entangled in a loop of cord; one moment I was recording, the next, being pulled along the bank. Some people make it look easy!

We were going through a period of mild weather but the past 36 hours had been wet and gusty. I had struck some young crack willows from heel cuttings and was planting them at the lakeside, 'helped' by Lesley, her three cubs, Susie and Sam. We all ended up very wet. If my young trees have survived that family, they'll survive anything. Sam ran off with my camera and, by the time I got it back any resemblance to a camera was purely accidental.

At first light the wind was surging through the barley, heaving, twisting and turning like sea swell. Waves rushed one after another, joined up, then petered out. The velvety surface seemed to hide a living beast. The white houses of the far village showed clear amongst a misty background of field upon field of green.

Waiting for me at home was a copy of the Badger Report, on the increase in badger digging and baiting and the need for strengthening legislation, compiled by the Royal Society for Nature Conservation. The publication of this report coincided with the Report Stage of the Private Members' Bill introduced by Dr. David Clark MP to close loopholes in the Wildlife and Countryside Act 1981 and to strengthen protection for the badger. I decided to photocopy it for Steve as we, like so many others, were hoping it would stop those caught digging at badger setts, excusing themselves by maintaining they were only after foxes.

The next night was the first clear, starry sky for a long time and very mild. Everything in my area was growing, including badger and fox cubs. The four young badgers were big and sturdy. Of the foxes, Josh and vixen had six cubs, while Sandy and his vixen had five.

Lesley dug out yet another entrance that morning well after first light and again it was under the bole of a chestnut coppiced long ago. The three entrances, much nearer Briarmead Lane, that Jude had dug out some weeks back, had been re-dug by him in the mild dampness. Susie was accepted by all the badgers of this sett, particularly by Lesley, which seemed to contradict observations made elsewhere of a pecking order amongst sows. However, all these animals were young and there was plenty of food and room here. Susie dug out an entrance and played briefly with Lesley's cubs who had found an empty lemonade can. When the tawnies began calling nearby, she decided it was time for bed after which the cubs lost interest and went to earth. But a short while later, as I sat writing on the Old Cherry, one cub came out again, spied the can, shook it in her jaws, obviously enjoying the rattling noise it made, and carried it to Susie's entrance, where she stood a moment on the spoil heap as if listening. Then she dropped it, whined softly and went back to earth.

It was my final day at work. After this morning I no longer had to hurry home. If I was uneasy about the badgers, I would be able to remain till I felt things were safe.

In the last week of June, Barry had cut some of the grass ley for hay. Even from a distance it smelt incredibly sweet. Lesley, the Clifford sow

29

and the four young cubs were foraging on this field as voles, mice and young rabbits, are often killed on such occasions and provide an easy meal for badgers, foxes and crows.

There was something about the Clifford cub; I had become rather fond of her. She lacked the boisterousness of Lesley's three, though physically she was robust enough. Indeed, she was her mother's daughter, very gentle and placid. When the others had gone home across the lane to the wood, I played with little Missy in the hay, rolling her over and over and tickling her till we were both hot and breathless and covered in damp wisps. I peacefully sat in the field with her in my lap and the mother came up against my legs and groomed herself. The grey sky was turning a rosy pink to the east with the Morning Star clear and bright above. The quail in the barley beyond the sett called once, twice, thrice . . . the perfect moment.

Later that day Steve brought his replacement, Inspector Tony Gould, to see me. I would miss Steve. I had such a lot to thank him for and couldn't have carried on eighteen months ago without his help. He was pleased with the Badger Report and also that the Amendment to the Act had been passed. Amongst other important matters, it put the onus on those found digging at occupied badger setts to prove that they were not after badgers.

Again I was out early that evening, and well before dark. The hours of darkness were brief and hardly dark at all. The great compensation was needing no thick clothing or anorak, although boots were a must for the long grass was nearly always dew laden.

At 4 a.m. the yearlings and I passed single-file through the barley, up the bank and on to the lane. On the opposite bank they played 'in and out' the damson trees amongst the lush grass and cleavers, the excitement mounted so I got out of the way as one ran full-tilt into another. They were quite strong animals and had bowled me over several times recently. Later a patrol came up the lane so they disappeared. One of the constables told me that Inspector Hogarth had left Oakley. I was sorry to hear this as we had got on well.

The first night of July was warm and overcast with superb visibility. The fox cubs were beginning to hunt for themselves in a small way. Their parents still fetched some food, but now left it a good distance from the den area for them to find, so encouraging them to discover their own as well as explore further afield. I was made much of by Josh who, I suspect, felt I was too engrossed with badgers. He sprang up, brush waving and as I stroked I noticed how fast he was moulting. His coat had a streaky look and my hand brought away tufts of fur which made him scratch. Sitting on his haunches, a hind leg scratching his neck, he sent drifts of fur floating on the still air, then he stood upright on three legs to rake with the fourth at his belly. His thick undercoat must have been irritating on that warm night. I left him rolling, rubbing his shoulders and squirming and twisting on the stony ground to release yet more of the loosening hairs.

Night-flying insects are everywhere at this time of year. Lacewings, cockchafers, moths and an occasional dorbeetle, blundered into me as I passed. Lesley and her three cubs caught up with me, their coats all shiny and wet, so I knew they had been foraging under the irrigation sprays. I intended to run away, which is easy when they are full of worms, but I waited along the path for the family to catch up. Badgers eat quite a number of moths and Lesley jumped to bite at three in quick succession, then the cubs followed suit, their jaws making a resounding 'snap'.

Later that morning I sat in the shade of the trees wondering about the future of this countryside. Twenty years on, would someone still be able to sit in this sun-dappled wood with birdsong all round? Would the quail still nest in the field over there and the badgers jump for moths? Or would their world be still and silent and these creatures no more?

The third night of the month was warm, after a day of brilliant sunshine. The Clifford badgers had been carrying in bedding under the full moon. Hay is a badger favourite as the sweet-smelling grass makes the softest bed.

The following Saturday of all mornings I woke up late for the first time ever. The wretched anaemia and virus infection I had contracted would be the death of me . . . or rather, the badgers. As the sky was growing light I tore out and ran through the streets, but already I felt tired and knew I'd take ages to get there. Then I met a patrol coming out of a side road and they gave me a lift to the woods right along the Wildflower Path to the sett. Fortunately all was well.

By Sunday night, Barry's hay was baled and piled in neat lines across the field. A tawny was using one such pile to hunt from. Under a clear and starry sky with a waning moon I watched the Clifford sow and her cub take in bedding.

Much later, amongst the beeches above the slope of the Old Cherry Sett, I crept up on Sam, noisily worming in the leafy wetness there. A big, grey rump and a snorting, snuffling, rustling with the occasional tearing of fibrous roots, then a sucking-up and chopping. Intermittently he sat down, scratched, belched and then had another go. One worm resisted his pulling; Sam jerked back as it broke, bit it into several pieces and swallowed what he had in his mouth. Then his flexible snout snuffled down again and searched out the rest. I stayed unseen by a beech watching the spaghetti gourmet find twenty eight more in that small, wet place. He went to earth at 4 a.m.

One warm night I watched all twelve badgers worming on Pete's land under the sprays irrigating the lettuces and in the wet earth which had been watered the previous day. The well-grown cubs at 22 weeks were proficient wormers by now. When the sprinkler saturates the earth, worms rise to the surface and are quickly sucked up by the badgers. It's surprising how long some worms are, two or three bites and a bit more sucking up, two or three bites more and a swallow. They are not quiet 'spaghetti eaters' and several badgers doing this make a surprising amount of noise.

That night I realised why Sam headbutted my legs when the others were about. He was jealous of my paying them attention. So I took avoiding action by sitting down smartly (not very smart as the lettuce field was wet) when I saw him coming. Purring loudly he climbed into my lap, nuzzled my face with a worm-mudded snout and curled himself round, still purring. The cubs came up but something in their father's slow stare made them abandon any idea of sharing his place. Lesley suddenly looked up from grooming herself, spied Sam on my lap and came purposefully towards us. I felt him tense as he lowered his head submissively, while his mate growling, brought her face close to his. Sam jumped hastily down and off, whereupon Lesley climbed aboard and settled herself in his place. It was clear who was boss in this family.

I was still far from well, breathless and exhausted, and having great difficulty getting to my area. One morning I just didn't make it, which worried me enormously. The next, I made the journey in easy stages and was sitting on a post at the top of Briarmead at 4 a.m. when a lone patrol came up and its driver chatted to me. Later, as I was walking into the wood from the top barley field on my slow way to the Old Cherry Sett, another patrol went up to the top of the lane. I was extremely glad they were around.

Dawn was gradually becoming later and the badgers were returning home later as a result. One morning when I was sitting on the 'Old'

Cherry trunk, Little'un appeared chittering and licking my face. I sat with my arms round her till I felt a wave of heat pass over me and sweat break out. The foxes and badgers I know here seem to sense if I'm unwell. Little'un settled herself on the trunk beside me and against my legs, her chin on my knee. Every so often she turned her head slightly to look up at me, then settled down again. 'Who's protecting who?' I asked her, and stroked her glossy head.

By the middle of that month I was fit again and had the unusual experience of going to sleep in the wood with Missy, the young badger from Cliffords Bank, tucked into the front of my plastic anorak. It came about like this.

Sometime after midnight I had been playing with the yearlings on Pete's land and we all ended up in a clump of thistles. The spiney leaves didn't seem to bother them, for their rubbery skin can take most things, but it was extremely uncomfortable for me. Sis stood with four paws squarely on my prone body, staring down into my face, almost asking what I was doing there. I wondered wryly why I ever started this playing with badgers, for I always seemed to come off worse!

For the preceeding couple of hot weeks, their night pattern had been consistent. The Clifford animals, as well as those from the wood, regularly wormed under whatever sprays were working on this farm, then the adults would usually sleep off a full stomach while the youngsters played, before going their separate ways. The Clifford sow and her cub might forage awhile (often now at a distance from each other), on the cut hay field or at the wood edge near their sett, bring in bedding or mutually groom. The Ashcroft badgers, in ones and twos, wandered back through the wood, foraging as they went. There were logs neatly stacked where coppicing had been done earlier that year and the light gained by the tree felling had encouraged invertebrates galore, as well as wildflowers and brambles. At night with a heavy dew, slugs would crawl over the logs in search of food so the badgers had a change from worms.

That night started mild and breezy after an evening of thunder storms and I was watching badgers worming in the newly irrigated field. Suddenly a storm erupted with thunder and lightening simultaneously overhead and there was a mad dash for the wood. Badgers don't like to be caught out in the open in such a storm, though usually they are not so bothered if deep in the wood. I trotted after their galloping bodies, not too concerned for myself but little Missy kept close to me and was clearly frightened. I picked her up (she was by now quite a weight) and sat against the old yew tree that grew out of the bank just inside the wood. Rain hardly penetrated its dense foliage. The roots and curving bole made a fine seat and the trunk, as it turned skywards, a comfortable headrest. Missy snuggled down inside my anorak and I could feel the warmth of her stocky body through my pullover. Her head was tucked hard against my chest while the storm's increasing ferocity continually lit the woods. Even through closed eyelids, the scene was as clear as day. Daylight penetrated dimly here, yet the bright, white lightening showed every detail. Each time the thunder crashed, my little companion jumped. But the torrential rain never touched us, and with my head cushioned against the ancient trunk and my body curled up protecting the cub, we both fell asleep, secure and warm, as the storm slowly passed into the distance.

A sudden clap of thunder woke us as the storm returned. We both jumped and Missy, urinating in her fright, made me very wet. I couldn't help seeing the funny side of that, as I had carefully kept out of the rain! The storm eased after nearly an hour and together we went through the wood. I saw her safely over the lane, for though the patrols were careful drivers, others were not.

The following night was dull, damp and windy and I came across three young foxes eating cherries blown down by the gusts. The barley next to the path there was almost ripe and home to many small creatures.

Above the wind soft-blowing the dry stalks, a fox cub heard a sound. Those large ears turned as he stood poised, then pounced on to a very young rabbit. His companions approached, but he snarled and they retreated to the verge.

Little'un and Sis had moved to the Bank Sett, which was a great relief to me. With so many badgers at such an accessible place as the Old Cherry Sett (one can drive a vehicle with ease to the bottom of the slope), it was very worrying. Now at least they were spreading out, yet I could see anything move at the Bank from the Cherry Sett itself. The yearling twins were very excited that morning when I came to inspect their new home. They had worked hard re-opening old entrances and turning out mouldy bedding. I decided that the next night I would take the earth and hide it to disguise the badger activity. If I had the energy, I would treat them to some of Barry's hay still lying by Cliffords Bank. It was too far for the badgers to carry back, but not for me.

Missy, helped by her elder brother Jude, had been digging out Tossy's old sett just inside the wood that was across the hay field and facing Cliffords Bank. This sett was dug out years ago by the badger diggers and the deep trench they made was still sizable though earth and other debris had been washed into it.

I was still regularly checking the Crawfords sett, which was occupied and unharmed, and often met Uglybug in the nearby garden. He would slip through the fence, tail wagging, and come up to be stroked or have a game. There was an old tyre hanging out of his reach by a rope from a yew branch, under which he would stand and growl in his frustration. Weeks earlier, I had discovered it could be lowered and on doing this, I pushed it back and forth. We had a wonderful game together but I was always careful to keep my hands well clear, recalling that he had been bred as a fighting dog, hence the terrible scars around his head and neck. He had immense strength in his jaws, head and shoulders, his teeth burying deep into the thick tyre. The game over, I would raise the tyre again and make a fuss of him, invariably having my face washed by the old dog. He apparently accepted my badger/fox smell as part of me now and after a quick sniff, took little notice of it.

The following was a warm, dry, starry night, ideal for renovating your home! I carried a huge armful of hay down Briarmead Lane for Sis and Little'un, causing great excitement, as they had to quarrel over it of course. Meanwhile I trowelled their fresh earth into an old peat bag I brought with me, took it to the Chantry and spread it about under the brambles. I repeated this nine times, till all the fresh, bright earth was gone. I made a comfortable bed of my coat and pullover, rested awhile, then returned to the hay field at Cliffords Bank and choosing the very best of the soft, sweet-smelling grass, bundled it into a great armful and returned down the lane. The 'girls' met me, jumping up and falling over themselves as they tried to take it from me. I was determined, however, to give it them only when I reached Long Field, as I'm never very happy about the badgers carrying bedding down the lane. Vehicles can come up so quickly that the animal would have no warning till too late. Putting it down at the bank end of the field, I spread it out to let them sort out their share. No quarrelling this time for there was plenty for each badger and I watched them repeatedly carry back and disappear backwards into their respective entrances.

All too soon, the sky was lightening and the stars grew pale but for Venus, clear and bright, where later the sun would rise. The tired twins went to earth and it was time for me to check the area for vehicles, so I returned to the top of the Bank where I had made my makeshift bed much earlier. My old, old coat was still there, though covered in dirty pawmarks, but my new, soft, wool pullover had vanished. I felt like taking back my hay!

As I crossed the plateau of High Ridge on my return home, I heard a volley of shots (semi-automatic?) from the scree slope below, shattering the quietness of the sunny morning. I ran to the edge and started down just as two swarthy men were coming up. Booted, with camouflage clothing almost obscured by the ammunition slung across their shoulders and around their bodies, they walked with guns at the ready, like freedom fighters from the Spanish Civil War. Both were dark haired, thickset men with moustaches, the leader medium height, in his forties, with a long, fresh, red scar above one eye and an aggressive manner. His companion was short, in his late twenties and looked embarrassed. I continued down the scree slope, recalling I had seen these men before, quite a time ago, shooting here with two others. There was no one else this morning and checking the area for cars, I found just one, a grey Chrysler. There was nothing to prove it was theirs – no gun cases lying on the seats, though they could have been stored in the boot. Later I contacted the owner of High Ridge giving him the number. He said he was anxious to stop shooting on his land, but unless people contacted him, as now, there was little he could do. I also mentioned the affair to Barry, who knew all about them. He had encountered these two some weeks before on his hay field at the back of High Ridge. The leader had what appeared to be an open razor slash over one eye. This time they were strung around with shot birds of all descriptions including finches, as well as ammunition, and offered to pay the farmer £1,000 a year for shooting rights over his land. When I expressed surprise at this sum, Barry just laughed and said that was nothing compared with what had in the past been offered by others. He told them to get out and stay out, and they meekly left. How I wished I had Barry's persuasive powers!

The producer of my *Badger Lady* programme on Radio 4 contacted me to discuss all the mail we had received and what he planned to do about it. He wanted me to give some sort of acknowledgement (to be read by someone else, fortunately) to the letters and the concern they expressed. The most common cry had been 'What can we do to help badgers? Is there a badger group locally and if not, how can we start one?' The same query came from Wales, Cornwall, Northumberland, the Midlands and the Home Counties. I had never imagined this sort of response when the interviewer sat asking me questions and recording my answers in our living room. The producer asked me what advice I would give and I said people should contact their local RSPCA inspector and the police would explain the law, advise and collate the information gained from sett-mapping and the noting of numbers. But most importantly, people must work with police backing and not alone.

After he had rung off, I contacted the RSPCA at Horsham to ask Steve Hammond his opinion. He pointed out that the police in my area were exceptionally helpful and recommended that people should contact their RSPCA inspector who, if he was worth his salt, would advise, explain and make any necessary police contact himself.

That night I discovered that a badger had been digging-out in the Chantry at Old Joe's Sett. I fetched my trowel to hide the earth under the beach leaves wondering which animal it was, when Jude came out of a sett entrance to investigate what I was doing with his spoil heap. He nosed the earth as I tucked it away, breathed in and exhaled sharply, spraying my hand and wrist with tiny droplets. I stroked his face gently and he nuzzled my face in return. My badgers accept what I do without protest, merely looking at me with gentle eyes. I went on to Pete's land, following Jude who collected hay for his newly dug sett, carrying it backwards at speed across Little Chantry Field, and along the tortuous trail through the Chantry itself.

As I walked home up Brairmead Lane, the banks were alive with bees, birds and insects round the flowers and seeding grasses growing there. This is a beautiful piece of countryside which in summer is a colour pattern of fields interlocked with each other and the woodland curving round. The pea fields were still green, as was the wood. The oilseed-rape had a lumpy brown-streaked look, the barley and wheat were flaxen and the sky, a vivid blue. I was surprised at the two oak track by Sandy's little vixen stepping out of the barley. I squatted down and she put her face close to mine, then together we strolled along the path to where it cuts through Cliffords Bank. Her well grown cubs denned under the old straw bales stacked amongst the rape. Barry had told me that he saw them sometimes as he drove through his land, sunning themselves on top of them. At the Poplar Row the vixen continued on through the orchard, whilst I turned towards High Ridge and home. My foxes looked scruffy now but by September they would be superb again – and, unfortunately have pelt value.

The third week of July brought hot, hot days. Some evenings there was thunder in the air and occasional rain spots. The nights were warm and dull. One such night Lesley met me in the company of Josh and his vixen. The foxes slipped away and together we walked to Briarmead. I sat in the hedgerow there and made much of her, my lovely badger. She musked and fussed me, then I followed her through the damson trees and on to Sandpit Field. First she tried running the wheat heads through her jaws, standing on hind legs to do so, but it wasn't quite ripe enough for the grain to drop into her mouth. Then, with the badger's character-istic sideways swipe, she sent some stalks to the ground and stood holding them down with her front paws, biting at the grain. Badgers certainly do a certain amount of damage on farmland, though Barry had said that here they do too little to take into account. A problem some years ago had been the undermining of the farm track and field above the sett in Cliffords Bank. It was then a wheat field and the farmer and his men had been forced to cut several acres by hand that season. They had tried infilling the offending entrances with flints and earth, but to no avail as the badgers had simply dug them out again. Later that year I suggested filling the holes with rags and newspapers soaked in old diesel oil and then infilling with earth. This had been completely successful, the badgers made new entrances along the Bank where they did no damage and we never had the problem again*.

The sky was overcast, so it was still quite dark when Lesley went home through the wheat to the Old Cherry Sett. Part of the great trunk was covered with broken cherry stones that the hawfinches had cracked. I noticed that the squirrels ate the cherry flesh, but seemed to leave the stones. It had started to rain so the light was still very poor. At the Crater Sett I watched the tawny fledglings flying and calling one to another until the parents came into the wood to roost. Owls hunt outside the wood once the foliage becomes thick, as they need a certain amount of light by which to see their prey. There was a great noise of caterwauling and kewiking before they finally settled down.

I had a look at my wild service trees then walked round sett-checking. I startled the Bank Sett badgers out playing in the edge of the barley on Long Field. They dashed up the bank and home. I sat halfway up the steep bank and emptied my boots of the odd bits and pieces that tend to drop into them. Next momemt I was bundled from behind and fell headlong into the corn, hitting my head on the hard earth below. Little'un looked down at me lying there, clearly wondering why I didn't play with her. I'm sure it was she, not Sis, who had taken my new jersey for bedding!

At the end of July I heard that Don Francis had arranged a terrier/lurcher show. Steve Hammond first told me about this annual event and had meant to go but left before he had a chance, so I decided I'd keep faith with him and go myself. When I arrived I was very glad it was so crowded, as I saw several familiar faces that wouldn't have been pleased to see mine!

I had never realised before just how many different terrier breeds are bred and worked for the sport. There were several beautiful little

*By the time this book is published there may be new regulations making this illegal, as pesticides, diesel oil, creosote etc. are now widely misused to exterminate 'inconvenient' wild life on proposed building sites, agricultural and recreational land.

coal-black Patterdales in the Lakeland/Fell terrier class. All dogs must be on leads at these events and since dogs are commonly bought and sold at such shows, Pit Bull terriers amongst them, this was just as well. The latter were not being shown, but were very aggressive towards any and every other dog, which is the purpose for which they are bred. Pit Bulls seem to swell up when challenging, rather than raising their hackles like other dogs. As usual it was the lurchers which held my attention. The matching couples were superb and I was soon engrossed. At one stage, I happened to look across the show ring and saw the young man I had encountered several times with badger-digging groups in Ashcroft Woods. This brought me up short, as the most recent occasion had been that April when his companion broke my arm. An equally familiar face was that of a man showing a lurcher. I knew him as a digger with terriers in our woods, but this would suggest he also lamped. I caught snatches of conversation from both sides. On my right two men were discussing the gameness of a Patterdale belonging to one of them, who proudly recounted a recent fight when it had been put to a badger, and pointed out its fresh scars as evidence. On my left were two friends who apparently bred fighting cocks, one was taking orders at the show. I had never realised how openly these things were discussed and wished that Steve could have attended with me. I had no power to do anything; a plain-clothes constable or RSPCA inspector could have mingled so usefully with that crowd, but everyone had been too busy elsewhere.

I was determined to keep the Patterdale and its proud owner in sight and was quite successful for perhaps half an hour, until I became aware that I was being followed myself, by three men, two of them strangers and one I had certainly seen before. I left the grounds and took the first bus that came along; it was going in the wrong direction but perhaps this was just as well.

Chapter 3

August began with heavy showers, it was very warm and there was thunder in the air. Every badger here was digging out and whichever sett I approached, I would hear grunting and snorting from below, or see a grey rump as its owner backed out with the earth. Throughout that first week there was a fair amount of this activity, but one night even the cubs were digging. Very old, long-disused entrances were opened up amongst the Scots pines growing in the area between the Felled Logs and Crater Setts and the edge of these woods. Bearing in mind that they are connected, (though for convenience I label them as separate setts), this part of Ashcroft Woods must be honeycombed with underground tunnels. It was at the Felled Logs that Lesley's father Joe, as a young badger, turned out the glazed fragments of a Romano-British tile on to his spoil heap. By now, two of Lesley's cubs were denning at the Scots pines. Unharassed and with good feeding, some cubs quickly gain enough confidence to be independent, though I have noticed they are likely to rush home to their mother if things go wrong.

One wet, dull dawn I came round to the cubs' new home just as two jack russells backed out of their entrance. One started to go down again, so I grasped it by the collar and neck with my left hand. It set up a snarling as it twisted and turned, whereupon its companion bit into my right hand and thumb, hanging on grimly. To dislodge it, I had to let go of the first terrier. Fortunately I wore wellingtons, as by now both animals were trying to bite my legs. Then one tried to go back into the sett again, and picking up a piece of branch, I stopped it. There was no sign of their owner, though the noise made by the thwarted dogs must have carried quite a distance. I stayed long after they had gone, just in case they might return, and wondered how the badger cubs had fared. Twenty minutes later, I heard someone whistling, so it could have been the owner out walking his jack russells and only bothering to call them when he returned to his car. As it happened, both the badger cubs seemed no worse for their terrier encounter and were firmly entrenched in their new home. The incident had served to remind me, however, just how vulnerable they were on their own, for terriers could find their way into that sett at any time.

When next I met Barry Hains I told him about the terriers. He knew of one dog owner who regularly sat reading a newspaper in his car, parked by the wood, until his dog reappeared. He wasn't quite sure whether it took itself for a walk or whether the man got tired of calling it! Barry sees a lot more of what goes on in the day here than I do. We discussed the lamping problem, as neither of us were happy at the prospect of autumn. He said last year he saw adverts offering £25 a fox pelt; this autumn the price would probably be up. This led on naturally, to my visit to the terrier/lurcher show and the 'familiar faces' seen there and I asked him if he ever went to these events. The farmer shook his head, laughing, and remarked that he had enough problems without looking for trouble, adding 'I bet someone found your face familiar too'. I didn't like to admit that they had!

The following night saw a crescent moon struggling through ragged clouds; by 3 a.m. we had rain in full moonlight and I almost expected a rainbow! An hour later there was thunder and lightening directly overhead and Lesley and her cubs, who were with me, made a dash for home. In moments I was soaked to the skin in spite of my plastic anorak. It was one solid sheet of water as if poured from a bucket and I had never known Briarmead so deeply or extensively flooded. There was no more thunder, just torential rain and it was difficult to keep upright as the woodland paths were surging streams. I couldn't clear my eyes of water, for as fast as I rubbed it away, more rain ran in. Then I heard a whicker and there were Little'un and Sis in the undergrowth. They came out and went with me, shaking themselves, dog-like, every few yards. At the old yew tree we parted company, they to their sett in the bank, while I struggled homewards across Pete's farmland. No need to guard the setts that morning!

By the next dawn it was cold and windy, though the rain was easing. Everywhere the grain was dropping from the sodden husks and all the fields of barley and wheat were ripe and spoiling. Leaves and branches had been blown down in the wood and both foxes and badgers were finding the dead squirrels an easy meal.

As the nights passed, the two young badgers at the Pine Sett seemed quite happy and settled. Their mother Lesley, together with her other cubs (all sows), were denning at the Felled Logs. Scots pine grows abundantly in this part of the wood and several were dead, some with large 'plates' of bark coming away. I watched Lesley rear up and pull off one such piece, using her teeth and claws. The beetles and insects beneath surprised me by their numbers. Lesley wouldn't let the cubs investigate her piece of bark but, turned on them, growling , so they pulled off their own pieces from another dead pine nearby. She was making them find, and fend, for themselves.

The police still patrolled the lane when they could and that morning the WPC I had seen several times before here, stopped her car and we stood talking. It was reassuring to know they were about. Walking round the wood at 7.15 a.m., I startled a young tawny. As he flew up I 'called' and he perched halfway up a silver birch and tried hooting back. At the Old Cherry Sett, a second flush of small, but bright foxgloves were in bloom and fungi had appeared everywhere with a preponderance of stinkhorns. I also found my first blackberries and wondered if the badgers had discovered them yet.

Steve Hammond came one evening. He had promised to call whenever he was in the neighbourhood. Inevitably we talked 'shop', progressing from badgers to dogs, and discussed the number of 'phone calls to the RSPCA from people who had been stopped whilst walking their bull-terriers and asked if they would care to fight them for a good fee. One such dog owner was stopped on Brighton beach! It was tempting to suggest that plain clothes RSPCA officials try dog walking, but obviously the lost man hours would be prohibitive. Members of the public had offered to take up such suggestions in order to find out times and locations but Steve said the dangers in this were considerable.

That evening I phoned John Shaw, asking if he would let me know as soon as he noticed lampers on his land. We both agreed it was inevitable, but at least, with no job to go to now, I could be out all and every night to try and catch them.

Going out early on Sunday 18th August, I was nearly at the far end of my street when a van passed just ahead of me and went on under the railway bridge. I crossed the road and started along the next, when I happened to look back in time to see another van go in the same direction. What was being delivered at 3.15 a.m. on a Sunday?

I reached the old house about ten minutes later and stood in the shadows by the sheds, watching them unloading the vans while the owner of the house supervised from the doorway. The long, thin, crates seemed very heavy and needed both drivers to carry one between them. These were taken indoors and I remembered the cellars of the old place. There was a movement just ahead and I spoke softly as my friendly guard dog came to my side. By now the activity had ceased; the door closed with light showing from a window and the two vans parked nearby. I decided to take the vehicle numbers and was almost close enough when the bull terrier by my side began to snarl. Instantly answering barks came from the nearest van. I disappeared up the bank and under the trees as the front door opened and a man's voice shouted. Next moment my faithful friend was at my side again, still grumbling to himself. Then a moist nose was pushed under my arm which I put round him, stroking the far side of his face. I could feel the pucker marks under his jaw and muzzle and for the first time looked really carefully at his scars. One on his throat and another at the side of his neck were not the bite of a dog at all, but a grip mark and tear – the tell-tale scar from a badger. He pulled away a little as I felt an old scar on top of his head; he didn't want it touched.

The door re-opened and light flooded out. There were voices, but I was too far away to hear the words. One van drove off and after a few minutes the second van followed. I waited till the door closed, then slipped away through the trees at the back of the grounds. Turning at the barn, I saw a solitary white 'ghost' watching me go. I felt sorry for Uglybug and hoped I hadn't got him into trouble with his master. I recalled being told about the other dog he had owned. It 'had been put to fight and later, had been beaten and received amongst other injuries, a dislocated leg'. If the owner ever found his dog in my company, it would bode ill for the old warrior.

The Friday before August Bank Holiday had been a mild, starry night with slight wind. Lesley had kept me in sight ever since I first arrived at 1 a.m. I normally try not to be too involved with her three little daughters and hadn't named them for that reason, unlike Little'un and Sis, their 'big sisters' of last year. However, with their mother pushing her snout on to my lap this night, I had no chance to ignore them.

Later I went round to the Old Cherry Sett with Sam to find nearly all the entrances stopped up. This was the work of professionals – the earth from the top of each hole shovelled in and trodden down. Was that why Lesley had been shadowing me? The entrance that she and the others had been so busy enlarging, had sticks lying on the top of the soil. I assumed this hole was criss-crossed with them and the animals, finding the other exits blocked, pushed away the sticks from this as they emerged. It was August Bank Holiday weekend and someone wanted badger sport. They would probably return today or tomorrow to see whether the earth or the sticks had been moved and send the terriers down that entrance. Alternatively, perhaps they were disturbed yesterday whilst stopping the entrances. In theory a terrier would normally smell fresh badger where the animal was denning, but the badgers here had opened up so many entrances (eighteen in all) and were using them regularly which might cause confusion. I decided it best to wait there all day until it was dark, as that seemed the only way to protect the badgers. The immediate problem was to phone the police without leaving the badgers unguarded. I would stay well into the morning until there were people about, then go down the lane to phone. A man and woman in their thirties unexpectedly appeared and parked a car at the Briarmead end of the Wildflower Path. They walked past me as I stood along the winding trail of the Old Cherry Sett and said 'good morning' to me as they continued, followed by their black labrador. At 5.30 a.m. in Ashcroft Woods this was a very unusual occurance and I had never seen them before, though they obviously knew the place.

Finally, I ran down Briarmead and phoned Sergeant Warren Hughes from Newby Farm. Barry drove into the yard to feed the horses and gave me a lift back to the Cherry Sett where I showed him the filled-in entrances. The chestnut-bough one had a rotten branch pushed into it. Just then, Alfie brought the combine across the fields and his boss went off to help him finish the barley. Minutes later, Warren drove along the Wildflower Path and together we walked the area, checking the entrances and discussing possible routes by which the badger-diggers could come. He said he would draw a map and let the patrols have a copy. I explained that I would stay until it was dark, so he promised to leave a note for my family. He thought the hunters might spot the patrol cars, but then, they could spot me too, so it was something we had to chance.

Around midday the sergeant returned saying he had left the message and asking what he could get me to eat and drink. I hadn't expected anything like this when I had phoned him, so was very grateful for his kindness. A little later two youths on horseback cantered along the path below the sett. The WPC I now knew as Jane with a constable, drove up and chatted, parking their patrol car well inside the wood. A radio was mentioned and the constable suggested I should ask Warren when he returned with my 'rations'. This I did and was told that if there was a radio spare, the sergeant taking over from him would bring it.

All morning I had stayed well behind a chestnut standard at a short distance from the unstopped sett entrance and well out of sight. Amongst the overgrown coppicing, it was the only tree large enough to hide me. I decided to eat, have a drink, and stretch my legs. I ate some of the contents of a bag of crisps, then sat the bag against the roots of the big tree and walked to the top of the ridge keeping a sharp lookout for any movement. The wind was getting up and the sky darkening; the only sounds were the distant motorway, the nearer throb of the combine and the wind rushing and sighing in the treetops. I was hoping and praying I'd get the radio – how marvellous it would be to actually let some diggers start, then call in the patrol. I returned to the chestnut to find, poking round its bole, a little grey rump with a whittish tail – one of Lesley's cubs with her head deep in the crisp bag, noisily sucking up the last few pieces. I gently tapped the rump and a blue crisp packet looked my way. I picked her up and took it off her snout as she snuffled my face and hair, her sturdy little body cradled in my arms. In that moment – so unexpected, yet so intimate – I vowed I'd stay every day from pre-dawn to nightfall, Friday to Monday of the Bank Holiday if necessary – anything to save them being dug out. All seven animals of Lesley's family were now denning at this sett and she was Old Joe's daughter. They wouldn't suffer his fate. I failed him; I'd not fail these.

The badgers knew I was around and I expect they heard me speaking to the sergeant. I put the young animal down at the entrance, watched her go below, then I went back to the chestnut to keep watch. The hours passed, the rain held off and a wind blew the slender coppicing. Meanwhile, Alfie had finished the far field and taken the combine up on to Great Chantry Field. People were walking their dogs on the path below now, so I doubted if anything would occur for a while.

Some time later a car slipped quietly into the wood – the new sergeant with the radio. He showed me how to use it, gave me extra batteries, and told me I could probably keep it over the holiday and return it to the station on Tuesday. Stern-faced, the sergeant informed me that the radio cost over £250, then grinned as he added 'So I'll leave you with the words we get. If you're about to be assaulted, not to worry, but for Christ's sake, hide the radio!' and went off down the slope. I couldn't have answered for laughing – they really were great. I would have to go to the top of the ridge to make contact, I decided, as there were too many trees and hills between here and Oakley station.

Two hours later a young constable in a patrol car, with a photocopy of Warren's map on the seat beside him, told me he was getting to know his way around while it was still light. At 9 p.m. when it was quite dark I walked home across the fields.

On Saturday morning Briarmead was flooded to a depth of 12 inches. It had been raining hard since midnight and few vehicles could get up the lane now, but there were other ways of entering the wood.

By midmorning, I was soaked to the skin in spite of my plastic anorak and shivering non-stop so I went home to change into dry clothes and came straight back – to sunshine and a gusty wind and, best of all, to an untouched sett.

Before leaving home I had phoned Tony Gould of the RSPCA. He was in Steve's old house, but wasn't officially designated to this area till the end of the month. He apologised for not being able to do anything as he was still working his city area. I couldn't help feeling that I had fallen on my feet again with another dedicated RSPCA inspector.

That afternoon I sat behind my tree with the slender coppicing all around and watched the squirrels in the leafiness above, whilst the church bells of Warby floated on the wind like singing voices. A bank vole darted to my shoe, picked up a chestnut and holding it in its delicate paws, sat and nibbled, turning it to peel off the shiny casing as it did so. It stopped to listen, whiskers aquiver, nibble, nibble. Then a chestnut's prickly bur dropped down beside us and we both jumped – the vole had gone. The bells still sang, sometimes clear, sometimes faint, beckoning to the little church in the valley. They evoked its mellow stone, old chancel and crumbling graveyard. This coppicing reaching upwards were the columns of a nave; this wind sighing in the trees were its bells. My church is here in a wood which was old when that was built; my stained glass, the sunlight shining through its leaves.

Later I walked unobtrusively from sett to sett and came back to the Old Cherry to find a patrol car tucked away well off the lower path. It was Philip who had come to see me in April. He thought Saturday evening would be a likely time to look around as the diggers might think the police were busy elsewhere.

The following night I checked all my badgers. I found twelve healthy animals full of high spirits and a certain endearing little Miss checked me (probably for crisps), then purred loudly into my face. Lesley's family were beginning to use some bramble-hidden entrances over-looked by the men who had stopped up the sett. Sam tried to dig out the rotten branch protruding from the chestnut-bough hole; he couldn't and it would need all my strength, but I decided to leave it for now.

I timed the two routes I would take to reach the places where I could make contact with the radio. I would have to go to the left, as the badger-diggers would be blocking me in on my right. It took three minutes up to the ridge as there was no path, only brambles. I spent an hour and a half making a proper path by dragging the brambles aside and raking the ground flat with the toe of my boot, so that I could now make it to the ridge noiselessly in less than a minute.

I was feeling drowsy and kept dropping off – literally – the result was rather painful but it made me stay awake. There were bees and brown butterflies on the wild marjoram; two gatekeepers and four meadow browns. There were so many colours, the vivid yellow and orange flowers of toadflax, the blues of the harebells and bellflowers, the black bryony leaves turning – the Wildflower Path was living up to its name.

By now my back was paining me so I went up to the top of the slope and stretched out on my anorak under the pollarded hornbeam there. I could hear everything from this point, but couldn't be seen.

This was the strangest Bank Holiday I had ever known. I hoped the diggers would come, then all the effort, especially of the constables, would have been worthwhile.

Bank Holiday Monday dawned dry and gusty. Later I saw Jane and a constable patrol on Briarmead. I had checked the badgers when I arrived. While I thought something had alerted the badger-diggers, I was loth to leave the area, although desperately tired. The harvest was unusually late here, so perhaps all the activity on the nearby fields had frightened the diggers off. They must have known that the longer they waited, the more chance there was of someone noticing the stopped entrances and reporting it.

I returned to the Old Cherry Sett. All was quiet there except for the wind in the trees. I didn't think the terriermen would turn up, but stayed until nightfall, just in case. Lesley, Sam and their family were unharmed and that was the main thing. I would always be grateful to the police for their backup that weekend.

Dusk found me lying on my plastic anorak in the undergrowth just above the main sett entrance, trying to ease the gnawing pain in my spine. I had been sitting still too long, but was anxious not to walk about as this was an ideal time for someone to come. Listening for any sounds of human movement I could just hear the faint sound of shotgun fire in the distance – and thought I heard a badger snuffle, but dismissed it as tiredness. Minutes passed then something damp touched my cheek and opening my eyes, I looked into Lesley's. I put my arms round her long neck and felt the vibration of her purring, the soft fur of her matronly head against my face. Like all the badgers here, she was beginning to put on weight for the lean months ahead. She snuffled the pullover showing above my coat collar, licked my face, then still purring, began to groom my hair. There was more rustling through the brambles and three small ladies were upon me, whickering, musking and purring, so I struggled upright with a lapfull of cubs. I could hear the shooting much nearer now and through the foliage I saw two young men returning home, firing as they went. Jumping to my feet, I led the badgers out of the wood, across the lane and into the safety of Barry's fields, from where I watched them amble off, their swaying figures disappearing amongst the stubble, foraging as they went.

Two mornings later I watched the rising sun cast a golden glow over the straw bales. The wall of trees surrounding Long Field were etched against a pale sky, dappled in pink cloud. Earlier, the badgers had been playing in and out of the bales – even the adults affected by the high spirits of their offspring. Bales have such play potential, climb on to a single one and you can dare your sisters to push you off; hide behind a stack of them or run circles round them. If a rustling betrays the presence of a mouse, then everyone gets excited. A lapwing flew down, intending to stay, but seeing the badgers it wisely changed its mind leaving the cubs staring after it in disappointment.

As I started checking the setts I realised the whole family, Lesley, Sam, their three cubs and the two yearling daughters – Little'un and Sis – seemed to be making a 'double' home, as they were taking in straw from Great Chantry to the Bank Sett, though all but Little'un and Sis were still denning at the Cherry. I imagined, this was due to the blocked entrances at the Cherry Sett. Yesterday, with some difficulty, I had pulled the rotten branch out of the chestnut-bough entrance, as having that one stopped, seemed to have bothered the animals more than all the others. Hadn't disturbed anything before then in case the diggers had turned up, as it would have shown that someone was aware of what was happening. Suddenly Sam appeared, his face and snout all covered in wisps, and snuffled first my left hand, then my right. I told him that if he was looking for gloves he'd need to wait a couple of months, then tweaked his tail, and he ran round me barking.

This was to be our last game together. The next night I found his body thrown under a hedge. He had been knocked down as he crossed the lane and must have been killed instantly. Sam's snout the most vulnerable part of the creature, was smashed to a pulp.

The last two days of August brought sunshine, cloudless blue skies with clear, cold, starry nights, full moon and early morning mist. Climbing about amongst the dead wood in the Chantry, I became aware I wasn't alone – a young dogfox was watching me with great interest with its head inclined, so I barked it up.

It jumped lightly onto my tree trunk and came towards me. Another young fox appeared and together we scrambled across the dead beeches, held slantingly upright by the living, like a giant game of Jack Straws. One pawed at a piece of loose bark and I pulled it off to let him devour the moths and beetles, as well as fungi, slugs, caterpillers and woodlice. Then my foot slipped on a moss-covered trunk and I fell headlong. As I lay getting my breath back, I opened my eyes to see two heads side by side silhouetted against the sky, large ears forward, eyes reflecting bluely in the moonlight. I wondered how people can call these creatures vermin. It could equally well be said of the foxhound, terrier or lurcher as they are all of the *Canidae* family and have so many attributes in common.

I had avoided the badgers since Sam's death and had no heart to play with them. But Lesley found me sitting on the Old Cherry when she returned that morning and settled between my legs. I stroked the smooth, sleek fur of her long neck as she thrust her snout into my hand. She had found her mate's body and I wondered what death meant to them.

In September I discovered the entrances of the Chantry Sett had been stopped up; Jude had dug his way out and joined the other yearlings, Sis Little'un and his sister Jet, in the Bank Sett between Great Chantry and Long Field. This sett is visible from the Old Cherry, so it meant I could guard all the badgers in this wood, (except Susie who had moved to the Crater Sett) whilst standing on its slope. The three young sows made Jude welcome with much purring and musking, as the young boar was coming into his own now that Sam's scent had vanished from the area.

One night the Clifford sow and her cub, Missy, dug out a wasp's nest, which had been formed inside an old rabbit burrow, on the wood edge. I was surprised they hadn't found it before, but possibly the wind had never been in the right direction. Several times I had watched the busy wasps pass to and from the great clump of common figwort a few metres away. To human eyes the nest was obvious, but the badgers located it by smell. Both sows went to pass along their usual route, but stopped short, snouts aquiver. They darted about scenting the air, looking far larger than normal with their fur fluffed up. Then both dug down, not into the burrow entrance where by day the insects emerge, but from above and behind the nest. In a few moments the ground was covered in fresh earth. They seemed to eat everything – grubs, honey and the nest itself, as well as its inhabitants. Belatedly, the wasps began to retaliate, but I suspect the suddenness of the attack in the dark was to the badgers' advantage. Some obviously stung the plunderers, but they continued to feed unperturbed, scattering soil and nest debris over a wide area. Recalling my past encounters in badger company with angry wasps, I retreated well out of the way. Much later, Missy and her mother were still licking their paws and curling their long tongues up over snouts to get the last remnants of sticky sweetness.

Autumn, the season of plenty was upon us – rowan, honeysuckle, guelder rose, wayfaring and elderberries, acorns, beechmast, cobnuts, crab-apples, damsons and sweet chestnuts.

Saturday 7th September was a cold, clear, frosty night with a waning moon. I was recording tawny vocalisation over an old tape of tawny song, when my finger slipped and the tape played back instead of recording. The hen owl in the tree above me began 'answering' the tape which happened to be of her mate. Her answers became more and more excited with less interval between each cry and the sound intensifying. She flew down to a branch just above me, so I held out the tape recorder and the next moment, she was perched, half on my hand, half on the source of the sound. She located the microphone immediately, soft-calling the contact call to it again and again – a lovely call interspersed with gentle, throaty cries.

I met Lesley and her cubs on the ridge and walked down to the Old Cherry Sett with them, our breath vapourising in the cold, moonlit air. Alfie had been liming the fields, so we all had white feet. I noticed a thick twig stuck down the main entrance, assumed it had blown down and wondered why the badgers hadn't moved it. Obviously they had emerged from another entrance. The crisp-thieving cub pulled at it half-heartedly but it didn't budge, and when I moved it I found it had been deliberately twisted into the opening. If Lesley had not been so apprehensive after the Bank Holiday sett-stopping she could have dug it out, but the badgers here were becoming wary, too much was happening to their sett.

The next night was cloudy and mild with a slight wind. I met Missy without her mother. They were probably foraging separately, but I wanted to check. At 3.40 a.m. Missy decided to carry back straw from the Top Field, Prossers Wood, where John Shaw and Rob had been harvesting the previous afternoon. I started to help her by bringing a load myself. When she had taken hers below, she returned to me and selected bits from mine. Clearly I was not a very good bedding collector, so I took the rejects back to where I had found them, rather than leave straw or hay lying above ground near a sett.

I stayed in the wood a little longer (carefully avoiding a shotgun enthusiast), and for a time watched squirrels and woodpigeons together, feeding on acorns strewn along a path. Already the leaves were beginning to turn, especially the beautiful red cherry leaves. Some were already drifting earthwards. The paths were dusty, though the undergrowth was still moist.

The Clifford sow was missing. I resolved to search the wood and fields for her after badger watch. It was a dull, mild morning and at 6.40 a.m. only a few birds were singing – turtle-dove, mistle-thrush and robin. In Glebe farmyard Rob was preparing the great combine for the day's work. They hadn't finished harvesting the previous evening till 8 p.m. He told me that he and his wife had been woken by brilliant light shining through their cottage window at around midnight. Lampers were working far upfield, but the beams could travel a long way and obviously, the lurchermen didn't realise. Rob apologised for not doing anything about them; he was too tired even to go across the yard and phone John. I mentioned the missing sow and asked if they could keep a lookout for her body, as they harvested the wheat below the sett Bank.

I decided to start my search in Prossers Wood, since I had seen Missy there that night and she had seemed rather loth to leave the area. I was inclined to divide the wood into sections, searching each thoroughly, but first went down to the flints and stood on top of the huge pile, looking around at the trees and undergrowth from this vantage point. The sun outside was dappling the darkness; it was going to be another fine day. I jumped down to walk round the flints, marvelling at the size of some of them.

Suddenly, I saw the old badger. She was crouched at the bottom of the mound watching me, her left paw trapped beneath a huge flint. I scraped around the flint with my penknife, pushing the blade further and further in and found some small stones to force into the cavity I had made, hoping to relieve the weight on the limb. Clearly this had eased the pressure, but the paw was still caught and her snout passed over my hand with an unusual dryness. I recalled the uneaten apple in my bag and offered it to her; two quick crunches and it was gone. The only way to release the paw was to try to raise the huge flint for a few moments. If however, the limb was too numbed for her to remove, it would be seriously injured when I had to let go. Together we worked at the leg, I massaging, she licking. Then I went above and gripped hard on the flint. Nothing happened! I took a deep breath and tried again. For a moment it stubbornly remained, then slowly, I felt it give and the paw slipped out; I heard a click of claws on the flint.

I left the sow and returned to the wood edge to find blackberries and elderberries. The sun was hot on my back as I picked. When I returned,

Missy's mother was busy washing the paw. As I laid the ripe fruit beside her, her snout quivered, her jaws passed over and it was gone. I stroked the head of a very hungry badger and wondered how to return her to the sett and safety. She followed me to the wood edge slowly, yet willingly enough, but the sun blinded her immediately. I wondered if she would stay for the daylight hours in the undergrowth, but no, she refused to go back. Fortunately, the paw wasn't broken and though she hobbled, it was the brilliant sunshine that distressed her most. We came slowly to the dying rosebay-willow-herb growing amongst the bracken at the side of High Ridge. She thrust her long head into it, then her whole body, and lay down. I waited with her anxiously. She couldn't remain there, where she was obvious to anyone passing by, so I stood up and began to walk on. Much as the sun worried her, being left behind worried her more. It seemed an age before we reached the sett, especially as I saw a man walking his dog, far behind us but coming our way. When we reached Cliffords Bank the sow ducked her head and disappeared immediately into the leafy darkness. I walked a short way picking blackberries and waited for the owner and dog to pass. When they had gone, I knelt down and laid the blackberries just inside the badger-path, hidden by the elmbrush. At the same moment a soft snout touched my hand and the fruit was gone. Stretching into the cool greenesss, I found and stroked her head. Then I got to my feet and returned along the side of High Ridge.

I was now going to my area early in the evening to check for lampers and staying over till the morning. The moon was a thin crescent, not rising till well after 1 a.m., so by the weekend we would have moonless nights which are ideal for lamping. I watched tiny vericoloured snails, some on the track, some climbing the tall grass stems. These banded snails are very pretty when you can see their colours before the sun gets high in the sky and they creep back into hiding. Watching them had attracted Lesley and her cubs and sadly there followed a series of greedy crunches. Apart from Crisp, I hadn't named these young sows, so decided to call the largest with the untidy fur Curly and the smallest one Candy. Curly went one better than her sisters and followed a slime trail to its owner on the track.

The Clifford sow seemed little the worse for her mishap, except for a bruised paw. She came purring to meet me that night and musked my shoes. I sat by the bank, took her paw in both hands and gently felt it all over to check that nothing was broken. Meanwhile its owner thoroughly washed my right ear, then decided my hair had some tatty bits. She and Missy were the gentlest of creatures.

All the badgers went gleaning grain fallen from the wheat harvested that day, then off to the old woodpile by the end of the Poplar Row to search for slugs. Next they wandered into the orchard and found some fallen pears. There were still some blackberries growing by the embankment and ripe damsons too.

Much later I was sitting on the old cherry listening to the tawnies and the wind softly passing through the trees, when Lesley and family returned, their snouts and paws all muddy, their backs shining with wet from the sprays of Colts Farm. Crisp looked as if she had been rolling, for her coat was thick with mud. They all made a fuss of me, then sat in the hollow, mutually grooming. I wished they had done it the other way round, as I had to go home through streets and now even my hair was muddy.

On Thursday 12th September I was with Missy and her mother under the pear trees in the orchard, when a beam shone along the Poplar Row, so near and so unexpected that for a moment I just stood, turned to stone. Then something thrust against my leg and looking down, I saw the old sow staring up. A great anger swept over me and turning, I ran to the railway, the two badgers following. With the trees between us, we had a chance. Along the chain link we went and so to the side of Top Field. We were cut off from the Bank, their sett and safety. The lampers hadn't discovered us, but the beam was like a searchlight spilling over the land, eating all in its path. Suddenly I realised we were at the railway crossing where the stiles, torn apart by previous lampers, were still unmended. The badgers had never crossed here; it is the limit of their territory – a totally alien world of gleaming rails and clinker. They just stood with the beam coming closer, as I tried to urge them over the rails. I ran back and scooped up Missy, who twisted and turned in fear, the green light up rail reflected in her eyes. She was heavy; I could never carry her mother; but we were across. As I gently put her down on the other side, I found the old sow had followed us over. We crouched in the bracken just in time as the beam snaked across our escape route and shone on to the field behind us. Then a hum grew into a singing as a goods train approached and passed slowly and heavily, taking its time.

(I have been known to bless British Rail before but never with such fervour.) The silence crowded in when it had gone, the vibration all about us. But the beam and lurchers were far away now, out of sight.

When we retraced our route to the Top Field, the lampers had gone. It would have been ideal to have tracked down their vehicle, but the badgers' immediate welfare had been my first concern. Animals recover quickly from a fright; I left the sows to their foraging and walked across the stubble, searching the hard, dry earth for any sign of fresh tyre marks. A van could be driven anywhere on to these fields.

Later that morning I spoke to Barry and told him of the lampers. It would seem that the vehicle was parked on the Briarmead track, so next time there are lurchermen and the badgers are not in the vicinity, I would check there. Vehicle numbers are of primary importance, though as Barry commented, they would probably be registered in a previous owner. The conversation turned to foxes. Barry is a keen rider and said that when he went on a fox hunting holiday to southern Ireland some years ago, he found they had imported English foxes, as shooting and snaring for pelts had practically exterminated the native population. It is a pity fox fur is so popular and the price so good for a prime pelt.

By 13th September the Clifford sow was in fine fettle and her leg almost back to normal.

When the badgers had gone to earth, I sat on the old cherry trunk while an adult tawny called nearby. He flew a short distance and perched in a coppiced chestnut; then flew slowly round me and perched facing me. Next he descended on to the old tree itself, watching me closely. Deep in my thoughts I had taken little notice, but now calling softly, I raised my left hand and the owl perched on my thumb. I laid my hand against my thigh, partly to rest it as the owl soon became heavy. He examined my jeans, then moved on to them and walking across my knees, turned his head at intervals to look at me directly behind him. His talons dug into the smooth material to get a purchase and I resisted a desire to flinch.

Shortly after midnight on Saturday, I met a lamper on Holmoak Lane, walking from one lot of fields to the next over the railway bridge. I made a fuss of his three beautiful lurchers and asked how he ran them. He was very concerned at me walking home on my own in the dark and offered to see me to the main road end of the lane, where there is street lighting. I replied that I was fine on my own, but he shook his head at me and said 'You just be careful love, there's some funny people wandering about'.

The following night I was under the trees of the two-oak track off Briarmead writing up my notes and just enjoying the company of Crisp and her sisters as I sat on the bank between these fields. To my right I had a good view of the lane, and to my left, of the farmland. The young badgers were playing up and down the little bank, inevitably involving me. They hid round me; used my lap for King-of-the-Castle, played tug-of-war with the end of my jacket and that great cub favourite, 'Let's examine Chris'. That morning, I had taken off my jacket, as a protest against tug-of-wars, so first a snout was pushed under my pullover (they love the feel of wool), then the owner's head and neck.

Jet reopened an entrance of the stopped Chantry Sett and chose to den there. I felt rather uneasy about this.

Just after midnight of Saturday 21st I was with the Clifford sow and Missy, when a lampers' beam shone out quite near us. There were two men, one holding a net, and two lurchers. We had just reached the sett, with the beam coming closer, when another light appeared below the bank and two younger men approached, with a net and a dog. Both groups clearly knew one another and had come on to the farmland from different directions. I wanted to avoid being seen so that I could sneak away and look for vehicles, as registration numbers were a top priority. They lamped above and below the sett; the dogs picked up the badgers' scent and became very excited. A beam nearly touched me as I stood at the corner of the Bank, so I crouched down amongst the nettles and long grass. Then a lurcher discovered me; and at that very moment a vehicle's headlights lit up the lampers. John Shaw in his jeep had come along without headlights and caught them neatly, just below where I was hidden on the Bank. He shouted to the trespassers to get off his land quick! The four men and their dogs ran towards him, clearly intending to overturn the jeep (this had been tried before). John warned that if they came nearer, he would run them down, but still they came, one shouting 'Come on lads, let's roll him over!' True to his word John drove at them and the groups scattered. One man fell over me as he ran; another swerved just in time. As he turned to see what he had avoided, I jumped to my feet and took a photo. Someone said 'There's a kid here' and the man I had photographed (doubtless seeing me in the flash) replied, 'No, it's a woman'. Unfortunately the flash takes some time to recharge. I managed to take a last 'face' shot of one of the youngsters as he ran past me. Then they all turned their backs. Meanwhile John had driven off, not realising that I was there. The man I had photographed turned back and started talking to me, asking questions and justifying himself. Was that my man? What was I doing here? They were just taking their dogs for a walk when 'my man' had tried to run them down on a public footpath! I pointed out that they had shouted 'Let's roll him over' and that the public footpath was half a field away. They had pocketed their nets but couldn't hide their beams. Their short range lights weren't suitable for foxes as they would need to run to keep one in the beam. Fine for slower animals like badgers and rabbits – but for rabbits you don't need a net.

When they realised I knew they were lampers and that I had been watching them for some time the situation changed. I had a witness – John Shaw; I had photos; all I needed now was a vehicle number. I recognised the two older lampers, one had hit me last year, when I told him they were trespassing.

They began to walk across Top Field, towards the railway crossing and the broken stiles. Three lampers and dogs were in front of me, while the young lamper – the second I had photographed – was walking next to me, trying to grab the camera. We struggled together till one of the older men told him to leave me alone. The youth suggested they should set the dogs on me, but the older man said he had enough problems at the moment without that. He told them to get to the car, they would pick up the van afterwards. This confirming what I had thought, that the two groups had arrived separately. They crossed the railway with me close behind them, as I was determined to glean anything from their muttered conversation that might help. 'Has that bloke gone to get the Bill? . . . she's got photos . . . stick to the story . . . she can't touch us . . . was she in the car with him and hid on the bank before he switched on the headlights? . . . no, he wouldn't have left her like that after last time . . . she was nothing to do with him . . . well, why were they both there at the same time? Clearly they didn't want me this close and by now we had speeded up to what felt like a cross country run.

The car was parked just off the lane, on the track leading to the crossing. As they all squeezed in, I took down the number and tried another photograph, of the car parked on the track. I hoped the place would be recognisable as Steve had said that the number wasn't enough for a court could argue that it had been taken at a previous time and I had no witness to their vehicle. So a photo and a number were ideal. I waited for the battery to recharge and used the last flash trying to get a close picture of the occupants, but they ducked or turned away. I stood aside (I've been run down before!) waiting for them to drive off, as the police would want to know in which direction they went. But the other older lamper got out of the nearside front seat and approached me, smiling. Why didn't we all go home and forget it? No one had been hurt. Was I going to report them? Was that guy my man? I made no reply. Then his attitude changed. I had a picture of the parked car, but he would say he

56

had been there with his girlfriend and he'd make sure she corroborated this. He would deny all knowledge of the others and get rid of the gear, so I could prove nothing. He turned to walk back to the waiting car (by now, one of the lampers was shouting to him to hurry up or the Bill would be here), then spat in my direction. He got in, then it backed off the track, and turned right towards Barksham.

I re-crossed the railway, ran down the Poplar Row to the farmyard and phoned the police, giving them as many details as I could and warned them what the lampers had said.

When I returned after dawn watch that morning I phoned John. He was surprised that I had been on Cliffords Bank. He had the impression there was a whole gang around and our four lampers were only the tip of the iceberg. Driving to the Bank, he had encountered two cars near the railway bridge. One contained a courting couple who left rather abruptly, but the other car, parked further along, had been empty. He had also seen headlights over on Briarmead Lane and made out a vehicle moving without headlights across Newby farmland. On returning, he found the previously empty car now contained two men and made them leave. When he had gone back to bed, he and his wife heard a car drive along the lane from the railway crossing direction and stop. They watched a man get out and take down details from the farm notice there. During the night the phone rang three times but they ignored it.

Sunday was a mild, breezy, overcast night with wonderful visibility, I was in the orchard with Lesley, the three cubs, Missy and her mother, all of us eating windfall pears. The wind was rising in the poplars like a great sea storm and swallowing up the sound of the silos in the nearby farmyard, but there was no human disturbance. I was very tired and thought about going home. Suddenly we were bathed in brilliant white light and a lurcher shot past me into Curly, bowling her over and over with the impact. Before she could regain her feet, he was at her neck. I reacted without stopping to think, came up behind the lurcher, pressing my knee into its spine and grasped its jaws in my hands, forcing it to relax its grip. I didn't release the dog until the young sow had regained her feet, then I shouted at the lurcher, hitting it round the head. The beam went out abruptly and I picked up the cub, quite a weight now she was two thirds grown and stood there with her safely in my arms.

There was no sign of the other badgers, dog or man. It was a powerful spot light beam and they need not have been near at all. I realised I was within a few yards of the farmyard and John's phone, so I deposited Curly in the great barn leaving my woollen pullover to comfort her, and went to the office shed. I dialled Oakley police who told me to stay in the farmyard until they came. While I waited I prowled around like an uneasy tiger, wondering just where the lampers had their vehicle parked.

I found myself standing by the big combine I called the 'Yellow Peril' and on impulse, climbed up the ladder and stood in the cab, looking around. What a view from this height! But I could see no badgers, men or beams. Then I turned towards Rob's cottage to see a police car taking the bumpy corner round his garden and approaching quickly.

I explained the situation and we searched the far roadside, but there were no vehicles. This terrain was new to this patrol, but they were more than willing to drive over it, so we went round searching the side of Prossers Wood and High Ridge, along to the corner of Cliffords Bank where John Shaw, the lampers and I had met up the previous night. It was the first these constables had heard of this so they were very interested. We went past the sett part of the Bank, down to the two-oak track and on to Briarmead. There was no sign of the lampers, though once I felt sure I saw a beam shine out briefly on Newby farmland. But the patrol needed lights to drive by as this was new country to them, so their car would have been plainly visible. I found that sitting in the car with the headlights shining ruined my night vision. This is one of the drawbacks of having good sight in the 'dark' and I am even more easily dazzled than the average person if a lamper deliberately flashes his light in my face. The police were very cheerful, not minding their wasted call out, merely saying they now knew where to come on to the land next time. They drove off down the lane and I went checking for badgers across the fields. Missy and Candy appeared from under the elmbrush of the sett as I called from the bottom of Cliffords Bank. A rustle, rustle further along and there was Lesley, the old sow and Crisp. Lesley nosed me in an anxious sort of way. With a feeling of guilt I remembered her other daughter still shut up in John's barn. The slight rain in the wind now turned to downpour as I ran along the Poplar Row to the yard and pulled open the sliding door, expecting to see a plaintive young Curly come crying out. Nothing. In the near blackness of the great building I tripped over my pullover lying just where I had left it. I had expected to see equipment, machinery, tractors, but stretching up almost to the roof in a great, steep slope was a heap of grain which nearly filled the barn. Curly lay huddled up on a far corner, away from the heap, and didn't stir. Speaking softly, I stroked her flank and she opened her eyes. I looked at her neck, but the running blood made it difficult to tell the extent of the damage the lurcher had done. As I felt carefully round the wound she yelped and immediately scrambled to her feet, so I walked back to the Bank through the rain, the little badger padding after. Her mother and

Candy smelt her and began licking her neck. I looked at my watch, but it was too late to go home for hydrogen peroxide and return in time for dawn watch so I decided to leave that for tomorrow night. The other badgers would clean her wound for now.

After only 24 hours, I was shocked at the deterioration in Curly. The dog had torn a lump of flesh the size of a hen's egg out of the side of her neck. I liberally applied the peroxide, but infection was present and she needed antibiotics.

Later I phoned Steve Hammond at the RSPCA and told him how the lamping had escalated, and of the photos I had taken. He said to me that they were receiving reports of badgers being lamped either with nets as here, pinned down by the neck with a forked stick, caught with a snare on a stick or tube, or merely grasped by the tail and dropped into a sack. It was also known that when a badger was caught and dazzled in the beam, lampers were setting their dogs on to it for 'sport' but if the lurchers weren't game or were hurt, the poachers would finish the job themselves. They had reports of sticks or metal rods or tools being used to crush a badger's skull or simply to beat the animal to death.

Steve went on to tell me that they had been given a tip-off via Tony Gould that Don Francis was staging a dogfight on Barksham Common soon, so I promised to make some enquiries.

The next night I cleaned Curly's wound, applied the ointment the vet had given me and fed her an antibiotic capsule between two muscatel raisins. I had a very sick badger on my hands. If she was no better after one more night, I would see the vet again. I was not taking her out of her environment for treatment as she would probably die of shock. The animals here were terrified of people, dogs and vehicles. If she worsened, I'd ask Tony to give her an injection to kill her.

That afternoon I collected the photos of the lamping incident. Sadly, the closeup of the older man was blurred, but there were good pictures of the young lad who had tried to take the camera from me, of the men walking away with a lurcher and of the parked car. I sent them to Steve at Horsham.

That Wednesday there was a beautiful moon near the full, rising over Prossers Wood as I stood on Top Field. Everywhere was very dry again in spite of the short rainy spell, as the wind had dried up the water and the tracks were dusty once more. Lesley found me looking for her in the wood. Her daughter lay face down in the undergrowth, very near to death. I could only sit there with Lesley in my lap, watching until the unconscious cub ceased breathing and settled on her side.

As I walked out to the Briarmead side of these woods on to Long

Field, the moon gave a silvery beauty to the place. Where the plough had made a deep curve at the field corner, I laid Lesley's cub, pulling the high ridge of earth down over the body.

I phoned Oakley station on returning home and was told the lampers' car was still registered in the previous owner's name. It could be traced but would take some time. I promised to warn the Shaws, as the two older men would not take kindly to their sport being spoilt and might retaliate if they thought they had got away without being reported. When I phoned John I discovered he'd already received abusive phone calls and his wife had just answered a caller who said that she was next on the list. Clearly they were mistaking her for me and I felt responsible and anxious.

Thursday 26th was a misty night, with lampers from Warby rabbiting on Newby farm. The badgers were very fearful of lights now on their fields and I was glad of that.

I walked to the farmhouse after badger-watch to speak to John Shaw. I had been keeping an eye on the farmyard at night in case of sabotage as the grain in the granery could so easily be contaminated or even the machinery vandalised. But the police had been to see them and John seemed his usual cheery self.

That afternoon I had a phone call telling me that Don Francis was indeed staging a dogfight with the owner of Crawfords. The latter was leaving the area and it was in the nature of a farewell get together as the men were good friends. I couldn't get Steve at Horsham, so left a message for Tony.

Tony came later and we discussed the rumoured dogfight. I sensed my contact was frightened. If I pushed him too far for information, I might lose him altogether.

This was the first time I had really had a conversation with Tony and I promised to show him round Bourne Place and Crawfords when convenient. He had only taken over Steve's area on the first of that month, so a heavy workload had piled up. His new area was 20 miles long and 10 miles wide, taking in part of the city and extending to surrounding villages and countryside. He was bound to take some time just finding his way about, as there is only one inspector to an area. He had had a much smaller patch before, but a high population density with highrise flats. He was inexperienced with wildlife, but was obviously enthusiastic and had a sense of humour too, which was most important. Tony expressed great interest in the lamping problem and offered to come out at night whenever he could to help, a gesture I appreciated.

The first of October was a beautifully warm, mild night with a slight breeze and the moon just past the full but the next night the skies had clouded over with a slight rain in the wind, and I saw lampers below Cliffords Bank. Going to investigate, I encountered a look-out, complete with balaclava mask and sheath knife – then another. Making a quick exit to the wood I managed to lose them successfully in the undergrowth. Word does get round amongst poachers and my camera had probably more than a little to do with it. Watching from the wood edge, I saw two men walking in the direction of the Old Barn ruins and came out onto the meadow in time to see the red brake lights of a vehicle (but no headlights) going down the lane. The wire at the top of Briarmead had been cut and the van driven in and out.

By the morning a mist lay on the field above Newby farmyard, spilling through the six-bar gate in the high hedge and so on to the lane and Long Field. All else was clear sky and to the west, still starry. The male tawny kewiked as he flew close passed my face and looking down and across the lane from the Briarmead bank, I saw five badgers appearing on the smoothly sown earth as the mist moved away to reveal them. Lesley and family were leisurely coming home, foraging as they went. The eastern sky was turning pink as light crept into the morning. A thrush began a phrase, but stopped as the now distant tawny kewiked again. Then the thrush repeated its song to the new day.

Later I checked for parked vehicles and watched a small flock of Canada geese taking to the air near Cliffords Bank. Only the tops of the tall trees of the Poplar Row showed through the mist on the path below. Closer to the ground were scenes of activity; Jet was still digging-out at the Chantry, while Lesley and her cubs were working at the Old Cherry Sett, and the Clifford badgers on the Bank, all in preparation for the winter.

One evening I again met the lamper with three lurchers; two were on slip (on their slip leads), one walking beside. He asked me why I was out at such a time on my own, so I played my 'tawny tape' and explained that I studied owls, a subject which also fascinated him. I told him I was very interested in lamping techniques and he suggested I go with him on to the farmland to watch him 'on the beam'. His dogs were greyhound crossed with border collie and were perfect, both in obedience and looks. I asked him if it was his beam I'd seen in the little bullocks' field last week and he admitted it was, but he wouldn't be working that field again as the young animals were badly frightened. I was glad and mentioned that one of the mares in the adjoining field has foaled two nights ago so he promised to avoid that field too.

I liked this man. He lamped for rabbits and the odd hare as he walked across from Clearthorpe, two villages distant. This proved to be the first of several meetings during which he taught me a great deal about the practical side of the sport and was courteous and interesting. The relationship only terminated months later, when I encountered a lamper working the same area who set his dogs on another very young foal and I contacted the police. It seemed fairer to warn my friendly lamper off in case he was picked up too.

It is good to remember that there is this side to lamping and that not every lamper is hoping to meet a badger. While this man was trespassing, the rabbits he caught were 'food for his dogs and sometimes for him and the missus'. His pleasure was derived simply from the enjoyment of the sport and just being out at night – the same love of the night that I had.

On the third Saturday in October, I was on the meadow in front of the woods above Cliffords Bank. Near me in the long grass Jet, Jude and Susie were foraging while the other badgers were searching for pears in the orchard. A long, dark van containing two men came swinging up the Bank track without headlights, meaning I think, to park at the field edge behind the trees prior to lamping. It was an unusually long and streamlined vehicle for poachers and I remembered it from last season. Then they had taken the Clifford boar, (Missy's father) and I hadn't been near enough to stop them. This night the men saw movement as the two nearest badgers galloped off, so they switched on their headlights, driving after them over the rough, bumpy field. I ran up shouting between them and the badgers. As the animals rushed into the wood, the men swung the van round and tried to run me down. The third time they came at me I tripped, but rolled clear. By the feel of it, I had stumbled over a flint; I picked it up, intending to heave it at their windscreen as they came at me again. It was much too heavy for me to throw and fell short only smashing their nearside light. This was sufficient for them to swing round and drive off without stopping across the field and away back down the path. It all happened too suddenly, and the blaze of headlights was too dazzling to see the van number.

I reported the incident later that morning and found I was speaking to Philip. I noticed that he didn't ask me for the vehicle number and asked why. He burst out laughing and reminded me of a similar occasion when a colleage of his had asked me for the number and received a rather rude answer. It seemed I was acquiring a reputation!

In the middle of the month I paid a visit to the college where I used to work and spoke to a young man who had heard the Living World radio programme and recognised my voice. He and a friend were concerned that I had no one to guard the badgers if I was ill and offered their help. Thinking this over, it occurred to me that I was the only person who knew where all the badgers were denning. With the new setts dug out, this was worrying, so I arranged to meet them that afternoon to show them the woodland setts.

The editor of BBC Wildlife Magazine knew of my desire to get the knowledge of the lamping of badgers to a far greater audience and had suggested I write an article on the subject for the magazine. RSPCA headquarters at Horsham were helpful in supplying me with information and their legal department advised me to contact the police Wildlife Liaison Officer of Derbyshire's force who might also be able to help. Sergeant Charlie Parkes with the assistance of his training department, had just made a video called *Death of a Badger* intended initially for the police themselves and showing the badger, its habitat, the nature of digging and baiting offences and police powers. Sergeant Parkes was the first of several police wildlife officers I was to contact. I told him of the lamping problem in my area and on impulse, asked his advice. Was I going about the lamping on our farmland in the right way? He asked how good the relationship was with my local police, then suggested:

1. That we should attempt to track down all lampers irrespective of their intent or equipment.
2. When questioned by the patrol, if they said they were only after rabbits then the police could prosecute for being in pursuit of same without a game licence (very doubtful that they would have one).
3. If they had a rabbit in their possesion, then the police could prosecute for poaching also.

He clarified the law for me by saying: 'It is an offence under the Night Poaching Act 1828 to take, without permission, rabbits or game, e.g. partridge or pheasant, by any means, or to go in search or pursuit of game with a gun, net or instrument which would include a light. It is not an offence to search for rabbits under this Act, but becomes an offence if the pursuer does not have a game licence. The Badgers Act 1973 makes it illegal to take or kill a badger by any means, but it is also protected under the Wildlife and Countryside Act 1981 and cannot be taken using certain prohibited methods, which include lights. (This would also include a vehicle's headlights). This applies to certain other animals too, e.g. hedgehogs and otters, and to any wild or game bird. So the poacher who has a torch strapped to his gun barrel and is shooting pheasants at roost commits offences under two Acts. He would also commit the offence of trespassing on land with a firearm – Firearms Act 1968'. It is not of course, an offence to go on another's land without permission, merely civil trespass and the trespasser can only be sued for damage he has caused on the land. This, as my farmers know only too well, can be an expensive and not always effective remedy.

Tony Gould of the RSPCA offered to help with the lamping article and put me in touch with a friend and fellow inspector who, earlier that year, had secured the first ever conviction for badger lamping. Tony's friend was as anxious as I was to get the knowledge of badger lamping to as wide a public as possible. He said that most people knew of deer lamping and a few people were aware that the lamping of badgers was being carried on, but not of its true extent. He was going to the Annual Meeting of Badger Groups and sugested I write down all I knew from personal experience of the subject which he would make available to everyone there, the RSPCA and police officers as well as representatives from each of the thirty badger groups then in existence. All this was new ground to me as I had no idea there were so many people up and down the country mapping setts, patrolling a given area and generally learning about the badger and its habitat. Nor had I known that for the past four years they had met together to help and advise one another! This was perhaps the best morale booster I could have had.

Next I went to see Sergeant Paul Collins who had taken over from Warren Hughes at Oakley station. We discussed Sergeant Parkes' suggestions for the lamping, which our sergeant agreed to implement as and when the occasion arose. Regarding the lampers whom John Shaw and I encountered, that poacher was true to his word. His girlfriend was questioned and merely said they were in the car when some people ran by and I had taken a photo of their car which she and her boyfriend were in! There was nothing we could do about it by then and really I felt it was more a case of lack of communication, heightened by the length of time caused through their car being registered to the previous owner. The constable who spoke to her hadn't been told of the circumstances, so naturally took her at her word. But good had resulted from this. It had made me realise I was going about the lamping problem in the wrong way and had prompted me to ask Sergeant Parkes' advice. In future it must be a patrol, not I, who accosted the poachers. It also made us all take stock of the situation, with Sergeant Collins, who was new to the station, asking me if I would take him and the village constable round the farmland setts so that they would know their exact location. He was interested in the Derbyshire training video *Death of a Badger* and said they would obtain a copy for Oakley station.

I later phoned John Shaw to keep him up to date with events and to ask him about a safe that had mysteriously appeared on the farmland. Sometime the previous Friday evening, Rob saw what he took to be lamper's light on the fields. It appeared that the farmer, Roger Johnson, had his safe jemmied from his office wall and taken on to the field by the pear orchard. The thieves tried to open it, but probably decided they were too near Rob's cottage, so drove without lights over the two farms on to Briarmead and opened it on Sand Pit Field. The farmworkers felt they were lampers as they knew the lie of the land so well and their light appeared to be a handheld spot lantern. Whilst I was keeping an open mind, one of the points that has been made to me by police in different areas when I was researching the lamping article, was that poachers often check out the land for themselves or others. An area that lampers had worked might later have a spate of burglaries, stolen cars, barns broken into with machinery stolen, or sheep being rustled. So Rob and the others could have been right.

The leaves were slowly turning. The wood was full of soft sound; chestnut prickly cases and acorns dropping. Here and there a lazy leaf was gently drifting earthwards. The ten remaining badgers here – Lesley with Crisp and Candy; beautiful Jet and her brother Jude; the Clifford sow and Missy; Susie, Little'un and Sis – were in lovely condition for winter.

Chapter 4

You could hear the wind coming in Ashcroft Woods. I was standing amongst the trees with everywhere dappled in moonlight. But for an occasional leaf floating past, all was still. Then there was a distant moaning and a rushing that came nearer and nearer at great speed. The trees before me began to sway and toss; next moment, the wind was here. A great roaring gust blew debris into my eyes and mouth and leaves into my hair. For a few moments all was confusion – exciting moments – then it was gone. The branches ceased to sway and all was still again. Leaves like snow, fast falling for awhile longer and the moon crept further inwards – I love this wood and most of all at night. Lesley whickered up at me as I sat writing this, then blinked as a cherry leaf landed on her face. It dropped as she snuffled with an intake of breath, then she scrambled onto the old, dying tree next to me. There had been no lampers for several nights, possibly because of the clear moonlight, but there were plenty of rabbits feeding close to the hedgerows.

On the 3rd November a deep frost crunched underfoot with a clear half moon set in a starry sky. Jet and Jude seemed determined to den at Tossy's Sett just within the wood and opposite to Cliffords Bank where Missy and her mother were settled for the winter. The boar found me by the Old Barn ruins and together we followed the edge of the hay field till we reached the soakaway and the corner of the boundary Bank. In the elmbrush there near the bee hives, he crunched snails noisily, dug and used a dung pit, then purposefully, padded along the top path. I followed, his grey, swaying body a few yards ahead, feeling at peace with my world. We passed the Poplar Row and entered the orchard, where the three 'ladies' were eating fallen pears as if their lives depended on it. He was the only boar in the area now that Sam was dead. As I saw Jude and Sam mating long duration with several of the sows, there should be cubs next January or February. A lot of munching – very juicy, these pears. I enjoyed them myself, but checked for slugs first. The badgers however, weren't fussy like me!

One wet evening, with gale force winds, I came over at 10 p.m. as I was uneasy about my badgers. Jude musked my boots, followed by Missy, Jet and the Clifford sow. The wind parted their fur as we stood together in the meadow. They were all very playful; I stroked Jet's dark fur and she promptly grasped my glove – I seemed to see my Sam as I retrieved it. I left them foraging on the field below the Bank and went on to the Top Field by Prossers Wood, with Jude following. He chewed up chestnuts he found at the wood edge and worms that had risen above ground to feed on the field. The rain blew over in the noisy squalls.

A beam or rather, the top of a beam, flickered through the elmbrush of Clifford's Bank as its owner lamped on the lower field. Remembering that we had left the three 'ladies' there I was running down when a screaming came to me, blown on the wind, scream upon scream. Someone has described the screaming of a tortured badger as sounding like a woman being murdered. To me it sounds more like a child. I ran across field towards the sound. Then suddenly, it ceased; just the wind and the rain. I think they either clubbed her or killed her and I was sure it was Jet (though I couldn't have said why). By now I could see the backs of two men and a big lurcher in the distance; the men were carrying something between them. They passed through the track in the Bank and seemed to turn left. Suddenly I realised I was doing the wrong thing; I must go and phone; so turned and ran back along the Poplar Row, the wind in the great trees almost deafening as I ran beneath them. The officer on duty knew nothing of the set up so it took awhile explaining, but he said a patrol would check the main road, then meet me in the farmyard. I ran back to look for the badgers. I had noticed one near the pylon before I phoned. I located the old sow, Jude (who had probably come to investigate the noise) and Missy, who was hurt. There was no sign of Jet anywhere. I ran round the field calling, calling – then stood on top of the Bank . . . but the little black sow had gone. Keeping an eye open for the patrol's headlights along the railway path, I examined Missy, and saw that her side was pouring blood. As fast as she washed the wound, it continued bleeding, but I would have to leave her for now and return later. In the farmyard I met the village constable Alan Matthews, with another. They had been all round the perimeter of the area, but seen nothing. I explained what had happened and they left to check once more.

Missy had staunched the bleeding and let me look at her. Like young Curly, she had a piece of flesh ripped right out, but fortunately for Missy, it was from her flank and not her neck. At least she could wash it herself and it wasn't such a vital spot. Her snout anxiously followed my hand as I felt round the injury. It was easier to put my left arm round her neck and my face against hers, talking softly all the time, as my right hand examined her. Lurchers are reputed to inflict appalling wounds on deer when dragging them down. Now I could believe it. I would need to bring the hydrogen peroxide and the capsules that Curly never lived to be given.

I saw headlights go up Briarmead, stop and turn at the top, pause as if searching awhile, then slowly return. The lane is lower than the fields, but I guessed it must be the patrol car. I always seem to waste their time. Oh, for two-way radio! My watch showed it was already Saturday and 12.45 a.m. so I decided to return home for the anti-biotics, left the badgers and walked round to the side of High Ridge. It was still raining and gusty. Suddenly I stood stock still as someone came out of the gap straight towards me. He shone no light and obviously couldn't see me, but it was his dogs that had stopped me in my tracks. A very tall, rough-coated lurcher that was part wolf-hound, two terriers, one dark, one brindled . . . and an alsatian* This man had dug for badgers in our woods. At the same moment he shone a light and swore as he recognised me! Well, at least we both knew why the other was here. And the patrol was gone, long since. What a stupid situation. He told me to go away (but a little less politely!) and at his tone, the alsatian lurcher began to growl. The group moved on along the way I had come and I looked back undecidely, just as the man dazzled me in his light again and shouted. I thought it best to appear as if leaving, scout round for a vehicle and return to see what he was up to. As if I couldn't guess! There was no vehicle at the bottom of High Ridge nor over the railway crossing. By now a beam was being used below Clifford's Bank. This must have been one of those nights. I hadn't the cheek to contact the police again and felt that probably the badgers were safely underground, having had more

---

*I was later to encounter more greyhound crossed with alsatian lurchers, for this has become a popular hybrid. As one of its advocates wrote: 'It revels in hunting-up and catching hold of anything from a pheasant to a poacher or perhaps a gamekeeper, depending on which side of the fence you are actually trespassing upon!' It does indeed.

than enough for one night, but I would have dearly liked to find the vehicle(s) involved. By now I could see there were two men and five dogs; another lurcher and its owner had joined them. But the men were looking out for me and the whole situation seemed to be getting out of hand. There was probably not much wildlife about anyway after the earlier lamping. Just then, the heavens opened, the wind rose to a fury and the rain lashed down. Visibility was almost nil. I took shelter in the great barn, so didn't know what became of the lampers, but lamping was definitely out.

For 24 hours the gales continued until by 2.30 a.m. on Sunday the rain stopped. A thin-edged crescent moon appeared with stars between the clouds. I checked Missy's wound again and cleaned it. Badgers have almost rubbery skin which the teeth of a small dog have difficulty in piercing. The animal that had inflicted this injury, however, was large and powerful and a badger is no match for the likes of this. Missy had lost a great deal of blood, which was what worried me most. There was no problem administering the capsules, wedged as always between muscatel raisins.

Another bitter, frosty night, but this time it was far colder with the flooded lane a gleaming icy surface reflecting the starry, moonless sky. Inside the wood, as always, it was warmer and only frosty in the open places. Moles had been busy on the sheltered eastern slopes; the fresh, moist, dark earth showed above the fallen leaves. Outside on Long Field, the rows of sprouting barley were ranks of white tufts stretching away into the distance. The badgers had only been above ground late last evening and by 1 a.m. all but Jude and Candy had gone to earth. Missy's wound was not as yet infected, which I thought was as much due to her continual washing as the hydrogen peroxide. I had been bringing her a pound of raw mince and some milk each night, mince being the cheapest and most easily portable raw meat I could manage. I would only feed her until the wound began to close, as I don't really approve of feeding wild animals. However, I didn't want her to start living off her winter fat yet. It was far too early and the winter had scarcely begun.

Jude was missing his sister and I watched him pottering about Tossy's Sett that he and she dug out that autumn. Poor Jet. Was she killed here or merely stunned and saved for a lingering death elsewhere?

That same evening I heard that the Francis/Crawford dogfight had come and gone. The venue had been Laversley where Don Francis had connections. Was he afraid that word had got about? There was to be another around Christmas or New Year's Day. I'd been warned to watch out for trouble in Ashcroft Woods over Christmas, as sport was wanted for Boxing Day, and I wasn't surprised at this, recalling last Christmas morning. I wondered if I could ask for a police radio for that period; also for the coming weekend.

Friday was a great change from the previous few nights, for now it was raining and mild. The badgers, who had been less active in the iciness, were foraging eagerly again in the pear orchard and the ploughed earth of the fields. Missy's wound was holding its own. She pushed softly against my face as I bent down to look at it.

I phoned Sergeant Collins to ask if I could have police radio for the coming weekend. He said he had been wondering about this himself and would come round with a spare one later. Shortly afterwards, Tony Gould arrived. I had promised to go with him sometime that day to look at an area dug out on Barksham Common. This had apparently occurred about three weeks before, but no one seemed sure whether it was a badger sett and if so, whether it had been recently occupied. We both went into Oakley station first and spoke to the sergeant. He had tried his best but unfortunately, I couldn't have two-way radio. He had also tried to obtain a bleeper for me instead, but found that wasn't practical. It had been decided, however, in view of last weekend's lamping, that one of the patrol which came out then, PC Alan Matthews and the special constable I already knew, Dave Jones, would come out with me that night (Friday night/Saturday morning being the ideal time), in the hope of catching some lampers. It would be a moonless weekend, so a good one.

The editor of BBC Wildlife Magazine had lent me a copy of the Death of a Badger video and as our police hadn't yet been sent theirs, I left it with the sergeant for them to see. Tony would collect it later that week to show at a meeting of RSPCA inspectors, then return it to me.

We left the station and drove to Barksham Common; sure enough, it was a badger sett and in some parts, still occupied. Whilst we were there, the warden and a groundsman Tony had met there before, turned up and we chatted. They had never been sure it was a sett, but had recently noticed a man-made path leading from the area to a layby off the motorway just beyond. Then it was dug out and the warden informed Tony and the police at Barksham. I showed the men the difference between the used and disused badger entrances and the signs to look for. Sadly, it was apparent from the old 'crowning down' holes that this ancient and large sett had been dug for badgers in the past. Walking back to the RSPCA van, I talked to the warden who was thrilled that his area really did contain badgers and promised to keep watch round this part, to see they weren't dug out again. Considering there was just this one man to patrol 660 acres of common and woodland, I felt he was taking on something! We gave him our phone numbers in case a problem should arise and left feeling we had all gained something from the meeting. I certainly had, for it cemented a plan I had been mulling over for some time, to encourage landowners, not just local to me but anywhere in my county, to take an interest in the badgers on their land and help protect them. I never dreamed driving back with Tony that day, how many friends this was to make for me and more importantly, for the badger; how many families with their children would become involved plotting setts, recording not just the badger, but any wildlife in them, protecting them and, perhaps best of all, taking pride in the richness that was theirs and gaining in knowledge and pleasure.

By 10 p.m. that evening, we were all assembled ready for lamper-watch – Alan Matthews, Dave Jones, Tony and I. Alan had already seen the video. He said that the new Police and Criminal Evidence Act 1984, known as PACE, which was to come into force on 1st January next but was being practised now, would help in this type of situation; for example, stopping vehicles and questioning, although in some cases it would have its complications. (The new regulations gave power of arrest and search on suspicion). He spoke of a badger they had seen ambling in front of their patrol car in Arbour Lane, Warby, after he and his companion left me that Saturday when Jet was taken.

We arrived at about 10.30 p.m. and parked well tucked away near Oak Dell. It was a clear, frosty night once more, for the day's mild, damp weather had quite gone. I showed them the routes on and off the farmland, and exactly whereabouts in the farmyard the telephone was housed. We waited unitl 2.30 a.m. but there were no lampers. Thinking back to a week earlier, how ironic life was! In a sense however, I didn't think their effort had been wasted. PC Matthews had seen the place on foot after viewing it from a patrol car. I now knew another constable (who was very easy to talk to) and Tony had become involved with the local police just as Steve had been. Dave made us all laugh with his carrier bag of food and the relationship was good. Reception by radio was poor and I recalled that Sergeant Collins said this area was a blackspot. However, if it were tested out more thoroughly, I felt there were several places here where Oakley station could have been contacted with reasonable clarity, as I had found around Ashcroft Woods on August Bank Holiday last; but it needs time and patience. I asked Alan Matthews what the chances were of my being allowed the use of police radio over the Christmas and New Year period. He was very doubtful for it had to be agreed by the Barksham Superintendent. He did say, however, that in order to catch lampers here, he felt they would need to watch consistently for a period, and he promised to speak to the sergeant about it.

I left them at their car and went to collect the antibiotics as well as my Olympus camera left overnight, then tried to locate Missy. All the farmland badgers however, were very much underground what with the men backwards and forwards over it and the extreme cold. I could have gone home for an hour, but I felt restless and unsettled. Walking over Newby, I heard a fox call distantly and began to answer; I'd been too badger-orientated lately to do this. I harked it nearer and nearer . . . my fox was sounding on the move and knew me as well as I knew him! Next moment Josh was jumping up open mouthed, tongue lolling, his vaporising breath warmly touching my face (he'd eaten recently, for I could smell blood). Later, as we sat together, I ran my hands into the thick fur round his shoulders. What marvellous pelage these animals have. I hoped my foxes wouldn't be taken this winter. No one cares about foxes. The poachers snare, shoot and lamp them. But these mean a great deal to me. I can't expect anyone to appreciate that, but I had learnt so much from Josh, his vixen and their offspring and come to understand something of the way of the fox.

It is interesting that horses, like cattle, graze sporadically throughout the night even on deeply frosted pasture. A little owl was hunting over the meadow of the mare and her foal. I called Missy up for her capsules just before first light and saw that the wound was drying well. I also had my fingers gently nibbled! Although she was young, I had the feeling she could have cubs the following spring. She reminded me of Lesley in that both sows in their first year were very well developed, sturdy young animals.

An icy, frost-covered dawn turned to bright sunshine. I came from the Chantry Sett at 7.15 a.m. to see the backs of four figures at the Old Cherry Sett. Two were youths, one an Irishman sometimes seen rabbiting, but it was the fourth that horrified me – a big, corpulent man, near balding with a very long coat and just in the act of picking up a small terrier that has come out of the chestnut-bough entrance. I hadn't seen him for a considerable time, though I had known him for years either rabbiting, after foxes or directing operations digging out badgers. He used to come here long before the Wildlife Act and in 1979 used gas at this very sett. (As I have no name for him 'the gas cylinder man' is how I describe him.) His long coat is distinctive (what Inspector Hogarth called a poacher's coat). He must have had a vehicle for no one would walk about streets dressed like that – too unusual. In any case, I don't think he is local. He threatened me once and has a very soft voice. Now, with my knowledge of dogfighting, I would say he is a dogfighting man. He's one of the few people here that I really fear.

I decided a vehicle number was imperative, so ran round the Briarmead, cul-de-sac entrances of these woods, but with no luck. I resolved to go the far greater distance to those the Madden Lane side, then panicked. What was happening whilst I checked for vehicles? I came quietly up to the sett in the crater to see a closer view of the gas-cylinder man and heard someone else speaking below him from the hollow. I was tempted to take a photo, but only had the Olympus which has no flash attachment; it was dark under the holly tree and, after all, what would it prove? To be honest, I was also too scared. There was no one else about at all, though by now a good half hour had passed. I backed quietly away (fallen leaves tend to rustle underfoot) and waited as they moved off. I felt sure they were checking entrances. There was no sign of equipment though with a coat like that, there probably wouldn't be. If only I could find out the big man's identity. He's always so much in control and has authority over others. I decided to contact the police to look for vehicle(s) and ran down Briarmead, passing the field above the Cherry Sett. I heard men's voices, then saw movement at Barry's dump in the wood edge there. I phoned from the first house and waited for the patrol.

The constable arrived and I took him to the dump. The Irishman and two lads and their dogs . . . but no gas-cylinder man. They had a ferret down and were rabbiting, with three dogs, a bearded collie, a whippet-cross and a young jack russell tied to a tree nearby. When I asked the Irishman where his companion was, he said did I mean Davey? Like a fool I asked who Davey was; I should have said yes and acted as if I knew more than I did! I stroked the dogs whilst the constable interviewed them. When the Irishman approached me again, I asked about Davey, but couldn't get him back on the subject. He was very voluble, protesting his innocence. They were only after rabbits, which was obvious. He said they had seen another man at a distance and stuck to their story.

Although they were trespassing, the constable couldn't order them off the land without the landowner (Barry) being there. He could however, and did, warn them to leave the setts alone.

Later, I sat in the patrol car talking to the constable. It was he who had interviewed the lamper's girlfriend in the incident that John Shaw and I had been involved in last September and it obviously bothered him. The constable remarked that 'it's gone on too long' and I agreed it was much too late to do anything about that now. No, he meant that the lamping business as a whole had gone on too long and suddenly I realised he wanted to do something about it. I think he, Alan Matthews and some others had been discussing a concentrated effort to catch the lampers. He spoke of 'a hide or something out of the wind and rain'. The few times I had encountered this man, I have had the impression he was disinterested, regarding me as a nuisance and here he was telling me how he felt about the situation! In future, I mustn't judge by appearances. We discussed lurchers, lamping and field sports. I pointed out that I wasn't against field sports in general. Indeed, I didn't feel I had any right to be, but I was certainly against poaching and the illegal shooting that went on here. He had been Alan Matthew's companion in the car when Jet was taken and he too, described the badger they had seen later in their headlights crossing Arbour Lane. I thanked him for helping and walked home feeling a lot better about the whole situation.

That Sunday was a mild, wet, gusty night. I puffed the Aureomycin powder that Steve once gave me for Sam, into Missy's drying wound. It was still a big cavity, but now looked healthy enough. I wasn't feeding her any more as she was worming with the others. I inspected the brick built barn standing in the gap of the Poplar Row, as I thought it might do for the constables' hide. Sure enough, it was fine and dry inside and empty but for a few fruit-picking ladders stacked round the sides. There was no lock on the double doors, just a drop fastening. It faces up-field, towards Top Field, Cliffords Bank Sett, the railway crossing and High Ridge. It really couldn't be better sited. So if anything should come of that idea, I'd bear this in mind. I felt, however, that it was unlikely since Friday, Saturday and Sunday nights are always busy for the police with pubs, discos and parties turning out. Unfortunately, these tend to be popular lamping nights also. Ours isn't a large police station and badgers, after all, can't be compared with a pub fight or similar disturbance.

Dawn was very late this morning. Although the rain had ceased, everywhere was dripping and dank. The tawnies were only now sounding their boundaries. As a tree moved in the slight wind, showers of droplets pattered earthwards as if it was raining once more. There was a continuous drip, drip and occasional louder noise as a chestnut case fell. Thrush, blackbird, great tit and robin were fearfully 'alarming' as the owls called. I enjoy this sort of morning. No dawn is ever quite the same, nor morning sky. The sun clearing the horizon was white and moonlike, though unlike the full moon, it shed little light. How many dawns and night skies have I seen in the years I have walked this place? Lesley suddenly appeared and clambered on to the prone old cherry's trunk to attract my attention. She didn't approve of my day-dreaming; at least, not when she was around! Stroking her head, I recalled the gas-cylinder man. Thank goodness there was no job to hurry back to now, so I could stay well into each morning; I must remember to warn Barry when I next saw him.

Tony Gould came a couple of days later to return the *Death of a Badger* video. It seemed to have impressed both the RSPCA and the police. I must get round to seeing it myself! I told Tony about the gas-cylinder man and he suddenly asked me if Don Francis knew my address. I told him yes (which meant that 'Crawford' probably did too) and that sometime ago I had been warned I was next on his list. I hadn't really been surprised and was not bothered, but hoped one of his cronies didn't harm my son or daughter. We discussed a dogfight which had been held on primary school premises and organised by the school caretaker! Not as surprising as it seems, though the time it was held was unusual . . . all over and cleared away, bar a dead dog, on the Sunday morning when the police and RSPCA turned up. School equipment had been used to form a fighting ring and simply washed down and re-stacked after use. The officers noticed some pieces chalked with numbers 1, 2, 3, 4 that when assembled made the perfect shape. Tony doubted that the case would come to court though, as the dog died of natural causes – a heart attack; apparently it had only just started to fight when it collapsed. (Tony was wrong here, as the case did reach a court and the caretaker was convicted). The time of these fights is usually phoned round at very short notice and people often come from considerable distances. Many of these fights are videoed (like the sensational Enfield case), by the people themselves, to show how game their dogs are in order to sell their offspring for the highest prices. Tony said that the Enfield video turned up shortly afterwards in the Midlands as a private advert. They are also sold for private viewing to clubs.

Saturday 23rd was a mild, overcast night with rain in the wind. Visibility was exceptionally good for I could see to a great distance and in detail. Missy seemed well and her wound had dried up completely. She will always have a cavity in her flank which will be furless. You can't have a lump of flesh ripped from your side and have no sign when it heals! She seemed very well – and affectionate – in herself and only left me when Lesley appeared. She knows that badger regards me as her special property! All nine badgers were foraging under the orchard trees, like a crunching, munching flock of mini-pigs. Candy and Crisp had a game of chase; round and round, in and out. Candy did 'leap-frog' over her mother which started both cubs using the adults sideways on for this. In the end, all the badgers were playing and I got out of the way.

Jude moved to Cliffords Bank that night, forsaking the home that he and Jet had shared. Badgers are sociable creatures, and doubtless he was lonely. Lesley, her two cubs and Susie were together at the Old Cherry Sett, whilst Little'un and Sis had the Crater Sett. Some leaves still clung to the trees as if reluctant to fall, especially those of the oak and field maple. I had never known such a colourful November. Early in the morning there was a lone shooter in Ashcroft Woods, whom I carefully avoided.

On the last Sunday morning in November, at 6.45 a.m. I heard a quail call from somewhere between Briarmead Lane and Cliffords Bank. I had thought I heard it before (just two calls, last Monday), but told myself I must have been mistaken. I could only think it was injured and unable to migrate to northern Africa. The damp, gusty overcast morning still had a first-light look, with sleet in the air.

I came out on to the lower path by the Old Cherry Sett a few paces ahead of a man with a cap pulled down over his eyes. Behind him was a youth with two fell terriers. He promptly spun round, muttered something to the other and both went off quickly along the holly path. I followed at a distance as their reaction to me seemed so odd. I hadn't seen the older man's face because of his cap. Near the gully part of Briarmead that becomes a ravine, they were joined by another man, two more youths and a jack russell. I kept well out of the way, hoping they would think they had lost me, though I suspect they guessed I was still around. By the padlocked gate at the foot of High Ridge and Maddon Lane, they had a blue transit van parked. I stayed well back as they got in and read their number through the monocular. As they drove off towards Rendcombe I noted it had a sticker of a garage in the city on the back window. By now it was sleeting hard and if anything, becoming darker. This was the first of several appearances this group were to make in our neighbourhood and we never were able to trace the van.

What had happened that morning, coming on top of the warning I'd had and the reappearance of the gas-cylinder man the previous week, was worrying to say the least. The badgers had freshly dug out the entrances they were using at all setts here, so making things easier for the terriermen. That evening I discovered that during the daylight hours of Sunday, someone had checked the sett of Cliffords Bank. There were boot and paw prints everywhere on the field below, on the spoil heaps and leading up through the elmbrush, and the same again on the earth round Tossy's Sett; Jude of course was no longer living there but had moved to the Bank with Missy and her mother.

Tuesday saw a near full moon that by 2.30 a.m. had become overcast. Jude and the cubs, Candy and Crisp, were out and about, but not the others. It was mild and damp, but very pleasant.

At 4 a.m. Lesley and her cubs were digging out and playing. The youngsters had turned the dead leaves over round the Cherry Sett in their chestnut quest. I noticed that Little'un and Sis had forsaken the woodland setts to den with Missy, her mother and Jude on Cliffords Bank. Lesley had Candy with her at the Old Cherry Sett, whilst Susie and Crisp kept one another company at the Crater.

I met Barry Haines on Briarmead that morning and discussed the feeling that was building up nationally against farmers, with various anti-farming programmes and articles. He mentioned ITV's 'Cold Comfort Farm – a crisis that the British countryside and farming are heading for'. The Sunday Times ran an article on farming and conservation and Barry remarked if he had taken all of it seriously, he'd have gone out and shot himself! He said all farmers were concerned over the state of farming and many small farms were on the market, especially in Devon. Conservationists would like to buy up farms and let them go wild, but of course, this wouldn't necessarily mean more wildlife habitat or beautiful countryside. One has only to look at disused farmland to see that. He asked if I knew what had eaten the young wheat on the far field by Cliffords Bank. I said it was partly rabbits, but the Canadas and greylags had been feeding there too, as they had on Great Chantry Field. I brought him up to date with the lamping and terriermen's activities and Barry said he'd noticed there were dog paw marks all over the place.

November ended with a near full moon, savage frost and temperature −11°C. It was a fantastic world as I stood on the Ridge, beautiful in the moonlight. A tawny was hunting far over towards Top Field. The frost lay like snow shining in the lunar light. My vixen's paws crunched softly underfoot as she cast about beneath the gorse bushes. Her movements caused a soft fall of frost. Each dead stalk, each bramble-leaf had its glittering covering. My hot breath made my face ache as it cooled. The corners of my eyes and mouth split and smarted now in the sharp wind as the intense cold made them water. It had been a beautiful and a frighteningly cold November, I had never known the mouth quite like this. One good thing was that it seemed to be keeping the lampers away (and the badgers were less active in these conditions too). Foxes will hunt more at dawn or dusk though my present company belied this! She was lovely. I put my hand on her back and she turned, her head inclined enquiringly. I wondered where Josh was. I was not cold but my exposed face throbbed with pain and my scalp tingled. I never wear a hood (unless it's raining or sleeting hard), as it impedes hearing and vision. The foxes were denning below ground, unusually for this time of year but then it was unusual weather for the month. There was frost sparkling on my fox's fur and I saw it was also on my anorak, especially thick in the creases of the sleeves.

Even the eastern-facing slope of the Old Cherry Sett was frosted, like the paths and everything else; branches, twigs and finest twigends, covered in a frozen coat of glistening white.

A breeze stole through the petrified woodland and in its wake came the tinkling of a myriad tiny bells, a vibration of delicate cymbals amongst a multitude of trees. The music of infinite icicles touching on infinite braches as the sun rose in glory, turning all to fire.

Someone had expressed the opinion that lamping had far-reaching effects on all kinds of wildlife and gave, as one example, the fact that a light shone along hedgerows or below trees caused many birds to fly up startled from their roosts. These often blundered about in the darkness, unable to find a safe perch again. In the bitter winter, this meant certain death to small birds already weakened by the cold and rendered them vulnerable to predators. I knew from first hand experience that lamping caused stress in badgers and that stress affects reproduction so that implantation may not take place, or if it does, cubs may be stillborn. As I never use a light at night myself, it had not occurred to me before that birds lost their roosting sites. I decided to take a small torch on a mild night and prove this for myself.

December started, for me, with bronchitis. I had managed to guard the setts each morning, but that was all. Luckily, all had been quiet. The following Tuesday it was dark and windy (the ideal lamping conditions), so I was determined to be out that evening. I had missed not being there and it was so mild that I wasn't coughing much. I checked that the metal gate at the foot of High Ridge was padlocked and walked slowly across to the farmland above. I tried using the little torch, shining it along the ground and was horrified to discover the trees alive with birds flying upwards, outwards and anywhere. Some called as they went, others scraped the branches in their panic. A few were woodpigeons with their clapping flight, but most of them were titmice, chaffinch and siskin. Hastily I switched off the torch and thrust it back into my pocket.

Dark clouds were obscuring the waning moon, the wind sighed in the long grass and all was peaceful, until I heard sounds of 'niking' and Missy, Jude, Little'un and Sis came padding up, the smell of musk hanging on the warm air. They were all very playful and I found myself used as an object round which to race. Their gyrations made me giddy, for I felt none too steady as it was. I saw the Clifford sow near the Old Barn ruins, and left the youngsters to make contact with her; I squatted down, speaking softly, whereupon she stopped snuffling in the meadow grass and came up 'purring'. I sat down to let an earthy snout nuzzle my hair. The fresh smell of damp earth was indescribable. Time passed as I sat with the old badger on my lap, feeling drowsy and content with my world, when something made me look across field towards the Ridge. A spotlight beam was shining down to the sett in Cliffords Bank. I called urgently to the badgers, who were now scrambling about amongst the old beams where once the barn had stood. The anxiety in my voice was almost contagious; they sense my fear and I sense theirs. We ran on to the next field, the six of us doing our best to out race the others, then on to the track that goes through the Bank, so bringing us below the lampers on the field above. The badgers had barely gone to earth when a lurcher appeared further along. In a moment, it had picked up their scent and 'homed' in straight for the entrance down which Missy and her mother had gone. I shooed it away. It looked uncertainly at me, then ran through the elmbrush, back to the top of the Bank. I managed to avoid the light and reached the Poplar Row undetected. I decided to wait till these lampers settled on one field to do some serious lamping, then run down and phone a patrol giving their exact position on the farmland. But it didn't work out like that; instead, the lurchers worked back over the badgers' trail, back to the ruins, across the meadow, down through the pear orchard. Why they did this, I will never know, nor why the lampers let them.

I gave up waiting after half-an-hour and went into the barn to phone; I had barely been there two minutes, when the group went past outside! I never switch on the light because of this very possibility; once lampers realise a phone is housed here, it is bound to be vandalised. Whilst the station officer spoke to the patrol, I watched as the beam shone out along the farm road parallel with the railway line. I told the police in which direction they were heading, then ran to try and catch them up. If the patrol met them as it crossed the bridge, the poachers might run back and I would be there.

However, that didn't work out either. I saw them far ahead, cross the field halfway along, then disappear as the ground dropped. Were they coming full circle back to the yard again? I returned to the farmyard and looked all round. No sign of lampers, patrol cars or anything moving. Then suddenly, there were the poachers, complete with the two lurchers (one almost pure greyhound, the other tall, slender and shaggy with a very broad head), walking without beam, round the side of Rob's garden on to the field in front of the cottage! Once there they proceeded to lamp up field (Rob's dog made no sound, incredibly), and I moved close against the front gate as the lampers were less likely to turn their light towards the cottage for fear of detection by the occupants. I watched the shaggy longdog run the beam like an arrow and kill, but not retrieve. A tall, slender man (who I'm sure I've seen before), ran along the beam and picked the rabbit up. At that moment, the light went out and they were all running across field. Then vehicle headlights shone out to my left from behind the cottage, over the place where moments previously, the hunters and hunted had been. I took it to be a patrol, when the lights disappeared and I ran round the side of the garden in time to see its red rearlights going over the hill. I hadn't actually seen the vehicle, so wondered if in fact, other lampers had turned up only to find a group already here? This had been known!

I went back and phoned, then remained outside the barn. Two patrol cars and a dog handler's van converged there moments later, one from the Briarmead side. The track across the farmland was very muddy so he'd had to take care. The mystery vehicle had been police, though the driver hadn't known the lampers had only gone minutes before (not surprising really, and I knew just how exasperated he must feel), nor how near to the farmyard he had been. Behind me was Philip with the dog handler. No vehicles had been seen, but they would check as they returned and then go round the outside of the area again. I said I would go across the land in case the lampers were just lying low till the police had gone, which they could easily do in such a big area. I mentioned I had the small

torch and if I caught up with them, I'd follow closely showing the light so that the patrols could see the direction in which we were going. Someone asked rather drily what kind of fracture had I sustained to my arm last spring – greenstick or compound? We went our separate ways, but though I walked round the two farms and High Ridge for the next hour and a half, I saw nothing more of the poachers.

That morning I spoke to Barry to find he had encountered the blue transit van parked at the top of Briarmead at 10.30 a.m. last Sunday morning. On checking, he found it contained a shovel and other equipment, so continued on his rounds and discovered a group of people (men and boys aged 9–11), at the badger-occupied part of the sett in Cliffords Bank. They had with them an assortment of dogs (norfolks and jack russells) and a lurcher. Barry spoke to a 'thin, weedy, ferrety-faced chap' who said they had merely been out for a family walk and exercising the dogs, when one of their terriers bolted a fox into an entrance. I remarked to Barry that with two miles of Boundary Bank and the hundreds of holes it contains, how coincidental their terrier should have bolted a fox into one of the few badger-occupied entrances! I gather he had been rather sarcastic over a family walk including a van containing so much equipment. He told them to get the dog up, get off his land and stay off. Then he went away, for as he rightly said 'you can't call up a dog quickly once it's really onto something'. He returned later to find all the people in the van waiting for 'ferret-face' now armed with the shovel and about to dig for his dog. Barry pointed out that the sett was very old and deep and he'd better not dig his bank or else. The farmer again came back to find van, people and dogs, all gone. With five badgers now in residence there, I wondered to Barry if they did get the dog up unharmed – or indeed, if a terrier really was underground? Barry had heard no whining or barking and the sett hadn't been dug into.

I told him I had informed Tony Gould of my incident with this van and on checking with Oakley police found it had recently been sold by a city firm and hadn't been re-registered. Tony was told to ask again in two or three weeks' time.

I told PC Alan Matthews of Barry's encounter with the transit van and also mine. He was very helpful, saying that they would speed up the tracing of its new owner. The sooner this was known, the better for everyone. I would ask the farmers to keep a weather eye open, as I felt this van could be back before Christmas, now less than three weeks away. Not however, parked at the foot of High Ridge or on Briarmead, but somewhere well tucked out of sight. I confirmed with Alan that the police could escort these poachers off the farmland (and Barry's part of

Ashcroft Woods), now that the owner/occupier had told them to stay away.

I felt sure that 'ferret-face' knew my area, but hadn't been here for some time. He could be a man I know (certainly he knew me that Sunday) and I wished I had seen his face. It is quite possible that he is one of those who work a regular circuit taking rabbits, fox, badger, anything from one locality, then moving on to the next. As with my gas-cylinder man, it can be up to three years before they return. In theory, this allows for a fresh 'build-up' of foxes or badgers. In actual fact, of course, with more and more groups just as interested, these animals don't now have such an opportunity to do so.

I discussed with Tony Gould how children are taken with their fathers and older brothers on poaching expeditions. The RSPCA inspector said this is commonly used as a cover, as most people seeing children feel the situation must be innocent. Some children are very affected by animal suffering; others can be as callous as their parents. It just depends how they are brought up. I recalled the two men who lamped my very first badger here. The little lad I met at the van with them held the lurcher, whilst Roger Smith and his friend carried the badger between them. The child appeared quite unmoved by its piteous cries.

It had been raining steadily for twelve hours until 4 a.m. that morning, when it began to ease. The Cliffords Bank badgers were out briefly (though not the old sow), to do some worming in the temporary 'stream' formed where the water pours off the Bank and meets the field edge below. There woodland badgers seemed to have reversed setts. Lesley and Candy were now settled at the Crater Sett; Susie and Crisp at the Old Cherry. They too came out briefly and I even had a muddy game with Crisp and Candy! Then all was quiet but for Sandy's vixen calling from the Chantry and a tawny fluting. The bright crescent moon and stars were struggling now between dark clouds.

At 7 a.m. as I stood on the Wildflower Path looking over Briarmead and the farmland beyond, moving orange lights weaved in and out through the distant dimness as a city bound train moved through the landscape like a bespangled necklace. I stayed at the setts till 9.30 a.m. as it was so unusually dark and there was no one about. This obviously upset the calculations of a shooter erecting a hide at the far end of the Cherry slope and two more men busy making another at the Chantry! With their abuse ringing in my ears that morning, I came to the reluctant conclusion that it is one thing to have a bye-law prohibiting the use of firearms and quite another to enforce it!

Walking home I met John Shaw and Rob and asked the farmer if I could leave my son's security torch on the shelf above the office telephone, explaining that the next time we had lampers, I would take the torch after phoning the police. When the poachers switched off their beam and made a dash for it, I would follow with my torch shining so that the patrol could see in which direction we were heading and be waiting there when we came off the land.

I had been out from 9 p.m. the previous evening – a Friday. It was rarely worth making the hour long journey back after I felt this area was safe from lampers, for by the time I reached home, it was almost time to return for the 'pre-dawn' watch. It was a damp, very dark night with slight wind. My night vision was excellent. I was standing at the back of High Ridge and looking out towards the Poplar Row, when I heard a dog bark not far behind me. I stayed in against the trees, awaiting developments, but none came.

Later I sat in John's barn to write up my notes, just going to look from the door every so often to see all was well. Nothing had come of the 'hide' but I was finding it useful! This door moves open slightly, then stays in that position. Only a high wind will move it, for being solid wood it is very heavy. Something made me raise my eyes from writing, to see framed in the lighter background, a large pair of erect ears! Josh's vixen came daintily forward, cautiously followed by her mate. She came up in greeting, whilst he carefully scent-marked some stakes leaning against a wall, a pile of fruit-picking ladders and a crate. I realised as the pungent smell reached my nostrils, that John or Rob would notice next time they came in here – oh well!

Now my foxes froze, their ears turning, their gaze out to the lighter sky beyond the door. What had they heard? I went to the door as they silently passed through and on the instant, three shots sounded over the Top Field . . . but there was no light or beam. The foxes had gone, down towards Rob's cottage and away. I walked silently along the Poplar Row and close against the trunks with the memory of two other occasions when I had heard shots with no apparent lights there. I recalled the constable talking about image intensifiers as we sat in the patrol car on Briarmead that morning. But surely they were out of the price range of most people? I had almost convinced myself that there was some simpler explanation, when from a distance I heard men's voices talking quietly and there moving along the wood edge I saw two figures – and I thought a dog though the grass grows long there – heading in the Briarmead direction.

I followed parallel and behind them along the side of Cliffords Bank. There were no badgers around, fortunately. One man was firing and twice, thrice a dog retrieved. I could see a spark from his rifle. It was not a shotgun for it had a sharp report, but he certainly was shining no light. I moved closer though we still had the width of the field between us. One man glanced round and stood staring over to me, the other following suit. I saw that they wore what appeared to be motor-bike 'goggles' but somehow different. Surely they couldn't see me; and yet I felt they could. Next moment they had gone into the wood with the dog running after. I saw and heard no more of them nor any other people.

Later, I was told that these men were wearing image intensifiers known as 'tank-drivers goggles'. These night-viewing devices are used by military vehicle drivers, helicopter pilots, security surveillance and biological researchers. They have short lenses which makes use of any available light. The image appears green to black. At one time, they were priced well above the average pocket, but now a Dutch firm exports them at around £2,000. The man to whom I spoke is a naturalist, lecturer and photographer and has such a pair himself. He added that photographic developers use them all the time for walking about their darkrooms. Such darkrooms are vast in size and anyone could loan a pair, probably with permission, over a weekend to return the following Monday. He also said that infra red would show a more precise image, but a filtered spotlight would be necessary in conjuction with it. However, unless viewed head on by an observer, this beam would not be noticeable at night.

Just after midnight on a dull, damp, very warm night, Lesley and her two cubs, Candy and Crisp, found me tawny-watching at the top of Briarmead. I never liked the badgers being on the lane, so I walked over to the Old Barn ruins with them following and so on to the meadow behind the woods. Some while later we were joined by the Clifford sow and Missy. The latter had been foraging in the wood I think.

Candy started to dig out beneath a bee-hive, which inevitably began to tilt, so that I was afraid the whole thing would come down on her. I was trying to stop a *very* determined young animal from having her own way, when a shot rang out, then another loud and clear, just above us on the

field. Next moment the place seemed all badgers as the animals came rushing past us. I ran up in time to see the two men wearing 'tank-drivers goggles', with rifles but no dog this time, and chased after them into the wood, determined to get closer and find out more about them. However, the roles were reversed when they turned and started to chase me. This was the first time I've had to compete with others having good night vision. A rather sobering experience, especially as running started me coughing and once started, I found I couldn't stop. By now I was being fired at, the men swearing and shouting. I ducked under a holly and waited for them to run by, then followed at a distance. We were very near the Warby side and the well on Pete's land. Out in the open I let them get ahead in case they looked round. I searched everywhere for a parked vehicle but finally gave up and went home for an hour's rest before dawn-watch.

Out again at 5.30 a.m. I did my usual check for vehicles. I came on to the Old Cherry Sett slope well before first light and stood by a coppiced chestnut for a moment, idly looking down the slope and thinking of the night's events. Two shots sounded, loud and close and I jumped in surprise, lost my footing on the wet leaves and fell. I stayed there listening but could hear no movement, though the wind in the branches above would probably have covered any. I heard nothing more (except the tawnies parlying ten minutes later) and saw no one though I walked round sett-checking till 8.45 a.m.

At home I phoned Sergeant Collins to let him know what had happened. He asked me if we had considered buying a handset radio, one set for me and the other for one of the farmers. Feeling very exasperated and not at my most tactful, I pointed out that if we could have afforded it, I would have had it long ago. I should have thought he would have realised that. Did he seriously think I enjoyed the position I was in? I added that if the early morning shooter was one of the image-intensifier men, then they must know I guard the setts. Their goggles made it impossible to identify them.

The 17th December was a cold, starry night with no moon and a wind. The foxes were very vocal with much scent-making on the males' part. Lesley and Candy found me at 2.20 a.m. having obviously picked up my scent trail. I was greatly concerned to see the mother had an enormous gash running down her forehead and between her eyes, narrowly missing the right one. Like us, they have little flesh there, so it was open to the bone. It could not possibly been caused by a vehicle or barbed wire. I know the results of such injuries too well. My thoughts leaped to lampers; I had been her since 10.30 p.m. last evening and all had been quiet, but could there have been earlier poachers? Her injury was consistent with the cut I received from a spade once – but lampers don't carry spades. I returned home for the inevitable hydrogen peroxide. Lesley came quite happily between my knees to have the wound cleaned. Her trust shamed me; I felt I failed my badgers again and again.

It was a beautiful dawn, the sky all shades of salmon, cerise, yellow and blue. I walked round sett-checking and at the Crater Sett, where Lesley and Candy were denning, I found a length of raw (undyed) leather, lying outside an occupied entrance. It hadn't been there yesterday and the animals hadn't been digging out. There was no sign of disturbance; just this folded round handle of leather, the earth-stained end with still wet teeth marks and two indentations suggesting tie-marks, at regular intervals along its length. Obviously it had been used to cover the handle of . . . what?

At home, my son Ross suggested trying the leather 'handle' on the folding-spade I had bought from the field sports catalogue. It fitted like the proverbial glove, the slight bulge at the earth-marked end neatly covering the ratchet which holds the handle in place for use.

Tony Gould came later. I told him I had a phone call confirming that Don Francis' dogfight was scheduled for Boxing Day. I also knew he had a lot of dogs at Bourne Place. Both Tony and I didn't feel a dogfight would take place there now as it was too obvious. He asked me to let the RSPCA know if I did hear of a venue and time, even if only ten minutes before the start, as they might be able to move in before everything was cleaned up and cleared away.

A local man had told me that a fox had been found behind Rendcombe village with its leg broken in a gin trap. The police had been informed and the fox destroyed. Soon afterwards, a patrol car stopped the man's friend as he walked his dog in the lane, asking if he had seen a certain transit van parked and to let Oakley station know if he did. So it would appear that 'ferret-face' was still untraced and our police were doing their best to find him.

I told Tony about this and we discussed the poaching problem in the area. He offered to come out on the land any time to Christmas Eve if I felt that trouble was brewing; on Christmas Day and Boxing Day, he and his wife would be away. I wouldn't want to take advantage of this as I felt he had more than enough to cope with in his job as it was. Nevertheless, I was very grateful for his offer.

Two nights later it was damp and mild with clear skies. Susie and Crisp had dug out three entrances of the Old Cherry Sett. They had just finished, when Lesley and Candy appeared from the field above. These four sows, both young and adult, got on amazingly well and sometimes I had to remind myself that the cubs were in fact, Lesley's not Susie's. They all mutually groomed in a hollow which was fast being worn near the old tree's roots; the bare earth was becoming smoother and shinier as time passed. Crisp came to join me and decided on a game of tugging the bottom of my jacket, then hanging on with teeth well embedded! I promptly sat on the ground, spoiling her play but saving my coat, waited till she lost interest and went to earth, then walked on with Lesley and a now playful Candy. Play tends to be infectious I find! She didn't repeat her sister's game however, but restricted her energies to nose-diving piles of dead leaves and bundling my boots.

She too went to earth at the Crater Sett, so I took the opportunity of a few quiet moments with the mother, I sat with Lesley on the edge of the crater, examining her swollen face. It wasn't infected, as the other badgers (her daughters included), cleaned it for her. The 'peroxide didn't 'fizz' when I bathed it. The bone had swollen with the violence of the blow and her right eye was almost closed. She was well in herself and very affectionate, now purring and nuzzling my chin. Meanwhile, Candy had re-emerged and came up to us purring with head lowered. Next moment, she had dropped a large, solid object at my side – a hard, red ball, which had once belonged to my dog. I had quite forgotten I had ever brought it to these woods. Lesley took it in her jaws, still purring; Candy turned her head sideways and gently took it from her mother's mouth. The purring of the two sows was loud in the confinement of the hollow. I put an arm round each animal and in sudden affection for the two, pushed my face between theirs. The ball dropped heavy and solid into my lap as my badger ladies proceeded to groom my hair!

On Friday 20th I met Barry on Briarmead. Over the past two weeks, equipment had been stolen from their other farm off Burr Lane. Amongst other things was a very heavy anvil. Alfie had all his fourteen ducks and three geese disappear that Wednesday night. Christmas was coming with a vengence! He said that a farmer friend, not far from here, heard shots one night recently and on investigating, saw poachers firing at his sheep with six already dead. The farmer told his wife to phone the police and say he would follow their vehicle with horn blaring and lights blazing. He jumped into his car and did just that. The chase went through two counties, jumping traffic lights and causing other vehicles to scatter. He didn't dare get too close as every so often, one of the poachers fired at his car. Nowhere were they stopped however and eventually returning (in a circle as it happened), he lost them. The police reckoned they were probably trying to get back to the Laversley area.

However, Laversley police tend to feel their poachers come from us! Barry wasn't sure whether these people were lampers as it was a light night and the sheep would have been seen fairly well without a beam. I remarked that it puzzled me why poachers in our county don't seem to use silencers on their guns. They are cheap enough to buy and fit and I knew from researching the lamping article that silencers are commonly used in other areas.

Shortly before dawn on Christmas morning, the rain ceased for a few moments. It had rained countrywide for 36 hours with brief pauses and some parts of the West Country were flooded. But for the occasional sound of motorway traffic, it was very peaceful here. I was wet and very muddy, as the badgers had investigated me earlier. Lesley's face was healing well, though she would probably always bear the scar. In six more weeks she would be three years old! The hen tawny flew on to the old cherry's trunk, as I sat writing my notes, and stood looking into the water of its crevice-pool, one strong, taloned foot grasping the fissured bark. Her mate 'kewiked' from the trees somewhere behind us.

Twenty minutes later, at first light, a man came walking down from the field above. He stood almost next to me, looking around the clearing made by the great tree's fall, and didn't immediately realise I was there. He was a tall burly man, perhaps 35 years old, and was wearing a long jacket and cap with a close-clipped moustache and beard. He stared down at me for a long moment, then turned and ran back the way he had come. I followed him to the lane and he began to run up it, calling. A van coming down hill stopped and he climbed in next to the driver who sounded his horn several times as they sped off towards the main road, it disappearing over the curve of the tarmac before I could read the number. Another van came tearing down the hill behind me and I jumped out of the way only just in time – a long, dark van; there was not enough light to distinguish colour yet. I only registered part of its number and that it contained two men.

I walked back to the sett and looked about me with affection. The wood had a wet beauty as the dead leaves and young honeysuckle foliage glowed in the dampness. At last it was becoming lighter, though the rain was steady. I stayed well into the morning, sometimes coming on to the lane to look across at Cliffords Bank with Briarmead's wet surface a shining ribbon in the poor light.

As I walked home towards the gap in the Boundary Bank, I heard a quail, then saw it come out of the undergrowth there! No wonder it hadn't migrated with the others, for one wing seemed tiny and malformed. How had it lived though the frosts of November? I think perhaps the answer lay in the deep cover within the Bank. I stood there in the rain for a long time, watching it with great pleasure except for the certainty that it would die in our winter. Could I perhaps help it to survive?

By Boxing Day it had rained almost continously for three days. The Bourne had risen by four feet, threatening to flood out villages nearby, and farmers had been busy dragging sheep to safety from flooded fields. A week earlier, two trenches were dug through the bank of Briarmead allowing the water to gush into the field below, so for the first time in some years, the little lane wasn't flooded. I had brought a small plastic pail out with me with soft, dry grass inside and positioned it carefully in the hedge a short distance from the roosting quail. I made it tilt downwards and faced it next to a blackthorn trunk, camouflaging it with bracken. There was no guarantee of course, that the bird would accept it. I would like to keep it alive this winter.

The following day, I saw my 'quail pail' was occupied. The next stop was food. The special constable Dave Jones and his wife kept Japanese ornamental quail, so I phoned to ask them what seed they fed theirs on – they said they gave their quails chick crumbs. Our pet shop was out of stock, so Dave kindly brought me some of theirs. As I passed nearby the quail's roosting place well before first light, I could scatter some each morning.

The last night of December was cloudy with deep frost again, so I went out early in case of lampers. All was quiet, however, and by midnight the near full moon appeared sailing in cloudy skies. The lunar light, streaming from sky to earth, touched all with an ethereal radiance. Soon large, soft snowflakes were drifting slowly in the moonlight. I stood on Long Field, my gloved hand outstretched and looked at the moon's great disc through one such flake. The light was cut into patterns, each glittering facet reflecting the planet above.

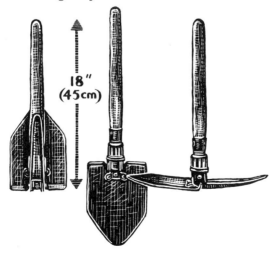

Chapter 5

I was on the land by 9.30 p.m. on New Year's Eve; a mild, windy night. I stood in the meadow behind Ashcroft Woods watching the firework display on the skyline and listening to the ships' horns heralding the New Year. The waning moon sailed from behind a cloud just as one of the three badgers at my side (Crisp, of course), stuck a long snout down the top of my boot. Her mother stood on hindlegs, front paws on my hip and looked up at me enquiringly when the ships' horns sounded. A deep snuffle, then a violent sneeze and Crisp's face reappeared. She bumped Lesley's upright figure and next moment, the three of them were playing chase, sometimes in circles, sometimes jumping over one another; a whirling mêlée of bodies. The game ended just as suddenly. Susie groomed Lesley's face and I sat down on the grass while Crisp made herself comfortable in my lap, lying against my chest, raking her belly with long-clawed paws, washing as she parted the fur. My hand came in contact with a moist, warm tongue. Now I was groomed, hand, watch; the tongue curled inside my coat sleeve, then outside. Someone's paws were at my back, then on my shoulders; now my hair was groomed. This had to be Susie as Les was by my right shoulder, washing my face. A tawny quavered from the distance as the fitful moon disappeared once more.

That past week, I had been checking my rather neglected foxes and confirmed what I suspected earlier – Josh was missing. The farmers said that for the last three weeks, there had been a great deal of shooting around dusk. I had found no body, so suspect they were right when they suggested he had been shot. Though the price of a prime fox pelt had dropped that winter, fox fur was still a worthwhile source of revenue. My foxes had become very wary of lampers and only went hunting in the evenings, especially during the deep frosts. Josh would have been seven or eight years old (I never knew him as a cub) and was slowing down, though his dark, melanistic fur was still very luxuriant and unusual, as was his size. He was the first fox to play with me, treating me as one of his kind. He had an unusually long life for a wild fox, and if he was shot cleanly, that was preferable to a lingering death as he slowed down. That was not to say I didn't miss him, I did.

Just after midnight on Sunday 5th January the deep orange disc of the moon slowly rose above Crosshampton, a very awe-inspiring sight. Later it began to rain heavily and I kept very still and quiet as Jude and Susie each quartered a patch of the field I was on, worming as they went. It never ceases to interest me how a badger can spend perhaps two hours in such conditions on one small area and find all its food requirements for the night.

At about 3 a.m. I saw figures walking up Briarmead. There were four men and two lurchers; I watched in apprehension as they took the two-oak track towards Cliffords Bank. The other badgers were foraging near the sett. I left my two animals on the field and followed after the poachers who were not using a beam yet. They walked through the gap, then followed below the Bank and passed the beehives. Then at the bottom of the great spoil heaps, they loosed a dog (a long-legged alsatian, probably a straight greyhound cross). Almost immediately it picked up the scent and streaked up the Bank with a lamper following. The next moment was chaos, as the rest of the badgers were on that field above. Three men had gun-mounted beams, whilst the fourth held a net. The idea must have been to keep one lurcher and lamper round the sett to block the badgers' entry, the others to aid the dog and dazzle the prey. One thing was abundantly clear. These men were after badgers, for disappearing rabbits were ignored by men and dogs alike.

Even as I ran to reach the badgers, I saw one, her scarred mask clear in the beam, turn and face the dog. The man with the net ran forward holding it in both hands ready to throw as I shouted. We stared at one another; he, since my appearance on the field was obviously unexpected; I, because I knew him. He was the man of Christmas morning at the Old Cherry Sett. I told him to leave the badgers alone and he warned me to get out of the way or else. Lesley and the dog were sparring, she giving a wickedly snapping sideways swing of her jaws as the alsatian tried to close in. I didn't want to get too near, lest I became 'pig-in-the-middle'. They would need to call the dog off to net her and then I could keep close and stop them.

There was a sharp shot from a beam-mounted rifle as something passed unpleasantly close. I ducked and went for the nearest man who promptly swung his gun-mount at my head. The place seemed full of men, dogs and badgers trying to get away. Something cannoned into me and I fell, tripping my attacker. I heard another sharp crack to my right and from ground level now, saw Lesley stagger – another shot – and fall. One of her cubs (Candy I thought), rushed by me full pelt, towards the Bank and safety, just as the collie-cross lurcher, running as only a longdog can, sent the young badger hurtling upwards to fall with a sickening thud. I scrambled to her and pushed the dog off, slapping it about the head with my hands. It backed off uncertainly and I set Candy carefully on her feet. She seemed to flop, then steady herself, but her hindlegs couldn't bear the weight and my hands were sticky with her blood.

I looked round to find the meadow empty. The badgers, Lesley's body, men and dogs all gone, but I knew in which direction the latter had headed and ran round to where the Bank turns at right-angles. There they were, hurrying along the path leading on to High Ridge; two carrying something between them. But crossing the Ridge, they saw me following and a succession of shots came my way. Where the lower scree slopes were cleared of bushes last October, I had to let them get well ahead, being a too easy target in the empty space. Thus I lost the group at Maddon Lane and wasted valuable time checking possible parking places there. By now the rain had ceased. I ran through the motorway tunnel then up the track on Roger Johnson's land where sometimes stolen vehicles are dumped and their tyres removed, but nothing was there. In the stillness of the night, I heard a distant vehicle driving away. I recrossed Maddon Lane and started up the motorway bank just as another vehicle drove away above me.

I returned to find Candy where I had left her with Susie by her side carefully cleaning the blood. Lesley's injured daughter could not walk, so I gently picked her up and carried her in easy stages down the lane. Faithful Susie padded at my side, occasionally looking up at us. I had great difficulty reaching the Old Cherry Sett, for with her accumulation of winter fat, Candy was only slightly lighter than an adult sow. I left her right up against her favourite entrance, though with her hindquarters so obviously paralysed, I doubted if she could go to earth. One thing was certain, I could never carry her home.

It was raining hard again as I walked round at 7 a.m. and found five teenage youths trying to sleep under a plastic sheet at the Crater Sett! They had been on a walking holiday and three hours ago had decided to spend the remainder of the dark hours trying to get some sleep, rather than walk on home some miles away. They seemed dry and cheerful enough beneath their make-shift shelter, huddled in sleeping bags. At least I needn't worry this morning about badger-diggers at this sett with five likely lads trying to sleep nearby.

Returning to the steep slope of the Old Cherry Sett, I found two bedraggled tawnies perched on one of its branches and both badgers gone. I would need to get something to destroy Candy painlessly for she would only die a lingering death like this. If a vet wouldn't help, I knew Tony would.

Heavy-hearted with the loss of Lesley, I had no great desire to return home for a while, so walked slowly about the lamping area, filled with regret. There at the foot of Cliffords Bank, I picked up a slip – the lurcher's slip lead incorporating its collar for quick release and recalled the long-legged alsatian off slip, leaping up the Bank hot on the scent. I crossed the railway and went under the motorway and round to the odd little piece of road leading to nowhere since the motorway was built. I surprised a resident working a bit further along on his car and asked him if he ever noticed strange vehicles parked at the end, late at night. Yes, he had, and no one in them. 'Not courting couples?' I asked. 'No, quite empty; usually vans and always gone by the morning.' Was this the answer to some of our lampers' mystery parking places? It was nearly 11 a.m. when I reached home, tired and disheartened, and phoned Tony Gould who as always, promised to help.

The RSPCA Inspector was on call all that weekend. I had said that late evening would be best, for if the badger could get above ground again, it would take her some time. It was still raining when we left at 10.30 p.m. There was Candy huddled against the old cherry trunk. She was trying to clean her fouled hindquarters and seemed quite dazed. I could almost read the question-mark in her brain. I didn't think she was in great pain, for the shoulder wound caused by the lurcher wasn't deep; but her hindlegs wouldn't do what she wanted. I picked her up and laid her on her back in my lap, as she often lay when washing herself. She raised her long snout as my hand smoothed the sleek throat. I don't think she ever registered Tony. She only gave the smallest start as the needle entered below her ribcage. A moment later, Candy's head settled gently down on my stroking hand.

Tony had to hurry off as he was still on duty with other calls to make.

I said goodbye and watched his van carefully negotiate the treacherous surface of Briarmead as by now the rain had turned to sleet. I took the young badger's body and laid it in one of the holes dug by the men who had searched in vain for her mother when she was left as the only surviving badger here, trowled the wet earth down on top and smoothed it over.

The following morning, the wet bracken glowed like fire under a lowering sky. I watched the squirrels in the bare branches above, as the sleet settled on my face and hair. This morning matched my mood. Only now was the enormity of my loss striking me. No Lesley. For nearly three years I had watched her, played with her and tried to protect her, in vain.

I took the Briarmead route home through the woods and had barely walked halfway to the ponds, when a patrol car caught up with me. In it were two constables I know well who asked me how the injured badger was now. Their indignation and sympathy, as I recounted what had happened, somehow eased my sense of loss. They said how dearly they would like to catch the lampers but without two-way radio, they felt it was virtually hopeless. They would ask their Inspector if I could be allowed use of it and I thanked them, though we all knew Sergeant Collins had already tried. They queried where the occupied setts were and getting into the car myself, we tried to reach that on Cliffords Bank. The track was far too muddy by now with the sleet, so we headed back to Oakley. One said he often patrolled across Pete's farm at night and I remembered how once I had said to him that badgers apart, a knowledge of the routes on and off Colts Farm would be of value. That farmland was an escape route for burglars, and farm equipment was sometimes stolen from the fields during the summer months. As he described the tracks he took across the hillside, I realised he'd taken my words seriously. I felt much less defeated by the lamping when we parted.

Two nights later, snow was lying thinly and only little Crisp was above ground, lonely and forlorn. She played with me, but there was no heart in it for either of us. I sat in the snow on the fallen cherry, she scrambled on to my lap, and I wrapped the fronts of my warm anorak around her body. How could I have imagined, that August morning when she stole my 'badger-guarding rations' that five months later, four badgers from this sett would be dead?

By the 9th, the snow had gone except around the well and its field on Pete's land and one or two sheltered spots in the woods. My quail was fine and perky. I forgot to leave his chick crumbs until I was on my way home that morning and found him waiting for them!

Sergeant Collins came that afternoon and brought with him a young constable from one of the villages, Mark Craig, who had trained and worked as a gamekeeper with deer for some time before joining the police force, so had a practical knowledge of shotguns, poachers and wildlife generally. He queried the weapon that killed Lesley and although I knew it hadn't been a shotgun, I really couldn't have said more than that.

We agreed on the touch formula for leading patrols to lampers' vehicles and though the sergeant was noticeably unenthusiastic, he promised to inform all the men that might be involved. He had done everything he could to obtain a two-way radio for me, but with no luck. I asked whether it was the price of police radios that prohibited my having it or whether it would set a precedent or might fall into the wrong hands. It was the last two, he said, not the cost, and this I could understand. Sergeant Collins had certainly tried his best and no one could do more.

The following night I was greeted by Missy and Jude in the field below the boundary Bark. Missy was very affectionate, stretching up on hindlegs, front paws on my thigh. Jude, not to be outdone, hung playfully on my anorak sleeve! All the while, a vixen was calling down near Glebe farmyard, but it was too far away to determine if it was Sandy's vixen or that of the now dead Josh. In this entire 800 acres of three farms, scrub area and woods, only these three foxes remained. Both females could mate with Sandy and, in theory, build up a new *Vulpes vulpes* population here. Something similar happened last year when Sandy's father was killed, though the shooting and lamping cut the numbers down again to these three! Certainly this area is over-hunted. Perhaps it was as well that I had finished my five-year fox study now, since there was little left to study anymore.

Later I found all the badgers on a freshly ploughed field at the Warby side, worming in the wetness. There were mole hills everywhere and I watched one after another being formed. So did the old Clifford sow. With a quick twist of her head, she threw the unfortunate mole high in the air to land next to Little'un, who made the most of a rare opportunity. The old badger hunted about for her lost meal in a puzzled sort of way, whilst the youngster looked on with an almost smug expression! Crisp was very clinging, padding after me as I walked back through the wood to check occassionally for lampers. I was quietly looking across Long Field, when she came up purring with head raised and there between her jaws was the old ball! How many badgers and foxes have played with that heavy, solid toy? It disappears, sometimes for a long while, only to appear again. For ages we played, I rolling it down the Cherry Sett slope, Crisp bounding after, till breathless we sat together on the old trunk with a tawny preening its plumage above.

Although I didn't know it at the time, much earlier this same night a patrol saw lampers working over on Glebe farm. A quick check was made for the vehicle and Alan Matthews with a colleague waited nearby and caught the poaachers on their return. In spite of their using a spot light beam 'going across the land like daylight' I was never at any time aware of lampers, which only goes to show the size of the area and the undulating ground. While the patrol waited, they saw the vehicle had a heap of straw in the back with a tube protruding from it. When questioned, the poachers said this was for the dogs and although they had only caught rabbits, the general feeling was that they had been on the lookout for badgers.

At 11 p.m. the moon, like a slice of melon, lay heavily on its back. As it set, it moved slowly down the Poplar Row to disappear below the distant fringe of Prossers Wood. All that afternoon and evening there had been a gale force wind that was only now beginning to ease. It had blown the roof clean off John's little barn that stood near the brick built one. The roof sat neatly over the path leading down to the farmyard, looking very bizarre. It was a beautiful night sky with clouds lying like the ripple of hair across a creamy brow. Frost was creeping upon us and our breath began to vaporise, as Crisp and I stood together in the meadow. She was a lonely little badger now for Little'un and Susie were feeling the stir of life within them and had no time for the yearling. Sis and Missy also seemed preoccupied and the old sow couldn't be bothered with a youngster. Jude would be friendly, but he seemed unwittingly to intimidate Crisp.

As the only male badger for the whole area, Jude was a vital animal in this colony. If he should be taken or die before mating this spring with the sows, it could spell disaster for all. Normally a sow is mated in her first year or soon after and due to delayed implantation, has her first litter at two years old. (Lesley's first litter was an exception to this.) Male badgers take longer to mature, usually in the early spring after their second winter when two years old and fully grown. So if Jude was to die now, any male cubs born wouldn't mate till 1988 and fresh cubs wouldn't be born till 1989. Much rested on this young boar.

Researching the badger-lamping article had far-reaching consequences, mainly because I contacted people I would never normally have had the courage to phone. The article, due to be published next month, might well prove a dismal failure, but what I had learnt in its researching had been an education for me.

The police realised that the Wildlife and Countryside Act of 1981, with all its provisions, was their responsibility to enforce, although the average bobby on the beat would have little knowledge of it. Someone with a genuine interest in the subject was required, to be a focal point for other officers in his force as well as for public organisations, to refer to as problems arose. Essex was the first to have such a Wildlife Liaison Officer, with West Yorkshire a close second. It is a voluntary, unpaid job on top of an officer's normal duties and for most, it makes deep inroads into their off-duty time. What impressed me about the Wildlife officers I came to know was their enthusiasm and concern. All countryside law is such an officer's responsibility, not just that of the 1981 Act, and as I had found for myself, the abuse of it often touched upon more serious crime.

Long after I finished the article, I was still researching. It had opened up a new world of intimidation and fear and I was very concerned, not only for the badger but for everyone. I spoke to farmers, gamekeepers and landowners who often 'looked the other way' if lampers were on their land, for fear that their barns or crops might be burnt down yet again or their wives and children threatened. Certainly what happened on our land was nothing compared to other parts of the country. Poachers are versatile and those that take deer, for example, may be found to have convictions for taking badgers, salmon, pheasants – or for burglary. Burglars not infrequently turn to poaching as a more lucrative, and safer, livelihood.

Later, I was invited on site to see how one police force successfully handled their poaching problem with a Rural Crime Patrol. Here I learnt that poaching is an offence, not a recordable crime, so it is not included in any crime statistics. If it was considered a crime however, with each incident recorded, there would be a national crime wave. Poaching occurs in every county, is increasing year by year and is not likely to go away. Badgers are just one of the lucrative pickings.

It was to West Yorkshire's Wildlife officer that I spoke of the lack of any centralised badger information. (West Yorkshire was unique in having, at the time of writing, the only police-initiated badger group in the country.) He told me that a National Federation of Badger Groups was going to be set up and one of its functions would be to collate all the badger information. He suggested I contact the organisers, which I did and was invited to a conference at Westonbirt in Gloucestershire that coming Saturday, at which the federation was to be inaugurated.

I was determined to go to Westonbirt, a big undertaking for me with a lot to arrange. The badgers here, if they were to survive, must always come first and this winter was the worst we had known for lamping. On

Friday morning, I spoke to Barry on Briarmead, telling him I would be leaving for the conference that afternoon. The college lads had promised to do Saturday morning's 'badgerwatch' for me and Mark Craig said he would come up the lane on Sunday morning and have a look around, in case I wasn't back. John Shaw, Rob and the police would look out for any lampers and I had to admit that I felt happier about the lamping, now some of the poachers had been caught. I hadn't left my area overnight for nearly three years; it would feel strange.

I spent the greater part of the overnight stay at Westonbirt writing letters and leaning out of my bedroom window, watching and listening to a pair of tawny owls flying round the hotel. This was my first visit to Gloucestershire and I was enjoying it. Having no breakfast gave me a good excuse to go for a walk before the conference started. Westonbirt itself seemed to consist of a few houses with telephone and letter box, a girls' boarding school and an arboretum. I chose the latter to explore; the dull, wet morning only served to enhance the winter colours of the trees. A place to remember. I returned to the hotel, muddy but happy, to find cars gradually arriving from different parts of the country.

The conference was a great experience for me and I met many dedicated and interesting people. For years I had been trying – unsuccessfully on the whole – to guard the animals on my patch. To meet so many people doing the same thing was a wonderfully stimulating experience. Their friendliness was heartening and I heard how they tackled their problems; problems often quite different from mine. I had never had to contend with bovine tuberculosis, for example, or with golf-course owners anxious to rid themselves of badgers. During the course of that day the National Federation of Badger Groups was formed, whose aims were broadly to learn, inform and protect.

I returned to Oakley too late that evening to do night patrol, but left home at 4 a.m. on Sunday morning, with chick crumbs for my favourite quail, who was fine. I wanted to check the badgers and although my family suggested I could safety give this Sunday morning a miss, strangely, I seemed to have been away far longer and couldn't wait to get back. At the Old Cherry Sett, Susie growled at Crisp (the first time I had ever known this – I was sure Susie was in cub), before coming and thrusting her long snout into my hand, Susie's favourite method of greeting. Lesley always liked to jump up on hindlegs, whereas Crisp runs circles round me! We all have our little ways. Even the owls gliding gracefully round my head seemed to have noticed my absence. On impulse, I called softly and put out a hand to each. First the hen tawny alighted on my right thumb, then her mate on my left.

It was a mild, wet morning with birdsong everywhere. The ground was strewn with hazel catkins stripped by the squirrels I was watching before dawn. Some of these creatures had young already, snugly tucked away in their dreys so clearly etched now against the blue sky. Little'un was settled at the sett on Colts Farm. I was sure she would cub soon and made a mental note to tell Pete's children.

Later that morning I had a disturbing phone call from a complete unknown. Well, at least now I knew why my contact never gave me the details of the dogfight scheduled for Boxing Day. He wasn't alive to do so. The caller had been a mate of his and was very bitter. I had never known my contact except by a nickname for safety. He had my christian name and ex-directory phone number. That was all and we kept it that way. He had gone to a rendezvous from which he had never returned. But that's how it can be if you inform, in the dogfighting business.

This morning might have been the dawn of creation. Above the slow, sweet curve of Great Chantry, a spread of pink, grey, yellow touched with blue, covered the sky. These barley-sown fields were deepest green and birdsong echoed all around. Below my feet the badgers slept – and Susie had her cubs!

When I last saw her briefly, two nights ago, she seemed very preoccupied and snapped sideways at timid Crisp who ran away into the undergrowth. This night I was sitting quietly on the chestnut-bough seat, watching the soft moonlight stealing through this wood, alone with my thoughts. No noise. No traffic, trains, owls or beasts, no dropping leaf nor whispering wind – when the clear sound of suckling intruded on my idleness. Susie was nursing her young just below and to my right. I sat in a daze of happiness until silence crept in again. Then there was movement in the hole beside my foot, something softly touched my leg, breathed noisily and there was Susie quietly watching me. I made no move towards her, but just sat looking at her. Then in one movement she seemed to flow out of the entrance and stand on hindlegs, her forepaws on my lap, to stare up at me, the sweet, warm smell of milk enveloping us both. I stroked the long, smooth sides of her head with both hands, putting my face into hers, then watched as the young mother washed round her teats, sampling milk as she did so.

First light came and went as the wet earth, a world of fragrance, seemed to intensify my world of scent. In silhouette against the sky, squirrels ran and leaped on the dark-etched boughs. A breeze came softly over the ridge behind me and moved the ivy tendrils clinging to an old birch trunk. By now it was nearly 8 o'clock as Barry's car went up the lane.

By the 24th, Missy too was lactating. I saw her briefly and made contact, checking by gently running my hand beneath her. It came away with milk on it, but in truth, I knew already by the smell lying on the heavy air. My sense of loss had eased and I felt a quiet contentment.

The near-full moon was occasionally visible in a cloud-strewn sky. John Shaw's little barn that lost its roof in the gale had been dismantled and carted away. I seemed to have missed out on my foxes mating this winter, but was sure by their attitude towards each other that Sandy and his vixen had done so. Josh's vixen was very much a loner now that he was gone. Suddenly this night, I seemed to have picked up the threads of my relationship with her. I checked that the batteries of my torch were in order which I kept on the shelf above the phone in Glebe's farm office. It wouldn't do to phone the police to come in for lampers, only to discover the torch not working! I left the vixen outside and when I came out again, found her lying doglike, head on paws, her brush stirring in the dirt at my reappearance. I would call her Watcher. We two were loners, communicating without words. I had noticed before Christmas, that one of the farm men had his chickens housed at the back of the open tractor shed. A dog was kennelled near them in this shed. It never growled as I went passed, but it did this time. Was it my fox company?

It was a cold, breezy first light with the tawnies tremulously hooting by the Crater Sett. Walking through the stand of birches above the Cherry Sett, I found myself enveloped in a fine haze gently drifting and falling. On close inspection it was made up of tiny, light fawn seeds encircled with a paler membrane, difficult to see with the naked eye, but made easier with the monocular. They were from the birch catkins that matured last June and had been gradually broken up by the redpolls, goldfinches, siskins and tits then finally dispersed over a considerable distance by this breeze. Looking closely, I saw they covered everything; bracken, grass, ground and still kept coming as the wind blew from the field. I was standing there quietly, when the bracken to one side of me moved and my vixen reappeared. Casually she came towards me, then moved to where a forked trunk of one of the old birches makes a natural waterhole and drank there, her lapping noisy in the quietness.

As I was on my way home a police patrol asked me if there was any truth in a rumour he had heard, of dead badger bodies lying on High Ridge. All my badgers were accounted for and well. He asked if I knew that the three lampers had been caught and I nodded; it had been well publicised in the local paper, partly to warn others off and partly to encourage people to be vigilant. With luck, perhaps word had got about and now the badgers would be left in peace.

The last two days and nights had clear skies with deep frost, every waterhole continuously ice-bound under a full moon by night and bright sunshine by day. This night, the frost lay on frost, ground iron-hard, breath a continuous vapour about my head, but I was not cold. I became aware of a shadow of a shade in the blackness of the overhang and my vixen slipped towards me, paws soft-crunching the frozen grass, from the shelter of the Boundary Bank.

She walked the setts with me this morning before dawn and caught herself a squirrel in the process and shortly after, a yellow-neck. It was a beautiful dawn, with no sign, sound, or sight of any human, the hazel catkins beginning to open in dusty, yellow clouds above my head.

A company contacted me towards the end of January, offering to put up the money (within reason) for a couple of hand-held radio sets, with two conditions. I must have two-way, not citizens' band, radio as some poachers we knew already used it here, and I must get police advice on it in order to find the best type for what was required. If anything came of this, I would also need someone willing to take responsibility for the receiver radio, but first things first.

Sgt. Collins put me on to the Technical Services Unit at police headquarters who told me, among other things, that private mobile radios cost from £200 to £300 per set and the licence required would be a further £80 for a year. The company was not prepared to pay up to £600 for two hand-held sets, so that was that.

A thin covering of snow lay over the countryside at the end of January. By morning it had frozen and was like glass in the bitter wind. Badger prints, Crisp's I thought, weaved in and out along the Cherry Sett slope. There was no sign of Little'un on Colts Farm. Had she cubbed? On the 31st she put in an appearance and seemed very quiet and restless. She was not lactating. Going home over Pete's land that morning, I carefully checked the bank where her little sett was. There amongst the brambles not far from her main entrance, I found two tiny cubs, still-born. They were covered with a fine, silky fur and seemed so pitifully small and vulnerable lying there that I didn't want Rebecca or her brothers to find them, so I buried the minute bodies just inside the wood.

Chapter 6

February started mild and damp. Susie, Crisp and Sis were foraging together on the Old Cherry slope, leaving snuffle holes everywhere in the soft, brown earth. Then Crisp cleared her entrance, the spoil heap bright amongst the still green bramble leaves. When Susie had gone to earth, I could hear the sounds of suckling again. Crisp appeared, her digging finished, the ball held in her jaws. She stood a moment looking at me, then cocked her head in the direction of the cubs' mealtime. She approached Susie's entrance, but promptly backed away, the ball still clenched in her mouth, but her long snout quivering. Susie scent-marked her cubs' entrance heavily this night; perhaps the yearling had got a whiff of it. Sows with very young cubs do this as a warning to the rest of the clan to keep away. Playing ball with Crisp was an exhausting effort for me at present. An abscess affecting teeth, ear and one side of my face had, as someone unkindly remarked, made me resemble an outsize hamster with one full cheek pouch!

It was a dull yet lovely morning. A crow cawed startlingly as it flew over the wood. Except for subdued traffic from the distance and soft bird sounds near at hand, the wood was quiet. Yet before the first week of the month was over, Ashcroft Woods had become a silent world of white. The stark, leafless tracery of branches above my head were softened by this covering of snow. Gone were the shoots of autumn-sown barley. Long Field stretched away, a smooth blanket now. I had just left my quail his chick crumbs and come into the wood before first light. Crisp came to her entrance, sniffed the cold air, sneezed, then suddenly shot out of the sett, scrambled across the snow and bounded onto the old cherry's trunk beside me, making the strange little 'greeting' sounds of a friendly badger. My arms were round her warm body. Only her stomach and legs were wet from her momentary flounder through the snow. As she settled on my lap I unzipped my anorak and brought her body in against mine. After a moment, however, Crisp scented something and scrabbled at one of its inside pockets. Puzzled, I took the contents out to show her lest her roughness tear the material. Not the spare tissues, recording cassette, monocular – just the chick crumb container. I unscrewed the lid and watched a long, moist tongue investigate its emptiness.

Later that week there were badger prints around Cliffords Bank and I briefly made contact with Jude, who looked bigger than ever in the snowlight with his fur fluffed out against the cold wind. I left my favourite quail his crumbs and didn't see him, but heard a peck, peck, peck on the plastic of his home. There were no badger prints at any of the woodland setts except for those of Lesley's young daughter, who ran circles around me in greeting, then dived into her entrance only to reappear with her ball. When I tired of playing, young Crisp dropped it down the snowy slope and slid down on her bottom after it! Dear, silly little badger, you eased the emptiness I felt at your mother's loss.

Watcher was denning at the disused Felled Logs Sett. As I walked round one morning at first light, I sensed eyes upon me and there she was; Watcher well named! Her prints were everywhere. Snow is such an appalling giveaway. I was praying nobody would send terriers down to get her underground. If they did, I felt I couldn't ask the police to interfere. I sat on a dead trunk, spoke softly and she rested her long, delicate muzzle on my knee. I stroked the thick fur of her shoulders, then her face. As an owl called hauntingly from the Chantry, her big, upright ears turned to catch the sound, her round-pupils still staring into mine. She was cat-like in some ways, yet so dog-like in others. She must miss her mate. Josh and this vixen spent many hours hunting, playing, mating, grooming and sharing in the rearing of their cubs. All her life she knew him, for the dog was much older than she. Watcher could have mated this January with Sandy (a dogfox will couple with more than one vixen in such a situation), but she showed no interest and did not.

At 6.15 a.m. on the 14th it was a poor light with the sky grey and leaden and more snow on the way. My quail was sounding from the snow-bound field. His wispy, haunting call seemed strange against such a background. When I left his food that morning, his head appeared briefly from the hay-filled pail. I was careful that Watcher didn't follow me. A quail meal is acceptable to a fox whatever the time of year!

That Saturday was sunny, but a bitter wind had tortured the snow into strange shapes and heavy drifts lay across some of the Briarmead fields. In the early hours of Sunday morning the temperature rose and, walking in the more sheltered wood, I discovered young Crisp trailing me. We had a marvellous game and I ended up so hot that I took off my anorak and hung it from the nearest tree. Then she decided to get a good teeth-grip on my chunky-knit pullover (badgers love wool) until I took that off too and hung it on the tree well out of her reach. We had a terrific game with her ball and both finished up breathless and hot.

By 6 a.m. she had gone to earth. The quail began to call across the fields, while from the distant Chantry came a tawny's quavering cry. The wind bit deep on this Briarmead side, yet on the eastern-facing slope of the Old Cherry Sett, most of the snow had melted, it was so sheltered. Here the badgers had been busy digging through the dead leaves into the softened ground. Indeed, anyone that morning could have dugout a badger with ease. The animals had turned up bluebell bulbs, also a small rodent's nest. On the patches of remaining snow, badger-prints were everywhere and in the beaten ice path that led from entrance to entrance, permanent pawmarks were preserved. Snow or not, I must still come out to look after the badgers here and in any case, I had my little quail to feed.

Three nights later, Jude was denning with Little'un on Colts Farm. There was a very strong smell of musk on the air, all round the sett and fresh pawprints everywhere. I thought he must have mated with her. Long-duration (and therefore, fertile) mating is common within a few days, or at most, a few weeks after the birth of cubs. This had been perhaps the coldest night for me. The wind ate into the bones of my face and made the branches groan and moan.

Later I found seven dead squirrels, all still warm. They must have been feeding at first light that morning and been killed by the force of the gale, which blew them off balance, altered the gap between branches in mid-leap, or crushed them as tree grated against tree. I left three with Susie at the Old Cherry Sett by simply dropping them one by one into her main entrance. The other four I carried across to Missy on Cliffords Bank. She could do with some fresh meat too, now that she had cubs.

I was standing on top of the fallen Cherry, which was still well-covered in snow, when Jude with Little'un in tow, came up to me. Jude was purring deeply; a very self-satisfied boar! He made me smile. He was very big and handsome, but he was fully grown now at two years old and 'monarch of all he surveyed'. Badger prints where everywhere in the snow. This winter made me think of Sam and how when Lesley had her first cubs, he followed me about. We played on the fallen birch and I snowballed him – it all seemed such a long, long time ago.

That morning Barry told me that Rob saw two men on Cliffords Bank by the beehives. They said they were ferreting and he told them to go away. Later, Barry himself saw a vehicle at the top of Briarmead, drove round and found no one, then had second thoughts. He drove back, got out of his car and went on to that part of the Bank where the badgers den. There amongst the elmbrush were several young men, actually ferreting in the badger sett itself with ferrets and dogs. Whether they were or not, there is of course, a problem in this type of situation. The sow badger sleeps apart from her cubs which are buried in a mass of dry bedding that retains the heat of their bodies. It is not uncommon for terriers to enter the sett and bring out such a cub without encountering the mother.

That particular day, Barry told them to go as it was private land and the men said they had been told it was all right to work the Bank here and also the woods. They had been speaking to someone in the Horse and Hounds, Oakley. The farmer's reply wasn't printable! But this was rather worrying as word had obviously gone round via local pubs that here was a good place and I didn't like the sound of it at all. Two points struck me about our conversation that day. Firstly, in spite of the farm men keeping an eye on things from the yard and Rob's cottage, it was easy to be hidden from view on Cliffords Bank. Secondly, Barry remarked that his neighbours (John Shaw and Rob) had always helped him and Alfie with any shooting or other trouble in his part of the woods that bordered the farmland, but none of them felt obliged to do so now, as Ashcroft Woods had recently been bought by the Parish Council. I could quite understand why they felt like that, for the wood and its problems had long been a headache for all the farmers adjoining it. Nevertheless, it was rather a blow for Ashcroft Woods as no one else could, or would, put in the time and goodwill of these men.

What surprised me though, was the combined determination of the farmers and their men to watch over the badgers here and protect Missy and her cubs against all comers. They had always been concerned, but this was something quite different. I was glad, for Missy, her mother and the cubs, needed all the protection they could possibly get if they were to survive.

On the 19th there was a north-east wind and penetrating frost. There were no badgers abroad that night, nor their pawprints anywhere, but some small prints of a dog at the Old Cherry Sett, especially around the entrance young Crisp had dug out a few nights earlier; also the marks of large size boots.

Watcher came to meet me through the snow, jumping where it was deep. The snow settled on her head; one ear twitched and the flakes were gone. She stood upright against me and I put my face into hers, touched by the beauty of this lovely vixen. Still upright, she began to bite at a forepaw; between the pads frozen ice was packed which can cause lameness if left unchecked. Nibbling and licking she freed the paw from its burden and tended her other feet. Her prints wound in and out of the Scots pines by her den but fortunately they would soon be hidden. She was digging through the snow to a nest; a long-tailed field mouse sprung into the air. A quick twist and a few chews as the bitten off tail slipped from the side of her jaws, a swallow and it was gone.

I left my fox still hunting amongst the snow-covered logs of her home in the Felled Logs Sett and returned to stand looking out on the Old Cherry slope. A green woodpecker that had been searching the bark farther along its trunk, flew up 'yaffling', then all was quiet. Woods and fields lay in a thick, white embrace. The tawny hen glided to her roosting place nearby, her wingbeats as silent as snowflakes.

On a frostless night under a clear half moon, I saw two badgers digging out their sett in the bank above the railway lines. There was very little snow on that part of the steep embankment, probably because this faced east. Occasionally dirt and small stones would shower down onto the rails below. At the noise, one badger turned and looked down mildly interested. I could see five entrances, three of which they dug out. The badgers here are intriguing as they cross the bridge to the fields on the far side of their territory. It is probably as quick as going down the steep embankment, across the rails and up the far side, and certainly much safer, for this line is electrified.

That afternoon, I had discovered fresh prints of a small dog and prints of two different kinds of boots at the Old Cherry Sett, both at the part where Crisp and Sis were denning and at the chestnut-bough entrance where Susie had her cubs. The same prints were evident around Cliffords Bank but not at Colts Farm bank, which sheltered Jude and Little'un. There were seven adult badgers and two cub litters on these 800 acres, but for how long? The snow couldn't last for ever, but at least it was keeping diggers and lampers at bay.

Next night I saw the old sow snuffling amongst the undergrowth inside the wood from her sett in the Bank over the meadow. I knelt in the snow to make contact with her, then her daughter Missy appeared. The latter seemed in very good health, though I couldn't say the same for her mother who was slow and ponderous. I wondered if she would survive this bleak weather. There was a ditch just within the wood-edge which was rarely frosty even on the harshest night and the badgers would often forage beneath the leaves there, as they were doing now. They didn't stay long however and soon returned to their sett on Cliffords Bank. It was very, very cold and the temperature was still falling. In the open field, the wind gnawed into the bones of my face like a living thing.

At the Old Cherry Sett, Crisp appeared briefly to say 'hello' by running round me in circles. Then she offered me her ball by dropping it between us, which I have never known her to do before. But she found it too cold and returned to earth quickly, taking the ball with her.

On the evening of Wednesday 26th, I was staying with Clarissa and Stephen while their parents went out. Stephen, aged 9, was interested in my Sanyo hand tape recorder so I decided to try and record some badger conversation to take with me when I went. The big questions were, would the badgers grace me with their company in this icy weather and would they be vocal? There was a possibility too, that they might take an unhealthy interest in the tape recorder. It seems to attract their attention when I'm using it, which makes me wonder if it emits high-pitched sound that I cannot hear, but they can. All went well, however, apart from a momentary lapse on the part of Crisp who decided that recorders had more play potential than balls! My badgers did all that could have been asked of them – purring, snorting, snickering and, in the case of Crisp, nibbling the cassette! The children would be well pleased. (As it happened, however, they were more amused by my voice telling Crisp she was a horror!)

By 3 a.m. it was snowing again – small, hard flakes of coldness blown on the wind – and my friends had gone to earth. At Pete's lake I jumped up and down on the snow-covered ice, but could make no impression on it; it must have been inches thick. That morning I checked the Yew Sett and Crawfords house; both appeared to be deserted with no prints or dungpits under the trees to indicate badgers in residence and no Uglybug or vehicles outside the old house. Later I heard that the burglar owed money to some of his gang, and had hastily moved away.

One lovely sunny day, I walked into Ashcroft Woods at Oak Dell. It was sheltered here from the full force of the wind. The tree trunks' vivid green, the blue sky with white snow beneath, gave this place a gentle beauty. Not many people had walked these paths. I saw my boot prints back and forth (they have a distinctive pattern), with Watcher's paw-marks, often side by side. There were the deep tyre marks of the coppicers' vehicle. Neat piles of trunks, some carefully split, awaited their removal. The coppicing had gone on despite snow and bitter weather. To my left, the Yew Tree Grove stood mutely exposed, looking strange. Where the path led on to Pete's field and the well, I counted forty-two recent mole hills created with the help of the sun's warmth.

Returning to these woods, I found yet another shooter's hide; their proliferation had been marked since Christmas. Poaching, whether it be by shooting, rustling, or lamping, seems to be the countryside's one growth industry. Parts of this wood had virgin snow still deep and quite untouched by any print, whether bird, beast or human. I wandered idly about with great pleasure and at 1.45 p.m. found myself at the top of the Old Cherry slope. I walked down towards the sett, quite unaware of the three men and their two norfolk terriers I had disturbed at the entrances there. They ran down to the path below and went off through the wood. I looked anxiously at each occupied entrance, then went to check Susie's further along the slope. To my relief all were untouched. I checked all round for strange vehicles but found none. Just a young couple in a mini that was stuck in the snow. After helping to push their car clear, I asked if they had encountered anyone else, but they had seen nothing. The north-east wind was bitter this side in spite of the sunshine and the drifts at the top of the lane were solid ice. No wonder their car had been stuck! I stayed till 3.30 p.m. in case of more trouble, any pleasure in the place quite lost in my concern. The snow on the cherry slope had largely melted and in places it was very muddy. Moles had recently been active and a rabbit was digging little 'scrapes' in its quest for food. Anyone could dig out badgers from this sunny slope on a fine day. It was not necessary to park a vehicle close by; in the past, poachers here have left their vans at a distance and walked. Later, one of their number would collect it and drive round to where the others were waiting with their catch.

The night of the blizzard, at −17°C on the exposed farmland, the wind raged so loudly that I could hear nothing. It hurt my face with a bone-biting rawness, and seared my eyes. Icicles had formed on the hair that protruded from my anorak hood and had stuck to the bare skin of my forehead and cheeks.

I struggled to Briarmead and crossed with great care. The lane seemed one long winding snow-drift. Going into the wood out of the worst of the weather, I saw something small lying dark on white and fast being hidden by more snow. I picked it up, felt a still-warm body and fumbling, unzipped the front of my jacket just enough to push it inside. I had a confused impression the bird was a tawny, but with my eyes stinging and watering, I couldn't be sure. Arms hugging chest to give it extra warmth, I walked on. The bird was still alive, for I could feel its urgent heart beat. There was no point in sheltering in the Yew Grove, for the recent coppicing had left the place open and vulnerable, so I made for one of my holly trees.

I stayed beneath the holly's shelter quite protected from the elements, sitting with my back against the triple trunk of the ancient tree and well underneath the sweeping foliage that hung to the ground. The curtain of branches and leaves was covered with snow, providing both insulation and clarity. Sound was muted; this part of the wood was protected and the blizzard seemed far away. My companion sharing my anorak, was quite dormant for nearly two hours. Then I felt movement and a pecking, first gentle against my ribs – then, ouch! Nothing wrong with its beak anyway! Gently I opened the zip and the tawny hen looked outwards towards the holly curtain. I spoke softly and her head swivelled round. Our eyes met, then she fluffed her rumpled feathers, opened her curved beak to yawn, turned her head back and (I thought), went off to sleep.

A rustling from the long dead and withered leaves on the ground perhaps half a metre away woke me and I felt the bird on my knees had tensed, then saw the mottled plumage become bars as her wings silently rose. The owl stretched forward and pounced. A shrill, high-pitched scream and there beneath her talons was, not a mouse as I expected, but a very young rabbit! My tawny stabbed down and the screaming ceased. Pulling off pieces, she began to feed. It would soon be light so I left her, ducked down beneath the protecting foliage and came out into the wood. The falling snow had turned to small, hard flakes. All was clothed in purest white, mystic and wonderful.

There was no dawn of course, merely a gradual increase of light and nothing to mar the snowy perfection; only my own footprints soon to disappear.

One night in March I stood on the Embankment Path off Holmoak Lane and watched three badgers digging out in the opposite bank. It was snowing slightly and the busy animals were making a considerable noise.

There had been much digging out by my badgers at the Old Cherry Sett, the Crater Sett and that of the Colts Farm bank. Briarmead was free of drifts now; just a little snow here and there, but free access up to the top of the lane. It was a cold, frosty morning, but very pleasant as the sun, a great orange ball of fire, climbed the bank of Great Chantry Field and shone all around me where I stood on the sett slope. It was an unbelievable orange, a beautiful sight. I watched two long-tailed tits collecting nesting materials, very pretty little birds with their delicate appearance. Pete's lake and the ponds in these woods were still frozen, but I thought they would be for some time. After the powdering of snow that night, we had a deep frost an hour before first light which had left a fine patina on the ground.

Susie, Sis and Crisp were digging out at the sheltered Cherry Sett before midnight and playing together. Susie had been rather on her dignity, for motherhood is a serious business, but she forgot herself and ran back and forth along the sett path playing 'pull-your-tail' with the others! By midnight, frost had crept unnoticed over the fields and by dawn was very, very thick. It had created a lovely morning, all clear-cut and sparkling and my breath in smoky clouds. This wood echoed to the sound of the birds – and a shotgun! Now dawn was that much earlier, I could usually leave about 7.30 a.m. That morning I walked down to Pete's lake, enjoying the sunshine although it was still bitterly cold; the barley was stiff with frost. The lake was still covered in thick ice and I managed to break some at the edges for the birds. There were many bird prints, amongst them those of Canada geese. In an energetic mood, I scrambled up the motorway bank and cleared most of the rubbish from it. I was glad that I need only carry it over to the farmyard bin, rather than take it home as I do the rubbish from Ashcroft Woods. The astonishing articles people eject from their vehicles never cease to amaze me. Humans are weird creatures and motorists are the most weird! Clearing motoway banks is a very exhausting job as you try to keep your balance on a steep and frosty slope, whilst grappling with some large object that has apparently acquired a life of its own. If I fell, I'd land right in the lake directly below, or rather, on the ice. At nearly 8.30 a.m. one tired, scruffy human with arms full of assorted strange objects, was trudging across Colts Farm. It seemed to have been a long day – but I must say, glancing back, the bank looked a lot better now.

Later that morning I spoke to Dr. Howard, the chairman of Warby parish council that had bought Barry's portion of Ashcroft Woods. What has always concerned me here is the shooting, its increase and the fact that now there were no farmers willing to chase after offenders. That very situation means shooting would continue to increase; indeed, the increase itself and the erection of so many more shooters' hides seemed to coincide with the publicity surrounding the sale of these woods. All living creatures are prime targets for the illicit shooter and with the approaching length of daylight, the badgers leaving and returning to their setts morning and evening would be at risk. The chairman promised to help.

In the early hours of Sunday 9th March, there was a deep frost with freezing mist stealing over the landscape. Visibility was fast becoming poor and it was icy cold though very interesting. Watcher was with me; she doesn't like these conditions as her thick coat, like my anorak and hair, becomes soaking wet, heavy and uncomfortable. Mist is exciting especially when it is dense and enclosed like this. It's a curious sensation and sound is muffled; a different world. By 2.30 a.m. the vixen had gone to earth at the Felled Logs Sett. The constant drops of moisture falling within the confines of this wood were the only sounds until little Crisp brought me her ball for a brief game. Then she, too, went underground.

The next night and morning were deeply frosty and someone had been firing a shotgun in Ashcroft Woods since first light. Walking into the Chantry, by chance, I came face to face with the shooter, a very tall, thin man I had clashed with several times before. He turned and ran, dodging in and out of the beeches. After a moment's hesitation I followed, pulling the little camera out of my pocket. A deafening report and shot smacked into the trunk at my side. That did it; determined to take a photo, I ran after him. The strides of this tall, long-legged man could easily outpace me in the open and knowing this he ran out and down the field edge of Great Chantry. The night's frost had made the once-wet earth slippery and he had barely taken a dozen paces when he measured his length on the field. I made my first mistake, letting him rise to get a good face picture and my second in not trying to dodge round him back to the Chantry rather than running off down the field. Halfway down I repeated what he had done and fell. He grasped the little Kodak with both hands, dragging me along the earth and finally wrenched it out of my grasp, then raced away.

Much later I found the camera where he had thrown it, the film removed and camera smashed. When I told Ross on my return he said cheerfully, 'Never mind, at least you weren't hurt. Glad it wasn't my camera though . . . it wasn't my camera, was it?' I had to confess that it was.

One morning at first light, I saw two men come along the lower path as I sat quietly on the old cherry trunk. The foremost started to climb the slope, his gaze straight ahead. Then he looked up, saw me and ran back, knocking into his companion and both raced off into the wood the way they had come. These middle-aged, thickset men I had seen before with terriers, looking round the setts. I couldn't have seen any dogs this morning, if they had them, as I was situated at the wrong angle to view below their waist level. I spent some time afterwards scattering dead leaves and pieces of twig over the earth the badgers had excavated at all the occupied setts. At least they didn't look so obvious now. Any terrier would soon scent a badger of course, but there was nothing I could do about that. I felt so helpless and useless.

The butcher's broom had its tiny, white flowers and there were hawfinches, two on the lower branch of a gean and one below on the Wildflower Path. Many, many finches were feeding on and around Cliffords Bank as I went home. This meadow behind Ashcroft Woods was raked with the zigzag harrow and half rolled the day before. Alfie had left the roller here to finish off this morning. The raking had pulled and dragged the loose grass into small heaps which Missy and her mother had taken full advantage of – fresh bedding is very acceptable. The early part of the night I had spent first with Sandy (I suspected his vixen had her cubs), then later with Jude and Little'un on the fields between the motorway and Maddon Lane. One of the tracks off the lane is always dangerously muddy except in the driest weather and in consequence, Pete's men had cemented it very neatly for some yards and covered it against possible frost with finely chopped straw, several inches deep. The moment I saw it my mind started working and the moment Crisp and Susie came on the scene, theirs did too – badger bedding! Raking it up with their long front claws, both sows soon amassed bundles of the stuff between long chin and chest. It's so unusual to find straw this time of year that I think the sheer distance from their sett had escaped the badgers' notice. The terrain too, would be almost impossible, yet they fell upon that straw as if it was a few metres rather than a good mile journey. I trotted along with them to the top of High Ridge where both rested and groomed. I took off my plastic anorak, laid it down next to them and piled Pete's straw on it, then bundled it up and carried it in my arms. To my amazement, neither sow made any protest, just looking upwards occassionally as they padded alongside.

On the Cherry Sett slope, I spread out the anorak. Crisp stood discreetly back, whilst Susie took her time selecting choice bits to bundle against herself. The moment she had disappeared backwards into the depths of the sett, I picked up the anorak and laid it down again in front of Crisp's entrances farther along. Like partners in crime we worked together – she raking my poor anorak, I picking up the odd bits and stuffing them into her bundle. The last I saw of Crisp was the gleam of her eyes, as with a snuffly snort she took hers below before the older sow returned to raise objections!

The 14th was a dull, mild, misty night when I had a brief glimpse of Susie's cubs. There were at least two and could be more. The long, slender spikes of dog's mercury were in bloom round Old Joe's sett in the Chantry.

I checked Colts Farm sett and wondered if Jude and Little'un would stay there long. They seemed to spend a good deal of the night in the other badgers' company and weren't digging out and carrying-in bedding at their sett like the others.

The following was a beautifully mild night. I had been out since the previous evening (a Friday), in case of lampers, but happily there weren't any.

During these mild nights, my badgers were obsessed with bedding. Missy was bustling in and out, still collecting bits from the meadow above. She emerged one time and a little face appeared behind her – then another, but she turned around and nosed them back. Now she was sitting on top of the great spoil heap that makes a platform before it falls to the field below and groomed herself. One, two, three soft shapes crept out to their mother. One, very timorous, hesitated, retreated into the entrance, then gaining courage, joined the others in the big, wide world of Cliffords Bank. Missy turned, nuzzled them one after the other, almost as if counting her offspring, then gave the smallest a quick wash. Only last November this badger lay injured by a lurcher on the field below and now she had three lovely cubs of her own. Missy was one of my few success stories. Long might she remain so. A cub, pushing beneath her, whimpered and tried to feed; then the others did likewise. Their mother rolled slowly and carefully onto her side and they suckled. A winged insect blundered by and a tawny called from the wood as the tiny cubs took their fill.

That morning a red-legged partridge started up as I passed by. There were plenty of them here as well as some grey partridge and pheasant too. My quail was fine and I supposed really, there was no need to bring him food now, but still I would do so till May. He certainly tucked into it and hardly waited for me to leave before he set to!

It was a mild morning with a blue sky, slightly misty in the distance. A stoat was hunting in the growing barley, stalking a long-tailed field mouse. It pounced and caught it. Near Crater Sett I had seen my first hedgehog of the year, making a great noise as it snuffled about in the dead leaves. It was here, too, that I came across Jude mating with Crisp. She had been nervous of him, but lately seemed to have matured. Jude and Little'un had left Colts Farm and were now in residence halfway along the Old Cherry Sett. They had dug out there extensively and taken in bluebell greenery, which had grown surprisingly so soon after the snow left us and was bitten off close to the ground by the badgers for their bedding. I noticed Jude and Little'un made no attempt to carry home Pete's straw.

That Saturday evening, some time after 10 p.m., I checked the Maddon Lane parking places as usual and crossed to the back of High Ridge. I have two access routes to the farmland beyond, both quite close to one another. The first I passed, as for some reason I felt uneasy, and walked quietly on to the next. As I came to step out from the scrubland on to the open field, a sixth sense warned me of danger. I had a momentary glimpse of a figure some way to my right as I jumped back. One shot, then two more, very close, and the faintest impression of green light. A figure crashed away into the undergrowth. There was no beam. Either my form had been against the light (later I checked this and it wasn't, not at that angle), or the shooter was using telescopic image intensifiers (the faint green light is only visible at close range). I decided to make a run for it down the Poplar Row to the farmyard and safety, for where there was one man gunning for me, there could be another. After all, I could have come out of the other entrance. My shooter had been waiting for me, I was sure. To be shot at by lampers doesn't bother me overmuch; it's something I feel I can cope with for I'm used to being the one with good night vision. I don't like others having better night-sight than myself though; that is a disadvantage.

At the farmyard, lights were shinning from the great barn. Rob, his son and a friend had just finished lamping from the tractor and were putting it away. They had let the police know they would be lamping this evening and had worked the fields near the main road the far side of the farm. Ironically, these two farms are overrun with rabbits in spite of all the trespassing lampers; but the latter aren't very interested in rabbits as they seem to prefer foxes and badgers. When I told my story, the friend turned to his companions. 'There you are, I *said* there were three shots, but you didn't believe me because there was no beam!'

I left them and decided to walk round, cross with myself that I had been frightened. Approaching Cliffords Bank, I made out two figures standing together in silhouette against the curve. I backed away before

114

they should turn round, so couldn't have said what they looked like, and retraced my route to the yard, where I spoke to the three men, now taking their boots off at Rob's cottage, and confirmed that they would be staying indoors for the next half hour at least, as I would ask a patrol to check the perimeter of the area for vehicles, and didn't want Rob's party to cause any confusion. A familiar voice answered the phone – Alan Matthews, who said he would come out and check. I thanked him, took the torch and ran up to the Bank. No one there. I ran to Briarmead and back. From the Bank top I saw a patrol car halfway along the Poplars stop, beam out slowly as it turned, making a circle to take in the other paths, stay a few minutes, then retrace its route. It was good of him, for it would put off anyone still around, but I took it to mean that no strange vehicle had been found.

At home Karen, Ross and I discussed the night-shooting without lights. Apart from the lampers with their gun-mounted beams, so many people seemed to be using the land and not all were hostile, though obviously, I was in the way. There was the group of military-styled men who appeared from the woods in camouflage gear with rifles (containing blanks, I hoped), who had used the farmland apparently to practise manoeuvres. At the corner of Cliffords Bank one night, I had come face to face with the 'sergeant' in charge who, quite unabashed, shouted, 'What do you think you're doing here? Get the hell out of it,' as he charged past, rifle at the ready! We felt it understandable that this group didn't use silencers as presumably, they were re-enacting a war situation. Why other men here didn't silence their guns, though, has always been a mystery to me. These 'militaries' appeared with their sergeant three times to my knowledge, that season. The badgers and I were merely in the way, not targets. The following winter, after a midnight incident in Ashcroft Woods with a jeepful of men and the same leader, I took their vehicle number. However, the owner of this ex-army jeep came from the city. This is covered by a different police force who were less than helpful, so the mystery was never unravelled.

Then there was a lone man who used the edges of both woods from which to shoot at anything moving on the surrounding fields. At first he was obviously frightened at my being there and disappeared for a week or two, only to reappear again. He was young and very local; probably his home backed on to the land. In time, he became vindictive and was accompanied by a friend. In fairness, this was possibly the one place he could practise his night-shooting undetected and he looked upon my continued presence as a threat to his anonymity.

This sounds straight-forward now, with the perspective of time, but it was very bewildering that winter. The two shooters waiting for me last night, however, had been something very different.

I went out early that evening in case of trouble. It was a very mild night again the crescent moon rising above Prossers Wood, shone through a cloudy sky. I walked round the edge of Prossers Wood just after 10 p.m. where the treeline curves. Round the curve and directly ahead, came a shot – no beam – I walked round, but there was nobody to be seen. Only the rustle of something moving farther in among the trees. I stood there for a long time in silence, unsure whether the shooter had been unaware of my presence and if it could have been the young man. If he knew I was there, well, I dislike games of cat and mouse, especially when I am the mouse, so decided it best to make myself known. I walked unhurriedly along the fieldedge, in the knowledge that anyone inside the wood would see me unaided by any artificial nightsights as a clear image against the sky. At the corner of the field, I turned and retraced my steps, reached High Ridge once more, turned and walked back, then continued on to the railway crossing. There were no stiles now, for the new ones had been ripped out almost as soon as they were put into position. I felt this evening's shooter was the young man and hoped he had got the message – I was here, I was not frightened and I was staying here.

Much later I met Missy, her mother and Crisp, all foraging in the meadow above Cliffords Bank. The old sow dug up a nest of young rodents (voles or mice, I couldn't be sure) and presently Jude appeared and snuffled into a fresh mole hill. This long sweep of field between Ashcroft Woods and the Bank, rises and falls as it follows the trees (always reminds me of sea swell), yet also drops down till it touches Cliffords Bank which runs three-quarters of its length, then the Damson Bank, to the Old Barn ruins. I was standing in one such dip with two of the badgers when a shot sounded from the wood-edge, then another and another. The badgers ran for home. I couldn't see the remaining animals, but was sure they would have done the same. I stared uphill towards the wood, but though I could see clearly, there was no human figure against the trees. The shooter had probably taken cover there. I took a deep breath and walked straight up to the wood edge, then along the outside till I reached Briarmead. I returned walking in the middle of the field slowly and deliberately (and looking carefully around), the entire length of the meadow. I knew I was the easiest of targets for anyone with a trigger-happy finger and a short temper, but also knew that if I once started to show my fear, it would be the finish of all I had striven to do here. To show fear would be to invite retaliation. This might just be the young man. It could be last night's shooter however. He had shot to kill and would have succeeded had I not jumped back when I did. No one would have known and the two men would have had all the night in which to walk off this land and disappear. My own family wouldn't have started to worry till mid-day Sunday.

Now, however, the element of surprise had gone. They would guess I had informed the police, so there was a need for caution. They would shoot more to frighten, though in the case of the badgers, they might shoot them to spite me. Missy was standing on hindlegs against me, her forepaws at my waist, when the shots rang out. If they hadn't been witness before to the relationship I have with these animals, they knew now. It was possible that last night's men were friends of the lampers who frequent this area, even perhaps of the three poachers caught by the police or the lamper with a grudge who had once spoken to John and Rob. I recalled the times I had seen lampers walking this land together, but not lamping since the poachers were caught. Lampers must have wondered what a woman was doing here night after night, carrying no light but seeing well. Now, perhaps, they knew.

Midnight came and went as the badgers one by one reappeared and began foraging. I continued on the move, walking the field and along the top of Cliffords Bank deep in thought. My night-vision can't compete with rifles equiped with highly efficient night sights. They must, of course, raise their rifles to see the area whether they wished to shoot or not.

At 6.45 a.m. the sun's golden light was touching the old cherry's trunk where I sat, transforming each gnarl and twist. It softly glowed on a hawfinch drinking from a 'pool' in the bark. On a nearby branch a robin sang close by me just as the two mallard flew above the wood towards the river. The sun was warm, sending fingers of tree-shadow across Long Field, towards the faint haze in the distance, whilst by my side hung lambs' tail tassels of pollen-laden catkins. The air was alive with birds; their song, flight, nestbuilding – a busyness of birds. There were clumps of tiny blue-eyed flowers, bright on the sandy earth of this wood; the early forget-me-not, *Myosotis ramosissima*.

A few days later, Tony Gould and I discussed the recent night shooters. The talk turned to lamping and how after my Living World programme, I had letters from people almost disbelieving that the activity existed. Such people thought badger lamping was 'just a story' and pointed out that their areas had plenty of badgers. I had kept in touch with them and quite recently was asked for advice because lampers had descended on them. This always makes me feel sad because you know that sooner or later it's going to happen to them; if only they would start keeping an eye on setts and mapping them when everything is quiet, it would save so many badgers in the long term. Be prepared is a good motto. To say 'it wouldn't happen to us' is akin to the man who has never had his house burgled so can't credit it could happen to him. People can't accept that when one area is denuded of badgers or gets too 'hot', then the poachers merely move on to pastures new.

Tony and his Chief Inspector were going to a local Badger-group meeting that evening. The county's police Wildlife Liaison Officer would be talking and showing the 'Death of a Badger' video. The RSPCA Chief had a badger-digging case from the Brockton area and would be citing it. I had to be out on the fields in case of trouble, so Ross would attend the meeting in my stead.

That night was beautifully quiet and mild. It had been raining since the previous evening; the type of fine rain that enhances scent, rather than destroys it. The badgers, and the foxes Sandy and Watcher, were all worming in these ideal conditions. I hadn't seen the other vixen for several nights and since Sandy was fetching back (part of a rabbit and also a skylark), I felt she had her cubs. When the rain is not too heavy, many animals are abroad and there is so much to learn and watch. Foxes are adept at following badgers to their feeding grounds, particularly where there are worms. Thus when badgers are quartering a certain area, a fox will often appear and forage until it comes too close to a badger who will turn, chase it off, then continue feeding. Foxes rarely go far when this happens and may be chased off several times before giving up and moving elsewhere. Occasionally, I have seen the badger come upon a fox worming. The badger is certainly the dominant animal and if persistent, will force Vulpes vulpes to leave.

That night the badgers very soon had their fill of worms, so there was plenty of time for digging-out, play, or just irritating Chris! I walk home sometimes, looking as if I've had a mudbath. No wonder I've a reputation for being an eccentric.

At 7 a.m. the rain had ceased and it was mild and pleasant, though everything was adrip. I like it after rain for it gives colour to things that otherwise appear dull. The faded leaves of the brambles were a brilliant red and green. The herb-robert foliage partly unfolded held drops of water, fresh and delicate and the stems of dogwood were like blood along the path. Many pools by now in the bark crevices of the old tree and two squirrels had come down within touching distance, to drink from them. That nearest me, leaned over with one front paw holding on the edge for safety and lapped the rain water, the sound clear in the quietness. I love this old cherry tree, so much happens here. The badgers still climbed over it, searching its bark for beetles and doubtless, Susie's cubs would learn the joy of playing here just as my Lesley's young ones did. Susie had definitely got two cubs, and Missy had three. They were eight weeks old now; in another few weeks they would be more adventurous and explore the area immediately around the sett entrances.

On Friday morning, after dawnwatch, I went over to Glebe's farm office to collect my torch. I had spoken to Sergeant Collins about the shooting and he had promised that while he was Oakley's Acting Inspector, I could have a police radio, though for how long this would be, he didn't know. All so very unexpected! I hoped that the shooters would be around this weekend for I doubted that they would be the next. By then it would be Easter and the full moon would give them little protection unless we had cloudy skies.

I collected the torch and met John and Rob by the great barn. Rob had noticed gunfire without lights last Sunday evening and walked out along the Poplar Row to confirm this to his own satisfaction. He had wondered where I was and guessed, correctly, that I was around. I now had two witnesses to this business. Tony Gould had stressed that others, prepared to testify, might be useful if a shooter was caught.

At home I had a phone call from a Charles Douglas who for some time had been quietly trying to help the situation. I had said in despair to him that now I rarely had the time or peace of mind to continue my studies of badgers. All my energies seemed to be geared to their protection. Even when things were quiet, I had difficulty settling down to serious work. If I did relax, that was the moment when something tragic might happen to my badgers and I was unprepared. I was also becoming physically exhausted due to the continued tension. This was a vicious circle and at times I felt my actions must seem stupid. Talking to a patrol who gave me a lift one morning, I remember describing it to him as being on duty every night and dawn of your life with no rest days in between. Twice walking home that week, I had gone to sleep still walking. The result could be imagined. The nightwatching that had been my greatest pleasure was fast becoming a nightmare.

Charles Douglas had made a great many phone calls on my behalf and enlisted the help of an army Major who promised to try and get clearance for one of their field range-finders for me to loan. Then Tony Gould or a constable could use it if they came out on the land with me and so track the local shooter back to his home. If it was a night that neither could be available, then I had a sporting chance of doing this myself. As it happened, the Major was unable to obtain the necessary clearance, though he certainly wasn't lacking in enthusiasm and was very apologetic when he couldn't do so. I could never say people hadn't tried to help, though as often happens, it is the ones at the top who have the final say.

Charlie went one further though and gave us both a badly needed laugh! He phoned two small arms dealers with a view to perhaps hiring a field intensifier. One arms dealer sold them from £1,000 upwards but did not hire. Another was at present low in stocks as he supplied Israel and was virtually reduced to two small tanks. Charlie laughed: 'How about those, Chris – one for you and one for the badgers? That would solve the problem for all time!' I had a vision of John Shaw's fields of barley after Operation Tank and sadly said I thought not! It showed how easy it was to obtain such equipment legally (and, doubtless, a great deal was black market, no questions asked). Certainly, I was beginning to learn a lot about life those last two years through guarding the badgers.

Then Alan Matthews delivered the police radio which, unlike the first one I was loaned, had a carrying strap. I had no intention of it being taken from me, so decided to wear it under my anorak. The first thing I would do that night would be to find where the best reception could be obtained. I had turned down Special Constable Dave Jones' offer to come out with me that Saturday, for I felt that if anyone was going to be hurt it shouldn't be him with a wife and small children. He had done more than enough for me already.

That Friday evening I came to my area and was immediately pounced upon by young Crisp! A very mild, still night with a moon seen through fitful clouds. I began to test the radio for the best reception, but soon realised it was a busy time for the police and decided to leave it on at low volume, note where on these fields I could hear conversation clearly, and test after midnight when they should be less busy. My badger was, at first, quite frightened each time she heard transmission (I had put the radio on before my anorak and then zipped that up for safety), but since I seemed unbothered, she accepted it after a time, though stopped whatever she was doing when it sounded. I slung my son's big torch over my shoulder, having first adjusted the strap so that a length of webbing hung down. This didn't bother me until I noticed Crisp's interest. She found the dangling strap very tempting with heaps of badger-potential! I told her sternly to behave and strode off hoping to outpace her. I had serious things to do tonight and playing with yearlings wasn't one of them. Transmission was good (at least from my point of view) in some surprising places. One was directly below the sett with the steepest part of Cliffords Bank looming up in front of me. Another was 100 metres from Briarmead in that sloping part of the meadow with two sides bounded by woods. I switched off. Later it would remain to be seen whether the station could hear me where I could hear them, which didn't necessarily follow. There was no sign of lampers or snipers, but since the radio, albeit at low volume, carried a considerable distance on the open farmland in these still conditions, this was scarcely surprising! If I had realised this before and been given the radio earlier yesterday, I should have come here in daylight to practise, but never mind.

My thoughts were dramatically interrupted when I was stopped in mid-stride and nearly pulled backwards. Young Crisp, fed up with my inattention, had made a scampering jump at the webbing, secured a good tooth-hold and was simply hanging on! I slipped the bulky torch off my shoulder and tried to persuade her to let go, but she refused to do so. I knelt down in the meadow and pulled till her snout was level with my chest, then felt with my right hand inside my anorak for the volume dial of the radio. Jane's voice from the control room, issuing directions to a patrol, came blaring on the quiet night air. My playful friend gave a bark of alarm, dropped the strap and with fur fluffed up like a giant peardrop, galloped for home. My eardrums felt shattered, let alone hers; I hadn't tried full volume before!

After midnight I began to test for reception. The first reasonable place was on Glebe farm above Prossers Wood, about forty paces into the Top Field. I had just seen the headlights of a vehicle come onto Newby Farm way in the distance and at an angle. Courting couples don't come that far on to farmland. The station told me there was no police vehicle in the area, so I went to investigate and found a dark van parked behind the Damson Bank at the bottom of the meadow, near to where the lampers' van had chased me and the badgers last October. The fitful moon sailed into a clear patch of sky so I daren't go too close. With the doors at the back of the van open, two men were bending over something on the ground. After a muttered conversation, they lifted a very heavy metal object into the van, closed the doors and drove off again down the path of Cliffords Bank towards the main road. The track was lower than the field edge and their ride bumpy, so it was impossible to see the vehicle number. I tried to contact the police by radio, but although I could hear them, they couldn't hear me.

For the next hour I continued testing and found that a spot 60 paces up from where the van had been parked had the best reception. Once off this very small area, however, it quickly deteriorated. There were also two good points between the Poplar Row and the railway, although from there it's only a short run to the farmyard telephone. The two most valuable spots, then, were at the limits of this land – the Top Field, Prossers Wood and the meadow 100 metres from Briarmead.

At 2.30 a.m. all was well, and I thought I would return home for half an hour, have a mug of hot tea, and come out in time for the dawn watch. I could just do it, as it takes approximately an hour to walk home from here and I needed to leave again at 4 a.m. to check for vehicles before first light. Walking across Roger Johnson's land I saw two lampers and their lurchers trotting alongside the railway in the direction from which I had come! I had seen these men working my area more than once and had never discovered a vehicle, so I suspected they were local. They only took rabbit and fox, it was true, but we had agreed to check on all lampers, irrespective of intent, and I had got police radio. I followed at a discreet distance.

They caught two rabbits en route, but obviously had a destination. I didn't want them to turn round and see me come over the fence by the motorway tunnel, so I gave them an opportunity to go ahead. Then I was over and running through Prossers Wood to Top Field. Their beam was parallel with me, but at the side of this field, so I couldn't risk them hearing the radio from this spot. I ran on down to midway between the Poplar Row and railway, when I saw another beam further over to my right and two more lampers! And I had thought it was quiet! The most sensible action would have been to use the office telephone but my pride wouldn't let me, after all my requests for police radio and the police time taken up this night helping me find good reception.

I took a chance and called up the station but though I could clearly hear the officer, he couldn't distinctly hear me. This was partly due to my speaking quietly. Sound carries on open land and even the normal speaking voice I was using would be clear. To raise my voice would be disasterous. I suddenly realised that the beam was out and the lampers were making off at speed. They must have known it was a police radio from the background noise and general tone of the voice answering mine. I hared after them as they ran the length of the meadow between Ashcroft Woods and Cliffords Bank, not using my torch as I wanted to get closer without them knowing I was following.

This long field rises and falls on its journey to Briarmead, in a series of little hills. The lampers and lurchers disappeared over one such hill and I happily followed, knowing we would soon be at the lane. Then suddenly they reappeared back over the hill, running even faster. I stood stock still in surprise, wondering at the unexpected development, torch still off and quite unaware that they hadn't seen me, for I could see them so clearly. One lamper cannoned straight into me with a yell of fright. He seemed unusually large and heavy but with one of his boots in my eye and my right hand twisted underneath us, I probably wasn't in a position to judge. The torch had been thrown a short distance off – thank goodness the radio was well hidden. The next lamper saw the torch lying there (although not switched on, the fluorescent tube shows clear at night), grabbed it in passing, ran a few paces and fell sprawling over his dog! I extracted my hand with difficulty (having noted that I knew these men of old), rolled clear, reached the torch and crawled with it out of the way.

As men and dogs crashed into the woods I stood up unsteadily to see the lights of a patrol car going away down the lane. That was why the lampers had turned back. Another patrol car carefully negotiated the muddy track of the Poplar Row, turned right and followed the railway line to Prossers Wood; it stopped beside me as it came down by High Ridge. In it was Philip, who was very good-natured over the whole business. Really, pride goes before a fall. If I'd phoned from the farmyard office, we almost certainly would have caught one lot. Those lampers had been terrified and no wonder. A police radio on the fields, a patrol car coming up Briarmead to intercept them and, lastly, falling into someone they didn't see. They must have thought these fields were swarming with police. I doubted if either set of poachers would return in a hurry.

Monday 24th was a wild day and night, with gusts of wind up to 100 miles an hour, some rain and very cold. I saw no badgers on these fields, but found Susie, Crisp and Sis foraging on the slope of the Old Cherry Sett. It was surprisingly still at ground level here, although the trees above were rasping together in agony. The north-west wind howled and shrieked on its nightmare journey across the farmland, hitting the trees on the Briarmead side with tremendous force. Many were down, either bringing others earthwards in their fall, or still held up by the living. I was standing out on Long Field with Watcher uneasy beside me. We earthbound creatures were fortunate; pity the birds and squirrels. Sleet, borne on the wind, lashed the bareness of my face. We parted, the vixen to the shelter of her den beneath the felled logs, the human to her shelter beneath the great holly tree.

First light was dry, with a bone-piercing coldness and a clear-cut beauty all its own. I had this world to myself; no bird nor beast would sound or venture forth. Just the living wind that plucked and cried as branches, catkins, debris were blown about with great force. This torrent of sound hurt my ears and, feeling myself near-hurled off my feet, I grasped a trunk. Both arms round the tree, head pressed against its strength, I heard the groaning and straining from within as it stood firm against the elements. No dawn, just an increasing greyness as I ventured homeward, hugging hedgerow and fence. To be caught in the open by such a blast would be to court disaster. Something brushed my face and scratched it in passing. Too late, I realised it was a bird, but could do nothing to help for by now, tossing and spinning, it was many metres away.

The sun touched the horizon like a great orange ball. Birds flew out of the wood into the dawning, and I felt it was going to be a fine day. Then as I walked into the Chantry, a shotgun was fired over my head. It was the tall man who didn't like having his photo taken. He stood there, shotgun levelled at my chest and dared me to come closer. I slipped the police radio slightly from beneath my anorak and turned to face Little Chantry Field and Oakley, inwardly praying that some sound would be emitted to impress him. What came out has probably made a lasting impression on the whole area! I had quite forgotten the height of the Chantry. The officer's voice came booming loud and clear and my unpleasant shooter disappeared at speed.

At home, my family suggested I tape some police transmission with various voices to sound more authentic, so that when I had to return the radio, I would still have an instant deterrent – and I wouldn't need to worry about reception! This radio had possibilities.

Tony came that afternoon. He was very pleased I had been given the radio, but felt the RSPCA should do something about the situation at night on the farmland. Since he was rushing around tremendously busy with all his day-to-day work, he was very good about my problems. Our area abounds in ponies and horses that are mysteriously put to graze in other people's fields all through the winter, with no other food. Grass doesn't grow in the cold weather and the RSPCA are left to feed the horses and try to trace their owners. When proper homes are found for them and arrangements made to transport them away, their real owners come and take them in the night. There are all sorts of legal difficulties to moving other people's animals and the ponies take up time, energy and patience of police and RSPCA Inspector alike.

Tony said he had a call from Oakley police to say a lady had phoned asking that two badgers be taken away from her back garden. A puzzled Inspector contacted her and was told one was green, the other blue! 'Green and blue badgers?' asked an amazed Tony, only to find they were budgies! He was not impressed, therefore, with his next call to a horse living on a fourth floor balcony of a block of flats. However, this was a case of truth being stranger than fiction, for on checking the flats he found a Shetland pony was kept there. Before he left, we agreed to try for the poachers after Easter, if I still had the radio and he wasn't tied up then. Secretly I hoped to have some success myself over the holiday and perhaps my right hand would be alright by then. I had damaged the tendons in last weekend's encounter with the lampers.

The last day of March was Easter Monday. It rained most of that day, but by dusk had ceased. The waning moon failed to penetrate the cloud layer. Missy, Jude, the Clifford sow and Crisp had a race to see who could reach me first. They were all very muddy and probably had been worming at the foot of the Bank where the water lays. After a game in which I became very giddy and was well musked, I wandered away from them along the Damson Bank to watch a tawny owl hunting from one of the stumps there. There were three pairs of these owls (and an odd one) that had territories in my area. This male was hunting not only for himself, but for his mate incubating her eggs near the Old Barn area. I stood for perhaps an hour, in which time the bird caught a vole amongst the deep grass of the bank and a very young rabbit that was unwise enough to venture well out onto the meadow. Suddenly, four shots from the wood edge across the field came very near me in rapid succession. The owl flew up startled with a harsh cry, out over the bank and across Briarmead, while the badgers, who had been foraging some distance away, rushed for the safety of the boundary Bank. There was no point in my running, as the sniper could easily have shot me so I stayed where I was, looking upfield in the direction from which the shots had come. There was no one visible, for the undergrowth and trees of Ashcroft Woods make marvellous cover.

Tony Gould was hoping to loan me an RSPCA field vision image intensifier after the Easter holiday and, with the help of the radio, if I still had it, I wanted to try tracking down these people. Meanwhile, I didn't want to frighten them off or aggravate the situation, so didn't radio the police.

Much later, I settled myself at the wood edge with Tossy's old sett just behind me and a good view of this farmland. Crisp, true daughter of Lesley, found me and clambered into my lap, curled round and went to sleep. She was warm, her belly tight with its fill of worms. I put my arms round her and gently used her chunky back as a cushion for my head.

I woke abruptly to see a small beam in the middle of the Top Field and two lampers with their dogs. I had left the torch yesterday morning at Glebe Farm office and would need it to lead the police to the vehicle, so I might as well phone at the farmyard. Crisp had disappeared into the wood, so I ran down the long way round to avoid being caught by beam or dogs and phoned, asking the officer to give me ten minutes to locate the lampers and try to follow them with the torch. If I lost contact, I would radio in later and let the police know.

By now the top of Cliffords Bank was being lamped with quite a small beam, switched off for much of the time. These dogs were obviously good scent as well as gaze hounds and the lampers were wary of a strong light being seen. The dogs were between me and their owners when they nearly chased a rabbit into me. One growled in surprise and the smallest, a norfolk terrier type, went for me, snapping at my legs; fortunately my boots give good protection. I had seen these dogs here twice last season, but on each occasion was dazzled by their owners and never got a good look at the men themselves. Now one man ran up with beam blazing to see what was upsetting his dog then, with a shout to his companion, rushed off with the other dog, a slender greyhound cross. By now I was losing them and the snapping, snarling terrier was hanging on to the sleeve of my anorak. With my free hand, I brought the torch down hard and it released its hold, though still going for me. I hit it again as it closed once more, then it was off, running down the track of Cliffords Bank. One man had gone that way, too, but the other, plus lurcher, had run towards the wood edge and now I had lost them.

Recalling that I had first seen the beam on Top Field, I ran on to High Ridge. Most likely they had a vehicle parked somewhere below. They only had to run along the Enclosed Path to get back unseen to the Ridge and so down to Maddon Lane. I might see them crossing down and even at a considerable distance they would be silhouetted against the night sky. But there was no sign of them. I returned to Top Field and made contact via the radio. The police told me that two men were being questioned at the Oak Dell entrance off Maddon Lane and asked what my two lampers were like. I was unsure, but I described the dogs, for I always take particular note of poachers' dogs. They are crossbreds and tend to be distinctive. I mistrust a terrier-type for lamping as it's not really a lamping dog, but good for holding a large animal at bay.

After awhile I made contact again and asked if I should stay. The police suggested I go down and meet the patrols at Oak Dell, which I did. I sat in the back of the police car as another approached and its occupants, a sergeant and constable, came over. The two poachers who were questioned had parked their vehicle just here and my description had fitted their dogs. It had come too late; their owners' explanation of what they were doing here was accepted and they had driven away. Asked if the dog had been deliberately set upon me, I shook my head. Had any attempt been made to stop it attacking? No. The police told me not to worry, for details had been taken and the men would be picked up.

One of the constables had been talking to me by radio on the far side of the railway crossing, but had difficulty hearing me. The sergeant exchanged my batteries for his as he was soon going off duty. We discussed the snipers and I explained why I didn't want them chased at this stage. The police were more concerned about me being fired at than about the lampers, but they did appreciate that I wanted the snipers caught. If they were merely frightened off, they would return sometime when I hadn't the use of a radio or image intensifier. I promised to let the police know if I was fired at again. One man said he would photocopy a grid reference of the area and give me one as he hadn't heard of Prossers Wood before. Local names are confusing and the new ordnance survey doesn't call it that any longer. As I turned to leave, the sergeant said, 'We worry about you; you be careful.'

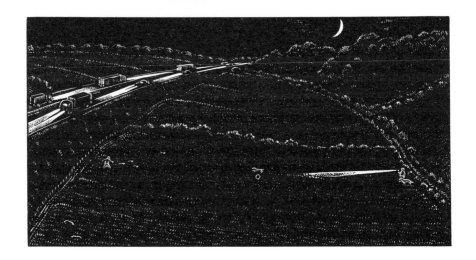

Chapter 7

Sometime after midnight on the 1st April, I saw a beam pass through the railway crossing and there were two men with an alsatian. Once into the field, they only used a small torch. I concluded they were probably walking home to Crosshampton. The field way is better if you know the terrain and definitely safer; no cars rushing along dark, narrow lanes. However, they did seem to hang about. The dog was let off to run loose and though it leisurely followed a rabbit or two, it clearly wasn't a hunting hound. Quietly it would be whistled back and obediently it came to be re-leashed. Eventually they disappeared down the Poplar Row path.

Perhaps twenty minutes later, I was myself near the same line of poplars, when I saw them again, standing clear against the skyline on Cliffords Bank, as if waiting. Did they have a *rendez-vous* with others who were late? They were burly, thickset men and as one turned my way to light a cigarette, he was somehow familiar. Or was it just that very few people smoke at night on this land? I was unsure. Then they disappeared into the elmbrush on that part of the Bank that houses the badgers. Dismayed, I ran up past the end of the elmbrush, across the meadow to the safety of the wood edge and a good vantage point where I could look down on them. Were they poachers stopping up sett entrances before they begun to lamp? Was that what they were doing?

Now men and dog stood out on the path again and a beam was sent up field towards me and the wood. Not very bright; I doubted if it could be seen from Briarmead. Then I noticed two things, looking through the monocular. The dog was actually 'on slip' not lead, so they were lampers, although the dog was not running the beam. And now the men wore balaclavas! I didn't know when they had put these on but by now I had to admit even to myself, that they were hoping to draw me to them. If the alsatian had been free it would have picked up my scent across the field, but fortunately it wasn't. I couldn't really bother the police; the strangers weren't lamping as such and had done no harm – yet. I decided to check for a vehicle and also stay clear of the area for a while. I crossed the railway, but there was nothing parked in Rendcombe Lane or at the dead end made by the motorway. So I returned, thoughtfully, to see far over Top Field that the group had reached the spot where I had been standing. The dog had its head down and was leading the men my way! I ran like a bat out of hell down the railway path to the shelter of Glebe farmyard and spent the next half hour in John's office. Now I realised why the cigarette smoking man was familiar. He was the badger-digger and lamper of April and May last year who came looking for 'young brockies'. This man always smokes, and has a way of looking sideways rather than at his companion when he speaks.

I found three primrose in bloom near the Crater Sett. It had been a cold, frosty night with clear skies and broken moon. Now the rising sun dappled the wood with light and the morning was filled with bird song. Quietly sitting on the old cherry, I watched a tree creeper living up to its name, as starting from the bole of a dying birch, it spiralled its way slowly upwards, searching for insects in the bark.

As I walked home across High Ridge, the two men and their alsatian of the night had the quality of a dream.

Charlie Douglas and Tony had both tried in vain to get me the use of a field vision image intensifier. I told them not to worry for I had not banked on having it and both had worked hard on my behalf.

One Friday evening I saw a lone tractor ploughing the fields near Holmoak, its headlights shining out across the lane. It was cold and starry, with the temperature falling fast. That night, Crisp and her big sisters Little'un and Sis were foraging near the stretch of waterlogged land off Maddon Lane. On Glebe Farm there were just Missy and her mother in the field below Cliffords Bank. Missy's two cubs were playing in and out the elmbrush around their entrance, till one slipped on the steepness of the slope, whimpered and went below, followed by its sibling. At 10½ weeks old, they were developing fast.

It was about 2.45 a.m. on Saturday when I saw two lampers and their dogs come through the railway crossing and begin working the Top

Field above Prossers Wood. They used the minimum of light, often switching off while their dogs were working. The men wore balaclavas, but I knew them from last season by the beautiful merle greyhound cross wolfhound of one and its companion, an equally tall greyhound cross airdale. Both are very distinctive longdogs. There were not many merles about my patch and this one was strikingly marked.

I couldn't radio from the field being lamped, of course, so went on to High Ridge above the motorway, sent my message and gave the map grid reference of the lamping area (for true to his promise, the constable had given me a photocopy of their map). Reception was bad, however, so I moved further over and tried again. Back on the farmland, I found them working the meadow above Cliffords Bank, both dogs chasing Missy who was heading straight for me. Normally, a badger will face a dog, but whether this sow had learnt from her previous experience of being dazzled and injured I can't say. She was on the exact route I had taken when I went to radio, so she could have been following my scent when the dogs discovered her. I swung her behind myself and crouched there confronting the dogs. Much startled, they veered off and back to their owners down field. Just as well, as I couldn't have held my badger for long without injury to myself. She would have bitten anyone or anything in the state she was in, for she had cubs and her instinct was to protect them. A lactating sow with cubs is the most sought after badger for baiting, with good reason.

The group disappeared, running round the corner of the Bank in the Briarmead direction as I escorted the agitated badger mum back to her sett. Then I took the same route as far as the two-oak track, but there was nothing in sight, so I ran through the gap and into the field above Glebe farmyard. A patrol car without lights was slipping passed Glebe Farm cottages and stopped just on the far side of the first barns there. I made radio contact and explained where I had last seen the lampers heading, but added that I still felt they would try to get back to the railway crossing. I walked down to the farmyard as the police car left to check Briarmead. I thought I would use John's phone to clarify the situation as reception at the station was evidently poor, though I could hear them well.

I walked by the big barn that houses the tractors and machinery and the little open-fronted workshop, meaning to go into the office. Something caused me to retrace my steps to the workshop and stand there for a moment. Though I carried the torch now, I was not used to one so did not think to use it. I was looking into blackness from the lighter night however, so walked inside – to see shadowy shapes and the reflective

130

shine of two pairs of canine eyes! Next moment I was bowled over in the rush as lampers and dogs made their getaway. Picking myself out of the mud of the yard, I saw they had taken a route out to the back of the barns and through the orchard in the direction of the railway crossing. They must have been there when the patrol car was stationed farther along. This was quite possible, for neither poachers or police would have been aware of the others' existence as they were separated from one another by several outhouses and barns.

Now a distant light caught my eye – the headlights of the patrol car searching Briarmead at my suggestion. I phoned from the office and explained. It was all taken in good part. Until now, lampers had tended to avoid the farmyard, probably because Rob lives so near. The men must have guessed that Briarmead, where they were heading, could be checked, so doubled back and hid until everything was quiet.

By now the temperature was well below freezing and the wet mud covering my anorak, hands and head was frozen. There was no sign of lampers, badgers or anything else for that matter, so I went home to change. My coat and jeans were covered in a layer of thick, frosted mud that began to steam in the warmer air of the kitchen. After a quick change I came out again in time for first light at the Old Cherry Sett in the woods.

One evening, I spoke to the ploughman sowing the fields off Holmoak Lane. I knew he came from a distance where he has a small-holding and makes ends meet by renting these fields. I thought perhaps he had turned to working here at night as the roads and lanes would be free of traffic to move his heavy machinery then, but that wasn't the reason. Youths and men from the nearby housing estate continually harried him during the day. It was also a walking ground for dogs, and an area where lads on motor bikes zoomed round. Last harvest time the barley was set alight in a circle round him as he worked. 'I was terrified', he confessed . 'The combine had a near-full tank and I was lucky to get out alive. I just can't afford to give up these fields. I have a wife and family like everyone else, so now I work here at night'.

It was a clear, starry, very frosty evening and an icy night with a strong north-easterly wind. There were no badgers or foxes out on these fields. They were hunting or foraging deep in Ashcroft Woods or on the leaward side. I found a rabbit killed on Maddon Lane and offered it to Susie. I had come upon her searching under the beech leaves above the Old Cherry Sett slope. (Sam liked this place too and always found a surprising number of worms here).

An hour before first light, the frost had deepened, till by dawn the cold was intense and penetrating. Just as the rising sun slipped over the bank and into the wood, something soft touched my leg and Watcher looked up at me. The sun's rays were turning her fur to fire and I saw a fox's coat as if for the first time – sandy, gold, red, auburn, russet – how many shades of brown make up my vixen's fur? The warmth increased and both our coats were steaming as the rising sun melted the frost which still clung to us from the night.

Going home along the Boundary Bank, I saw my quail huddled up in the bracken and dry grass of his pail. He didn't care for the change in our weather. I left him plenty of chick crumbs. Ours must have seemed a cold, inhospitable country to him.

On the 8th April, Alan Matthews came to collect the police radio as they were in very short supply. I spoke to him about the lampers and he suggested I contact Sergeant Collins. The sergeant said that the poachers they had caught had been served summonses and their cases were going ahead, but if they pleaded guilty, Oakley station wouldn't hear anymore about them. Only if their pleas was not guilty would a local officer be required at court. I mentioned the odd charactors, not necessarily lamping, that seemed to be hanging around the farmland. Whether or not I would be allowed the use of the radio again, Sergeant Collins had been very good letting me use it for those 2½ weeks.

Thursday 10th April was a squally night with rain. Susie had been digging out the four entrances used by her little family, while her cubs popped back and forth, generally getting in their mother's way. One of the three was smaller, but recalling Little'un I knew from past experience that didn't necessarily denote the runt of the litter.

On Saturday night Missy was digging at the Old Cherry Sett with the other badgers. I believe her old mother to have died underground, for when I last saw her five nights ago, she seemed shrunken in upon herself and feeble. It had been a long-drawn and harsh winter for the Clifford sow and the bitter winds of recent nights could have proved too much. Most badgers are at their lightest bodyweight at this time of year, but she had no reserves left. Watching Missy, I thought she might well move her twins into this wood. Jude would be the only badger not denning here then. He was restless and seemed to alternate between the sett at Barry's sandpit by the field edge and the Crater one with its communicating single entrance sett nearby.

Sunday 13th was a very mild night with clear skies and a crescent moon going down. I had been out by 9.30 p.m. in time to see Missy take her cubs on the first journey of their young lives. They followed their mother closely as she kept under the hedgerows, constantly stopping to scent the air with snout raised. It was a silent, cautious little band that stole along the trail through the grass of the banks till Briarmead was reached. There the cubs remained huddled together resting, whilst the big shape of their mother crossed to the broken gap in the soakaway fence. Sounds of her lapping, then silence till she appeared on the tarmac again. Missy nosed her offspring, purring very gently in reassurance, then the journey continued as two soft shadows followed a larger one over the lane and under the hedgerow to the safety of Ashcroft Woods. Only myself and the male tawny were present to witness their going and he had other things to occupy his mind. His mate and their growing family took up much of his hunting time.

I have often read that a lactating sow won't tolerate another sow with cubs in the same sett, yet again I was seeing this disproved. The Old Cherry Sett is certainly large, but Missy was permitted to house her cubs not far from the others. The two little travellers weren't so interested in their new home however, as in their new playmates, Susie's three offspring. All five cubs were cautious at first, as Missy stood, head held submissively low while the other mother approached. Then even I could feel the tension relax as Susie musked the other sow. Missy returned the compliment, then both mothers left the cubs to get acquainted as Susie went down to Long Field and Missy disappeared into her new home.

Selfishly, I was very pleased my badgers were off the fields and altogether here, for though they were bound to forage on the farmland of Newby and Glebe, they were undoubtedly less vulnerable from lampers, denning in the woods.

During this period I had several phone calls from different parts of the country. These areas had little or no trouble with badger-diggers, but sensibly, some people had been mapping the setts in their home range and generally keeping an eye on them. Now there was a spate of setts being dug out and in some cases completely destroyed, where the hunters had tunnelled long and deep and filled in entrances with the discarded earth. Digging for badgers is very common at this time of year when cubs may be present. On man described to me a pit about a metre deep and another had discovered a trench blocked off from the sett. Betting slips had been found and at one sett, fresh parts of a badger. The authorities had been contacted but had shown little interest. This was where Derbyshire's police video 'Death of a Badger' was proving its use over and over again. I sent a copy of the video with a note suggesting it go to the area's largest police station, made a phone call to the NFBG as backup for the people concerned, and checked to see if that particular police force had a Wildlife and Countryside officer – though usually if it had, this problem didn't arise. So often that year I was to hear the cry, 'Our local police think we are cranks and don't seem to realise there is a law protecting badgers. What can we do?' Each time the problem was quickly solved by this means; an interest and sympathy built up all round with police, RSPCA and public co-operating to the full. For speed as well as understanding, this video had proved invaluable.

The Living World programme I so lightheartedly recorded the previous June, had encouraged people (many of them young people) to ask either for help in finding if their area had a badger group, advice on starting one, or just how to learn about and protect their nearest badgers. This I think, gave me more pleasure than anything I had ever attempted. The RSPCA helped me at the outset and of course, from the NFBG. I now had a list of groups and emerging groups, whilst the chairman gives me any new information on the badger front. Since I researched the article on lamping and discovered the retaliation and intimidation suffered by so many farmers and small-holders, I have been asked for help on badger-related problems by these people also. Here on my patch, the badgers were slowly diminishing and I had at times, an overwhelming sense of failure and helplessness. Perhaps, therefore, is a very small way, I could help people and badgers elsewhere.

One mild, rainy morning at first light, a car came up the lane as far as the Wildflower Path and stopped partly hidden by the bank there, its headlights off. I suspected the worst, until, coming round and above it on the bank top, I saw it was a patrol car. We stayed talking and the officer told me he had seen a badger in his dipped headlights as he patrolled one night. It had scrambled down the bank and looked for a moment hesitantly at his car, so he switched off the lights and stopped a few metres away. The badger continued to stare, sniffed the air, but could get no scent that alarmed it. Then settling down on the tarmac in front of him, it began to groom! He described how it turned and twisted to get at its back, then seated on its haunches it raked its belly fur with long-clawed front paws, parting the fur and licking carefully and thoroughly with an occasional nibble at a tangled piece. Eventually, it got up, shook itself and ambled along a short distance, before going up the opposite bank.

I described 'up-and-over' paths, how easy it was to recognise them and how rarely they were directly opposite on each side of a lane, but normally like the one he described. The constable said he would go back off duty and try to follow the trail to the sett. He had an idea where it might be as he lived not far away and perhaps, could keep an eye on it.

An hour later, the sun had risen above the bank. Many trees were in tiny leaf and wood anemones speckled the ground like fallen blossom. The birdsong was tumultuous. Before I left I came upon a perfect set of badgercub paw prints, in the wet earth of a spoil heap on the Cherry Sett slope, which I obliterated with my boot. We didn't want that evidence around!

I had given a great deal of thought to something I had discussed with Sergeant Collins and Tony quite recently. A local man took his daughter 'badger-bashing' at weekends and it would seem this is a common practice in other places too. This information had come out because the 13-year-old girl had bragged about it at school to a friend. But the badger 'basher', as opposed to the digger, is difficult to detect since he merely digs a badger out, sets his terriers on to it, then drops the carcase into the crowning-down hole, covers it up again and goes home rejoicing. There is no badger taken home or exchanging hands and provided he isn't caught in the act, no evidence. Although I had been given the man's address, neither police or the RSPCA had the time to keep the continued surveillance that would be necessary. This I could understand, but it was unsatisfactory to say the least. It was all the more disquieting, as I had since discovered that 'badger-bashing' as it is quaintly called, is a popular pastime with those whose lives would otherwise be devoid of fun. The business of the schoolgirl worried me even more.

On returning home one morning I had a great surprise – a parcel containing two radios. They were beautifully made, very neat and compact with their own leads and plugs for recharging during the day. The accompanying letter said they should last 14 hours of continuous use, but naturally I must expect teething problems. A long time ago, I had been told a businessman was putting up the money for them, but had given the matter little thought for I had been disappointed so often. I stood a long time just holding them in my hands. It was difficult to believe they were real.

The same man had also tried to bug the setts for me, but this had proved impossible. Pete Williams of Colts Farm had offered to hold and look after the bugging receiver as he was living nearest to the wood, but there were factors against this. To bug a sett successfully, you need to have the receiver fairly near, otherwise the sound won't carry. We had not only distance to contend with but also trees and hills in the way. I had never seen the businessman or his friend, but it seems they had tried various things, most particularly from the Old Cherry Sett, all in vain. It was a shame, as Pete had said he would have the tiny receiver on him all the time throughout his working day, which he would need to do to hear anyone digging-out or attempting to do so. Considering he is a very busy farm manager, this was an extremely generous offer. However, we were well aware that badger-diggers apart, this particular sett and that on Cliffords Bank were much disturbed during daylight hours and originally, I had hoped to be able to hold the receiver myself so that I could monitor and record this. Had it been possible, it would not only have increased our knowledge on local disturbance within our area, but possibly been a guide to similar areas. Regular disturbance on foraging grounds (as in lamping) and around setts, causes stress in badgers which can inhibit breeding and prematurely age, so this tiny bugging device aimed at giving me a rest from sett guarding every morning and possibly allowing me an occasional holiday, could also have proved a useful field guide. However, it wasn't to be. But the radios certainly were!

On Thursday 17th it was still raining although not heavily. I watched the badgers on the railway embankment off Holmoak Lane digging out their entrances. Looking through the monocular, I suspected that one was a yearling sow and possibly the daughter of the older, lactating sow. A cub made a very brief appearance; younger than those of my badgers, it was probably 9 weeks old, whereas Missy's and Susie's were 12 weeks by now.

It turned very mild and showery during the night with my badger mothers digging out too (and young Crisp, who loves to join in). Jude seemed to have settled at Cliffords Bank, but made no attempt to do any digging. I have noticed before that at this time of year it tends to be the sows, particularly lactating sows, that have this urgent desire to clean out, renovate and generally tidy up, whereas in Autumn they are all at it. Now the Old Cherry Sett had twenty used entrances with well over fifteen disused.

It was a dry first light with a red-streaked sky at dawn. Primroses and wildflowers scattered the undergrowth, pushing up through the dead leaves. The birds called as the woodcock roded and the chaffinch sang on the cherry bough.

Monday 21st was a dry, very mild night with a hazy moon near the full. The leaves of the balsam poplars were unfurling; their scent pervaded the air. A blackbird sang in the briar behind me while I was sitting on Barry's gate. The pipistrelles' tiny shapes flitted round my head and skylarks were sounding from the fields. Every so often a wispy call announced its owner was up and about. Then I would have an inward vision of my plump little quail and smile to myself with pleasure. Crisp was upsetting the rabbits in the field to my right. It was the loveliest time, neither light nor dark and with the promise of a fine day.

Later I went to the station, taking one of the radios, and discussed recent events with Sergeant Collins. The radio's range would not go as far as my house, but Charlie Douglas would hold the other radio. Together we had tested it over the fields and for the most part, reception was excellent. We could talk very quietly to one another. Later, we would practise around the wood and the length of Briarmead Lane. The sergeant promised to let the other officers know what was happening.

The night of the full moon, escorted by Crisp, I tested the radio with Charlie along Briarmead and in the wood. The reception was marvellous. We could talk in whispers to one another as if in the same room with me being anywhere this side of Ashcroft Woods, and at the setts, either above or below and all surrounded by trees. Whether the dense leaves of high summer would make any difference remained to be seen. I was amazed by this, as I had been led to believe that it was mainly the wood which 'broke up' and distorted reception in the area. I told Charlie we should be professional about the radio, not give away recognisable place names (though I had been assured that no one could overhear us), and decide on a code name for each other. 'Code name?' querried Charlie. 'Yes', I said, 'You can be Charlie Foxtrot and I can be Charlie Foxtrot also, since there's only the two of us.' So Charlie Foxtrot was born.

My little badger was perfectly happy about this radio. Charlie and I have quiet voices and there was no static to hiss and crackle. In fact, when I was sitting at the Chantry about to answer Charlie Foxtrot, a long badger head came between me and the receiver so I found myself speaking to Crisp's smooth neck. The night was beautiful, the moon's rays pouring silver across the trees to stripe their great trunks. The villages were very clear with the distant bridge in sharp relief and the shimmering surface of the meandering river far below.

The following night was dry, but cloudy with the moon occasionally showing. The six little fox cubs were growing fast. The sounds of their play were reminiscent of dog pups, and also, at this age, of kittens. I believed their birth date to have been about 15th March, so they were six weeks old. Sandy's vixen was kennelling a short distance from her offspring and hunted in the near vicinity. Their father too, was hunting for his family well into the morning.

First light now was at 4.35 a.m. and dawn an hour later. A cuckoo displayed and called near the Felled Logs and Crater Setts. Jude was using both the Crater Sett and that on Cliffords Bank in which to sleep by day. Sometimes Little'un and/or Sis accompanied him on his foraging, but mostly he was on his own. There were fresh spade marks and other signs of disturbance by man on the Boundary Bank, which was puzzling as nothing had really been dug out, only half-heartedly started and then discontinued. I wondered if Barry or John had caught someone and stopped them.

Primroses littered the woodland floor like pale ghosts. Violets too, amongst the lesser celandine and coltsfoot and of course, the wood anemones were everywhere. Shafts of opening rowan leaves made a fine display; the sharply toothed leaflets are the softest of greens. I watched a pollen-laden, furry, solitary bee blunder drunkenly to its hole in the bank. As I walked home across the fields, the sun lay warm on the lane. High above, the skylarks' chain of bubbling song and a distant tractor were the only sounds. Then I stopped by the trackway through Cliffords Bank to see – yes, my little winter quail with a mate! I must remember to tell Dave and Margaret Jones that he survived our English winter, mainly due to their kind gift of chick crumbs.

Sunday 27th was a dull, damp, mild morning after a night of steady rain. Everywhere was incredibly green; even the tree trunks had a mossy, lichened look. Some birds were nest building, but also there were many already feeding their young. Young creatures were everywhere, squirrels, rabbits, birds, badgers or foxes. Missy's cubs were a sow and a boar, whilst Susie had two sows and a boar. They had been helping their mothers bring in bluebell greenery, running alongside the adults, bumping one another and picking up tiny wisps to carry back a short distance before dropping them again.

I took the long way home through Colts Farm and went down to the lake. Marsh marigolds were in bloom, their bright golden cups bobbing on the rippling surface. The goat sallow's plump catkins were just beginning to lose their pollen and the pale green willows' leaves were softly unfurling. I spent a happy hour clearing the spot of motorway rubbish, then stood near the bank top, arms full, looking down at the beauty of my private piece of heaven. The lake's clear waters, gently blown barley stalks sloping up to the crown of the hillside and topping it all, the ancient wood with its trees already a faint green. I decided that tomorrow I would have a good clean up of rubbish in the wood and made a mental note to bring some plastic sacks to do so. Trudging happily through the farmyard, I dropped my burden into the bin and there met Pete himself, hurrying to finish his chores early for he was taking his family out for the day.

I left the farm and walked out to the far end of Maddon Lane, my thoughts far away. I didn't cross the road as I normally do, but followed it along on the grassy farm side. There was nothing and no one in sight except a dirty white van, its engine running, apparently about to drive off. I crossed opposite it, then realised it wasn't leaving, hesitated a moment in the middle of the lane, moved to walk behind it, and suddenly saw the driver staring at me as if at a ghost. I looked at him and knew him only too well! He and his lamping companion netted my vixen and thanks to them I had a spell in hospital. They had also netted Lesley; I took a photo of them and in their efforts to take the camera, the badger escaped. In the last few years I had seen that face many times in a group or just with another companion in the woods. I had seen him also with two lads, one in his mid-teens and the other slightly older, a lurcher and at least three fell terriers. No wonder he looked so startled; I'm sure I did too. The van drove quickly away in the direction of Rendcombe village. I noted the number and also the fact that I had often seen that same muddy van (a firm's name and phone number printed on its side), parked outside different houses in the area. I always thought it a bad advertisement to have such a dirty van and had idly wondered, as I passed, if the owner lived up a long, rutted farmtrack. Now I knew why his van was so dirty.

Not far from my house was a police car parked with the driver obviously waiting for someone else. I knew him well by sight, so went over and gave him the van number. After this lapse of time there was nothing we could do about it, but at least we might have another name to go on. The constable said that when his companion returned from the house, they would drive that way and have a look around. I wondered if Tony had encountered the man in his work and if so, whether he would know the poacher's lamping companion.

Jude came upon the foxcubs playing that night and swiftly killed one. It made a high pitched bubbling sound for a moment as its companions rushed back into their den. The boar ripped into it, tearing the fur back and crunched up bones and all. Then he went on his way leaving the fur almost inside out and the tail with its white tip to tell the story.

The badger cubs were out playing also and I believed them to be weaned. On the muddy path above the Cherry Sett, leading to my holly shelter, I later found a set of cub and sow prints beautifully super-imposed; the cub's spore neatly fitting into the big pad of its mother's. Obliterating the marks with my boot, I felt I was committing sacrilege.

It was a lovely, sunny morning after a cold night with clear skies and waning moon. I watched the quail twosome and was so very glad my winter guest had a mate. His survival had been well worth it. The squirrels were eating the young sycamore leaves that were just breaking out of their buds. Many were left lying on the ground below the trees, quite untouched.

The radios had gone back to their maker for alterations as Charlie Foxtrot, who had his set switched on all night in case I should need to make contact, was getting taxi and other interference which kept both him and his wife awake. 'If you ever want a Chinese take-away at 2 a.m. Chris, I can tell you where to get it', laughed Charlie.

The last two days of April had brought a welcome warmth to these woods and fields. Now the cherries were 'hung with snow' and violets, daffodils, primroses, green hellebore and dog's mercury were on every hand. The five remaining foxcubs were pretty little creatures. Their parents had begun to moult. Both field woodrush and greater woodrush were flowering in these woods. The quail called lingeringly over the farmland and all was well with my world.

Little'un and Sis quarrelled over a dead pigeon they found one night and under cover of all the commotion, Jude ran off with it. The last I saw of the three contestants was Jude galloping across Top Field with girls in hot pursuit!

That night the Cherry Sett badgers had a massive bedding collection session and I seemed to be getting in the way as there was not much room on the winding trail along the sett slope. In the end, I sat up small on a chestnut stump and watched the world go by. First one badger backed along at speed, then another, then another. One stopped to rest and resettle its bundle of dry leaves and bluebell greenery, which stopped the rest of the line. The bedding was adjusted between snorts and snuffles and they were off again. It was interesting that they weren't taking these materials from directly around the sett entrances, but instead, going to the very top of the slope near the birch stand and collecting it from there. I picked up the dropped bits and pieces and offered them to the next along the line. This was a little cub with hardly anything left in her bundle. A quick check to see if my gift was worthy and yes, she would accept it. She snuffled away just as the next badger's rear appeared along the path. It was all go at the Cherry Sett.

The morning was full of birdsong. Before 5 a.m. I heard the Canadas sound and watched them 'lift off' from Great Chantry Field. I counted eleven majestically flying into a blood streaked sky. There is something mysterious about these birds in flight that gives me a feeling of awe.

Earthbound they are different and take their true form. The traffic noise was much earlier and heavier that morning for the Bank Holiday was with us. Everywhere the flowers of the wood and sun spurges were all in bloom. With their lack of petals and sepals, they are unusual looking flowers.

That evening, Charlie Foxtrot met me by High Ridge and gave me the altered radio. We had previously agreed to have as little contact as possible, since he has a wife and young family and people do seem to suffer for helping me. It was a beautiful evening with no lamping problems and I think Charlie and I felt rather disappointed! In another fortnight the lamping season would be at an end here, for already some of the barley was quite high and John Shaw's lovely field of oilseed rape was in golden bloom. I left the badgers below Cliffords Bank when it began raining heavily and took refuge in the brick-built barn by the Poplar Row. Wedging one of its doors open a little, I curled up on a pile of corrugated iron in the far corner. An hour later the rain had ceased, there was faint light to the east and a blackbird singing to the still dark morning. Everything smelt sweet and living in the freshly wet fields. A thin, fine moon climbed the clear sky and a skylark bubbled somewhere close on the ground. Another seemed to reply from a distance away, then came the lingering, wispy call of the quail. The new day had begun. I stayed until late into that morning, for the sheer pleasure of being there and walked home over the sunlit fields.

Sometime during the daylight hours, after I left, five entrances of the Cliffords Bank Sett and nine of the Old Cherry Sett were stopped up. When I returned to the area that evening, I found Jude had dug his way out of one and was trying, with difficulty, to clear another, so I collected the trowel from its hiding place and helped him with the rest. I left a very uneasy badger to his foraging and went in search of the others.

At the Cherry Sett, all was confusion. Susie had dug herself out and was frantically digging to her cubs. Before she finished, one had found its own way out via the mother's opened entrance, but the others called to Susie fearfully from their entombment, as she dug. Such stopping-up must greatly reduce the flow of air to the animals below ground. Once they were freed, their mother nosed them anxiously as they huddled close to her. There was no sign of the others though, as I began to dig out the well-trodden earth from Missey's entrance. The top of all these entrances had been broken down with a spade, then the loose earth jammed in with booted feet. Pieces of rotting branch had been pushed down the holes prior to the earth-stopping. Missy and I met halfway and I was greeted by a sweating and frightened sow with her cubs close behind her in the blackness of the tunnel. They must have found their way to their mother when they discovered their exit blocked. The badgers made no further attempt to re-open the other entrances but seemed anxious to quit the area, the mothers, closely followed by their offspring, hastily going off to forage.

Much later that night, the badgers returned and I noticed that Susie had difficulty negotiating the entrance she was using. I looked after she had disappeared down it and saw some way inside, a thick piece of rotting log had dropped in from the previous day's stopping-up. It was a good way down, so I lay my anorak on the ground and stretching out full length, managed to grasp and heave it out. It was much heavier than I expected, so I had quite a struggle. Sitting up I found a row of interested badgers regarding me, including Susie, who must have emerged from the cubs' entrance. Next moment I had a lapful of earthy cubs who clearly viewed me on the ground as good play material. Later, I went home for a quick change of clothes and a longed-for cup of tea, but was back on Briarmead by 4.30 a.m. in case of trouble.

The morning was cold, bright and windy. I walked round sett-checking and twice walked to the field below Cliffords Bank, but all was peaceful. The stopped-up entrances worried me and I was just wondering whether I should stay all day, when something blue moved on the path below and two lakeland or fell terriers came running up the slope of the Old Cherry towards me. The first growled, the second barked and the first joined in, just as a man's voice called out sharply and the blue vehicle made a quick turn and started back from whence it had come. The terriers obeyed the call, running under the great tree's fallen branches and out on to the open field. I had to chase round the longer way and came to the Wildflower Path in time to see a blue van driving bumpily on the rutted track, reach Briarmead and quickly disappear from sight. I only glimpsed a portion of the vehicle number but felt sure they were the dogs and people from the blue transit van last November.

I radioed Charlie Foxtrot, asking if the police would check for the vehicle around the Maddon Lane area while I ran across to Cliffords Bank to see if all was well there. Recalling my first encounter with these people I was fearing the worst. But all was well with the field sett and I made radio contact again to say so. Later, I left a message with Rob asking him to phone Oakley police if he saw anybody on the Bank that day, rather than accost them himself. The wind and sun had dried up the field tracks and a patrol car could drive with ease along the bank top. I didn't want Rob hurt and, recalling possible retaliation and his isolated cottage and family, I didn't want any terriermen to view him as an informer.

142

Back at home, I phoned the station. They didn't see the van round Maddon Lane, but promised to keep an eye on the situation during that day and the next which would be May Day. I thanked them, saying that I had thought of going out myself again later to look around, but was very tired. An amused voice on the other end of the line remarked that I was admitting it at last. He thought they were the only ones who got tired; it was nice to know that sometimes I did too!

During the past months several farmers and landowners, both local and farther into our county, had asked me to help with badger-related problems on their land. I enjoy doing this; it fosters good relations. I learn and they learn. I'm introduced to their wives and children, who become very enthusiastic about their badgers. Children's enthusiasm is infectious and it stimulates their parents. In next to no time you have a keen family of badger-guarders who take pride and interest in looking after their setts. Guarding and caring for my animals may have made me many bad enemies, but they have also made me many friends. Badgers have taught me a great deal, not least about my own kind.

One family, the Taylors, lived quite near Oakley in the village of Weldon. They owned 40 acres of scrubland, wood and open space and walking over it one day with Mr. Taylor, I found it contained at least three small badger setts, with a possible fourth inside a dense thicket. One of these was badger-occupied. They had discovered one sett just off the road blocked up the previous week after seeing some men with dogs leave hastily in a van. Mrs Taylor noted part of the number. Now that they knew their land contained badgers, they promised to report any such incident to Oakley police. They also had my phone number, as well as that of the RSPCA. They had bought the property some years ago and left parts overgrown, for the Taylors were keen naturalists. They had many birds nesting and recently, a long-eared owl. Mr. Taylor was delighted that he had badgers on his land, but wished he could encourage them to live where he and his family could keep a safer eye on them. We discussed artificial setts, how to make them and their siting. He promised to map the setts on his land for Tony and the police. More and more people I contacted were doing this. I hoped that in time, a network of mapped setts would be built up, which together with those the badger-group were doing and those I had already completed, should give us all a better picture of the badger community. Although this was progressing slowly but surely, one avenue, still unexplored, was on my conscience a great deal – the railway banks, miles and miles of them and a poacher's delight. I must try and get permission to map them soon, but I never seemed to have the time.

On Friday 9th May I was on the Embankment Path, looking over at the badgers busy collecting bedding. It's a very steep cutting here and several entrances were near the level of the rails, so bringing in bedding backwards was a much slower job than at the woodland setts. But theirs was the best nest material of all – hay! And where were they finding it at this time of year? Why, from the bales under tarpaulin that the farmer keeps for his horses across the lane! There was a big gap in the wire fence for his cats to come and go and it directly faced the stacked hay. The badgers backed down the field bank on to the lane with their bundles, then along the lane, over the railway bridge and so into the field above the embankment. A short distance along (no wire to negotiate here) and carefully down the steep sett slope. These cubs were younger, so did less work but made plenty of excited whickers and generally got in the sows' way. I imagine the embankment could be very treacherous after rain.

At 2.30 a.m. I was sitting on the Old Cherry, while Crisp padded about somewhere behind me in the branches overhanging the slope. The quiet night seemed full of rabbits. They rustled nearby amongst the dead leaves and wood anemones' tight-shut heads. Two were squaring-up to one another on the path below; there is a very rigid 'pecking-order' amongst wild rabbits; and far over on Long Field, many many, more were browsing on the tender shoots of growing barley.

The night was warm; my anorak and the radio safely hung from a broken branch 'hook' twenty metres away. A woodmouse slowly traversed the prone trunk; the deep clefts of its bark were steep steps to jump across. Within each hollow lay the remains of some past feast of squirrel, bird or mouse. Tiny fragments or near whole shells, with the tops chiselled out. The woodmouse disappeared into one such hollow and checked its contents. Then just as suddenly, sprung onto the rim and so down into the next depression to try again there. Now it was on a level with my trousered leg just below the knee. A momentary hesitation and I watched it flick on to my knee, almost at face level. It sat back on its haunches, one front paw across the other and I stared fascinated at its darkly protruding eyes, large upright ears and whiskers all aquiver. Pale legs and paws and long, long tail. How delicate and dainty with a faint shine of light through transparent ears. There were sounds of a badger approaching along the winding sett trail; a leap; and my mouse was gone.

Briarmead at first light was faintly scented with the damson blossom lining its bank. The sky that morning was spectacular, all dappled with red, yellow and grey as I spoke to Jane patrolling. The cuckoo called as it began to rain. The squirrels here were biting off oak twig ends now;

the tender young leaves were still creased from their birth in the bud. Walking home, Tuesday was a breezy, dry, cool night. I was sitting on the lower bough of the old cherry with Jude. In his ways he reminded me so much of Jet his sister, but not in looks; her extreme blackness was like no other badger that I've known. He left me after awhile and began digging out a long forgotten sett entrance just ahead of me. Big, hard, clods of heavy earth were excavated with the finer sandy soil, the former rolling down the spoil heap to come to rest below my feet. An hour's steady work and a great heap hid the bluebells. It also covered the branch of a small elder that grows lower down this sett slope, so that part of it sweeps the upper earth.

The tawnies were vocal at first light, one serenading the other. The male still hunted for his mate and their young. The damson and cherry blossom offset the vivid greens and birdsong filled the air. Sadly, that grandfather of trees, the old cherry, was now dead. No sign of living bud, blossom or leaf, while all around, its small progeny were bright with softly blown blossom and tender leaf.

A few days later I discovered that children had been picnicking at the Old Cherry Sett. The lovely old tree makes a marvellous seat so it is a natural stopping-place. Children had been trampling the spoil heaps of the sett entrances; their footprints were everywhere in the soft earth. Sticks were pushed down too, but the most worrying aspect was the trampling. This is hard for badgers to tolerate and causes them considerable stress.

That evening I had a phone call from the chairman of the NFBG. Among other things, we discussed the new section of electrified railway line between Tonbridge and Hastings. This was opened at the end of March and within a few weeks killed nearly 200 badgers. British Rail were concerned and it appeared that sections of the conductor rail could be removed without endangering the trains. Now it was a question of surveying the worst affected part to find the regular crossing routes. This won't however, help the cubs of badgers already killed; these must have died of starvation long since. Since badgers follow regular scent trails to their feeding grounds, whole colonies of these animals must have been wiped out, all for the want of knowing. Another section of line was to be electrified, this time in the chairman's own locality. British Rail were working with the RSCPA and the county trust to survey the area for badger crossing points, so that breaks in the live rail could be made.

I would soon have to give these badger cubs names, if only to identify them when writing. When you really get to know wild animals, it's surprising how individual they are, both in their behaviour and coloration. For instance, one of Susie's cubs had a brown tinge to her greyness and a very white tail. Her sister was extremely quick and would continue playing long after the others had given up and gone to earth. If they wouldn't play, well, she'd have a game on her own. At this time of year the badgers are still above ground in good light, so she chased a blown leaf, then an indignant blackbird who was disturbed turning over detritus in his quest for food. Lastly, she choose a solitary bumble bee – not a wise choice perhaps. But she merely sneezed at its angry buzzing and begun grooming herself instead. The badger's striped mask is another useful identity sign as quite often the pattern is irregular, narrow or unusually wide. One cub may be more timid, aggressive or bold than its brethren. But when all are madly whirling together in play, their bodies seem to weave in and out, over and under in a continuous flow, making it impossible to determine which one is which.

The 21st May was a cool, bright, breezy morning after the thunderstorms and torrential rain of the previous day. Jude had dug out on Cliffords Bank, whilst at the Cherry Sett there were mounds of bright earth amongst the bluebells and paw prints everywhere in the fresh, wet dirt.

Watching my eleven badgers, I realised how lucky I was. West Yorkshire's Wildlife Liaison Officer had told me that a survey had been made of the badgers in his force area, a countryside of 500 square miles. The badgers there numbered no more than a hundred animals with only forty setts now occupied. Yorkshire was the first county in Britain declared by Parliament in 1979 to be a specially protected area for badgers, but the badger-digging had continued. This officer had initiated the county's badger protection group for there, as he reluctantly concluded, the hunters must exceed the animals upon which they preyed. So the animals in my study area numbered more than 10 per cent of West Yorkshire's total badger population – a very sobering thought.

That evening I contacted the NFBG to enquire about reflector posts as a 'possible' for the badgers that regularly crossed on the Ledwell Road. Between 1977–1981, I recorded seven badger deaths on this stretch, though I have never gone there on a regular basis. Then, no one cared about these animals; their bodies were merely thrown into the ditch, and such posts were unobtainable. Mr. Taylor and another resident had told me of such a death the previous February. Obviously, it was still a regular badger route, though how many animals had died there over the years it was impossible to say. Most motorists wouldn't notice the bodies unless they were actually on the tarmac. I wondered how many had staggered away to die, or been sent flying into the verge by the impact.

On the Ledwell Road, I looked for signs of badger crossings, but unfortunately, this was an up-and-over path between high banks where the reflector posts would not work. The Clwyd Badger Group had taken the lead in the testing of these. There is a Dutch model which reflects light from the opposite side of the road and is made of mild dimpled steel. The Austrian model reflects light from the same side of the road and is made of red glass prisms set in angled casing. Both types need to be fixed into posts and regularly cleaned. They may be vandalised or stolen and are of no use under certain circumstances, including sodium lighting. These reflectors were originally made to deter deer and reflect the light of oncoming vehicles on to the animals' paths leading to roads. There were still mixed feelings about the effectiveness of these reflectors and more experimenting with them would be needed to evaluate their efficiency. I collected badger-hairs from the barbed wire and, climbing the farm bank, saw that a barn was built into it on the other side so that the badgers actually crossed the barn roof to the bank and Ledwell Road! Since I was in the vicinity, I went to see the Taylors and together we checked their land. The sett just off the road that the terriermen had stopped up was now badger occupied with the entrances freshly re-opened. They had the locality's only elm tree, untouched by Dutch Elm disease. Perhaps it had a natural immunity. I had quite forgotten the appearance of the elm in its full glory of unfurling leaf.

Sunday 25th was the night of the full moon. The wind was blowing in the poplar trees and at the moment, it was dry. The sky was clouding over, however, and soon the moon would be obscured. The barley had grown tall and the flowering rape even taller. I could smell the barley. Everything was living and growing.

At 2.40 a.m. Watcher appeared from out of the rape. I hadn't previously seen her fetching-back for the five cubs of Sandy's vixen, but had a suspicion she might be helping to feed them. The cubs were denning now at the farthest end of the Old Cherry Sett. This of course, is a sett of considerable length containing many, many holes on its slope, so they were quite a distance from those of the badgers. Watcher had caught a rabbit by Cliffords Bank, ate part of it including the guts and chest, then carrying the hindquarters, took the field path that runs parallel with Briarmead, till she reached the trail through the barley, and so into the wood. The cubs were above ground playing in the bluebells with no sign of the parents, but they displayed no hesitation towards Watcher, so I felt they were used to her. They swarmed around as she tore off pieces and as fast as a youngster secured a portion, it ran off with the prize to eat away from its siblings. Clearly, she had done this before.

She groomed herself, wads of loose hairs blowing away along the slope. Years of excavated earth had created platforms outside many entrances and upon one of these she lay with the pups playing all over her. Her belly fur was investigated I noticed, but no milk there! Although they were weaned now, nevertheless, all young animals indulge in a little wishful thinking. Then off she went. I met her at the slope top in the birch stand and together we passed round the wood edge, across the lane and back along Cliffords Bank. I think Watcher felt she had done her good deed for the night.

I had a problem now with the rubbish in Ashcroft Woods. I had always collected it as soon as it appeared and taken it to the depot in Maddon Lane as I went home. That depot was now closed. Plastic bags and litter, I could carry home bit by bit, but glass bottles, especially when broken, were a different matter. I didn't feel I could rightly fill Pete's bin in Colts Farmyard with rubbish not coming from his land. I didn't mind collecting it, but taking it away was now another matter. Rubbish encourages further rubbish to be thrown down, just as dumping and fly-tipping encourages more.

On my way home I checked the Yew Tree Sett and Crawfords. The sett was still unoccupied, but there was my friendly guard dog wagging himself in half! His owner was now in prison, having done one burglary too many, so as he was 'resting' I really didn't need to worry what went on here, for his family seemed harmless enough. I still wondered about the two vans unloaded at night last August. The patrol I had spoken to left me with the strong impression that I should stick to badgers, however, and leave surveillance to them.

In the early hours of one morning, Little'un dug out along the Bank Sett at the side of Long Field. And what did she turn out on to the earth of the spoil heap? My lambswood jersey from last year! She snuffled it a bit when I picked it up. It was indescribably dirty, with dead leaves entwined and big holes chewed in it. I looked at Little'un and as she looked at me, I shook it at her, which was a mistake, for she grabbed hold of it and we ended up having a game. With her teeth embedded in a sleeve and me holding an end, we pulled up and down the slope, until finally I let go. She stood with her end still in her jaws, looked at me sitting there laughing and took it back underground!

That morning the whiskered barley had a pinkish tinge; it is for me the most beautiful cereal of them all. I must make the most of these fields whilst they are still farmed as Barry tells me that pressure is being put on farmers to cease growing corn and indeed, to cease farming. I recall all the apple orchards once here and the imported foreign fruit we have to buy. Many conservationists want farmland to revert to the wild; but without care and attention it won't revert to anything except weedy wastes and barren land. It's frightening how really ignorant some are about the land, yet they state their dogmas with authority. Man is not in tune with the land any more; few really love the land or have a unity with it. Management is no substitute for love, as any child knows.

The last night of May was a Saturday and a mild, overcast night, with a crescent moon in a cloudy sky. All the badgers were worming under the irrigation sprays on Pete's land between Maddon Lane and the motorway. They were well spaced out on the two fields there. The ground below the motorway is perhaps the most popular, as where the bank meets the field, it is particularly wet. At 2.45 a.m. I was standing looking towards High Ridge, with one of Susie's cubs some way in front of me and Susie with her other two offspring a short distance behind, when I saw a lamper working the field side of the hedge at Maddon Lane and two lurchers running his beam – a tall, light coloured lurcher and another with a linty coat. Even with the length of field between us, his build, way of walking and his dogs, were all familiar. It was the young, thickset man of about 25, who walks over from Rendcombe village, lamping as he goes. He used to work his dogs on Glebe and Newby until the police began helping me on those farms. He just had a hand-held beam – no one uses a spotlight hereabouts now, at least the lamping fraternity have learnt wisdom there! Suddenly, one of the dogs overshot the beam and came like an arrow, straight towards me, probably seeing something larger and more interesting – the cub, up field. I shouted out to the man and tried to call up the young badger who was in front of me. I yelled and yelled, but apart from switching off the light, he made no attempt to call his lurcher back. Fortunately, the cub came running towards me and I bent down and scooped her into my arms. I had never attempted to pick up any of these young animals (though when sitting down, they scramble all over me), so if I had been bitten, it wouldn't have surprised me. But instead, she promptly urinated and hid her head under my arm! Next moment, Susie her mother rushed from somewhere behind me, through my legs at the lurcher which by now was very close. Really the sow never had a chance. Anyone seeing a longdog twist and turn to catch rabbit or hare would know that. All Susie had to attack was four long, slender legs which nimbly jumped over her as their owner buried his jaws in her neck. The screaming was Jet reincarnated; that appalling sound going on and on as the dog dragged the badger along in a vain attempt to shake its kill and break her neck. Susie is a hefty sow and something would have to give. Indeed, this is how my badgers end up with egg-sized chunks of flesh ripped from them.

With my arms full of cub I shouted above the screaming for the lamper to call off his dog and kicked at the lurcher with all my might. At the third blow it cried out and released its hold. I approached it threateningly, still carrying my burden to send it back to its master. It limped across field to rejoin the others and they disappeared hastily along the hedge. Things had happened so quickly and in the sudden quietness, I registered the motorway traffic high above. And I had imagined the lamping season to be over! How many badgers end this way with no one to know? I just happened to be with them, but not expecting trouble could have been anywhere else on these 800 acres, so both the cub and her mother might have been killed. I knew from past experience that this man views such happenings as a joke. The radio wouldn't reach to Charlie Foxtrot from this farthest side of my area, especially with High Ridge between us.

At 4.20 a.m. Susie was with me at the Old Cherry Sett. She seemed shaky, confused and shocked, standing there with her head lowered. Little'un and Crisp had tried washing her neck which was so swollen by now that her whole face appeared mis-shapen. It was difficult to tell just how bad the injury was. Thank goodness her cubs were weaned. I would come here early that evening and wait for her to emerge.

I phoned the station on my return to report the badger lamping. The officer I spoke to was very sympathetic and said they would keep an eye open for the young man after I explained that quite often I see him walking the Holmoak Lane area by day with his two lurchers. Then he takes an old jack russell bitch with him too. I think he checks the lane for holes. I mentioned that the Embankment badgers were also at risk from him and his friends. Once over the railway bridge into the far fields, they were easily trapped. This apparently surprised the constable, who hadn't realised that badgers lived in the steep railway embankment.

Later I spoke to Tony who was still extremely busy, involved with various cases of birds being taken illegally from the wild. Branches are limed and seed or a decoy bird in a cage is placed beneath the tree. Birds, especially finches, see the food or decoy and fly on to the lower branches to check all is safe before alighting on the ground. There they are stuck and taken to be sold. Often their feet are permanently injured. The branches are frequently left limed, so other birds, alighting some time later, may die a lingering death. A wildlife liaison officer who has handled many such cases, told me that one man caught by his rural crime patrol had made a lucrative living out of wild birds for 27 years without ever being questioned. So it is an old, old trade; but at least there is more awareness of it now.

Chapter 8

Susie remained in a dazed and shocked condition for 48 hours, with the damaged area of her neck swollen and hard. All I could do was to feed her antibiotic capsules between muscatel raisins and bathe the wound with hydrogen peroxide. There was no fizzing, so it wasn't infected, probably due to the other sows washing it. Her cubs were frisky enough; the little female, no worse for her fright. The mother wasn't foraging when she came above ground. Not that she stayed for long, but spent most of the hours of darkness inside the sett. I tried to hand feed her with raw mince and she did swallow some before going below.

On the 3rd June it was a relief to find her out of shock and much brighter. The adult sows continued to wash the wound. They were doing such a good job that I decided not to touch it anymore, merely feed her the antibiotics.

The weather was very mild and damp with everything green, lush and growing fast. The wayside, meadow and woodland flowers had a beauty all their own. Crisp and Sis were busy digging out at the Old Cherry Sett. In consequence, all but a couple of those entrances that were blocked last August Bank Holiday by the hunters, had now been dug out by the animals here in the past few months. One was the entrance in the 'play-pen', the place where 2½ years ago, the badgers were dug out and taken and later, Lesley made the trench and hole a nursery site for both her cub litters. That hurt when it was stopped-up, though I can't quite explain why it did. Somehow it seems a violation – a dumb animal's

151

struggle against human interference. The fact that in spite of everything, she had re-dug her home and borne her cubs there twice, only to have the place completely sealed again, the spade marks clear, hurt a lot. Now it was becoming overgrown but some badger, some day, would, like Lesley, open it again.

Early in June I had a telephone conversation with Dr Howard of Warby parish council. He was as concerned as I over the illegal activities in Ashcroft Woods and most especially, with the motorbike riding and shooting. The bye-laws were in process of being amended and we discussed the new notices publicising them, that would be erected. He solved my immediate problem too, by offering to take away the plastic bags of collected rubbish.

A few nights later it turned very cold for June, with a bitter wind blowing the rain away almost as soon as it fell. I had been on the farmland between Maddon Lane and the motorway for the greater part of the night with the badgers. The unexpected lamping incident had unnerved me, for there seemed no safe time or place for these animals. So where they go, I must go too. The cubs were really beautiful, very healthy and full of life and Susie was improving night by night. I gave her the last of her course of antibiotics. After eating them and the muscatels, she snuffled the palm of my hand, then began to groom first my hand, then arm and finally, of course, my hair. What was happening in other parts of the country? How many badgers were falling foul of lurchermen to be taken, or merely left to crawl underground and die? My area wasn't unduly bad; only I was here to see, while others slept. With my face against her furred one, I gently felt the teeth marks of her wound. The area was raised, but there was no infection and although stiff-necked, she could now forage with the others.

First light found me walking round under the trees, simply enjoying the place. It was all quiet except for a few tentative twitterings from some 'earlybirds' and the rush and sigh of the wind high above. The fox cubs were growing fast. I saw Watcher without her knowing as she hunted amongst last winter's coppiced stumps. The tawny owls had chosen to hunt there too, rather than move out on to the farmland.

At 5.15 a.m. walking up Briarmead, I met a patrol coming down. The two young men said they had parked their car in the wood for about 45 minutes while they walked round. They had found all quiet, but the birdsong great! They had done this before and found the setts in the wood from the map I had originally given Warren Hughes. Thus they had got to know the lie of the land and the general atmosphere of the place. I thanked them, for, as in the case of the Rendcombe lamper, you

152

think things are quiet, then suddenly it happens. I rarely came out into the open as I had the radio, so that we now had a chance of catching badger-diggers, therefore I had no way of telling if the lane was patrolled or not, unless conditions were right for recent tyre marks to be visible on its surface. The driver asked me exactly where the badgers were denning in Cliffords Bank and the best route to follow to get there. We discussed the recent lamping incident. I mentioned that I had been invited to go on site to another police force to see how their rural crime patrol coped with poachers. Did they think that whoever was on duty that morning would check the Old Cherry Sett for me about 5 a.m.? I would have to leave very early to catch my train. Though everything was quiet digging-wise, I felt it would be just the badgers' luck if on that particular occasion, something was to happen. They readily agreed and said they would tell Sergeant Collins.

At 7 a.m. I met Dr Howard as arranged, at the top of Briarmead. It was the first time we had met and with his dog we went to look at a 'log cabin' camp some youths had made in these woods. It was a well made and permanent structure created from off-cuts of the winter coppicing and at first when I found it, I had been inclined to admire their ingenuity and overlook the havoc they were causing. A clearing had been made for their camp by the cutting down of young saplings. At first they had been tidy, keeping a careful eye on the fires they lit. The badgers and I passed close by almost nightly, going through the wood to Pete's farmland beyond. The youths never heard us on the trail through the trees. But soon the area became strewn with rubbish and the empty whisky bottles thrown into their fire had burst, sending glass far and wide. Last week-end, they had come with friends on motorbikes. Tents were erected next to the log cabin and the periods of their stays in Ashcroft Woods were getting longer. Next they were glue-sniffing and, recalling some campers years ago who accidently set fire to the undergrowth here and ran away leaving me to cope, I had visions of this lovely wood razed by fire. What they were doing at the moment wasn't illegal however, except to bring motorbikes or cars here, but the bye-laws were being revised, so perhaps now was the time to make it illegal with a view to the future. Later, the doctor drove me into Warby and I met his wife. Just as he and I have a love of the woods in common, so his wife and I found we had a love of local history. Indeed, it was the ancient earthworks within Ashcroft Woods that first aroused my curiosity twenty-five years ago and was the start of my affection for this place.

The next Friday night and Saturday morning were mild and damp. I was watching a woodcock feeding in the wetness of the irrigated field off Maddon Lane, when there was movement just behind me and the bird took to the air. It was Susie and her three cubs – no, there were five cubs, so Missy must be somewhere about too. The youngsters snuffled in the disturbed earth left by the woodcock's probing, whilst their mother musked my boots. Then she stood on hind legs to stretch upwards against me in greeting. I was able to have a good look and feel of her injured neck under the pretext of fussing her. We were standing together like this at the wood edge, when I happened to look up and see a man's head and shoulders in the distance, as he walked along Maddon Lane. Then he jumped up on the field bank and shone his beam towards us. There were two lurchers. It must have been about 3 a.m. just another half hour and the sky would begin to lighten. I couldn't be certain that this lamper was last week's man and didn't wait to make sure. I shooed the badgers back into the wood, but the trees grow sparsely at first and I wanted them well amongst the undergrowth or nothing would save them from the dogs. I saw them disappear into the thicket and then ran to the hilltop as I was well beyond the radio's range. I switched it on to contact Charlie Foxtrot to alert a patrol, only to find to my horror that it was quite dead. I had forgotten to recharge the battery, a daily occupation that is normally automatic! Leaving the radio and the rest of my gear in a bundle, I ran through the wood and across the two farms to John Shaw's office and the telephone. I explained that if the lamper was the person I thought, there was a good chance of intercepting him on his return via Holmoak Lane and the railway bridge there. The sergeant said he would send a car to the spot right away and I thanked him, hoping I was not too late.

Coming out of John's little office, I saw the martins were now flying by the Poplar Row and the skylarks singing from the fields. The sky was paler as first light crept across the land. I saw three leverets, but couldn't stay to watch them as I was anxious to make sure the badgers were alright, and, caught up with them before they went to earth. They seemed fine and no worse for their fright.

I phoned the police on my return home, but the patrol had seen no one in the lane. Then I contacted Charlie, who groaned; quite apart from my bungling of the battery, we had never before had problems on this extreme edge of my area, where there was no way we could make contact. Charlie and his family were going on holiday for a fortnight, so we agreed that I should collect his handset on Thursday and Ross and I would see if we could get reception from our house to the Maddon Lane area. Barring bad weather (the Rendcombe man is a weekend lamper and he doesn't like rain), he could turn up again the next Friday night/Saturday morning. Susie and her cub were very lucky to be alive. I didn't want this to happen again. Come the winter, we could have lampers from far and wide if last season was any judge. But this was just a local lamper; at least, I assumed he was local as he disappeared over the fields in the Rendcombe direction. It could be, of course, that he simply had a vehicle parked there.

Sandy's vixen had moved her cubs to Tossy's Sett at the wood edge. Their old den was becoming very fouled. On my way home that morning, I stood by the soakaway looking up field and watched them for a long while as they played in Barry's meadow. All five had survived and were sturdy young animals. There were lots of bickering, gruff barks and running to and fro. That morning, too, the six hives all had swarms of bees busy in the sunshine. Yet a fortnight ago, these hives appeared deserted.

On Sunday night I watched the crescent moon going down in a starry sky. There was mist in the hollows and frost in the exposed places. I had slight pleurisy and the pain was not greatly helped by coughing, but being here was worth it for the peace of mind.

It was a bitterly cold night again, with my breath vaporising in front of me and by 3.55 a.m. I was sitting in the wood on a coppiced stump with birdsong all around. There were two young badgers playing at my feet and Missy with her snout down the top of my boot! I didn't know if the sow was looking for something in there or whether she had dropped what she was eating. These animals have a habit of chewing away at a morsel, then decide to investigate my footwear – dropping inside what was in their mouths. I took my wellie off, turned it upside down and found a large, squashed bettle. Missy promptly lunged forward and gobbled it up. Sometimes, on reaching home, I take my boots off to clean them and discover the oddest things, like worm portions, that could only have got there in this way.

Susie's neck had healed, though the area was still raised. All the fur, both guard hairs and undercoat, had come out, leaving a neat, bald area.

Probably it would grow again. The badgers were in the process of moulting and I dare say as her new fur grew, so would this patch. The scars of the lurcher's teeth were clearly visible.

The sun was rising and everything – grass, corn, the Briarmead banks and trees – were adrip with moisture. I was terribly cold and couldn't stop shivering. The sun was a hard, orange disc in an all grey sky and it had the look and feel of a winter's morning. Mist lay in long streamers along the valley and on some of these fields. When the sun had climbed well up in the sky, a long snake of mist moved steadily across the hedge by Barry's gate, over the tarmac and so onto Long Field. The sun pierced it through with rainbow colours. Everywhere else, including the top of the barley, was almost grey with moisture.

By the following weekend, Ross and I had practised with the radios and found there were just two places in my area from which we could make reasonable contact. Both were on the slope of High Ridge above the motorway. These radios were specially adapted for the Crosshampton side, with sloping fields and the river, and worked marvellously well in mist and rain (unlike CB radio). But on this side the terrain was quite different, the distance greater and, most important, there was the high bank of the motorway. I had told Sergeant Collins what we were doing. Running at present was not my strong point, as the pleurisy was still making me cough. Privately, I hoped the Rendcombe lamper would lie low for a while, at least till I was better and Charlie Foxtrot was back, for we could now have a lamping problem on the Crosshampton side! Barry and Alfie were cutting the grass of the meadow above Cliffords Bank; a very long field stretching from Briarmead, all along the back of Ashcroft Woods and High Ridge. Perhaps a third of it was completed and lay in sweet smelling swathes above the badger sett. With the badgers' love of hay for their bedding, if lurchermen walked their dogs here by day, they would see the lamping potential.

On Saturday 14th I had been on the Ridge since midnight, but the lamper hadn't appeared. Occasionally I walked over to the farmland and the cut hayfield beyond, but all was quiet. At 2.15 a.m. a patrol car with dipped headlights passed quietly below me along Maddon Lane, then disappeared out of sight on to the farmland, its lights off. I am rarely on High Ridge at first light, so sat resting on the stony scree, trying hard not to cough! It had been a very mild night. After a while I told myself that I must make a move and walked through the woods. This is the loveliest time of all, neither day nor night. In the open places, white campion enticed insects to visit its clove-scented flowers, while high above in the tree canopy, honeysuckle sweetly pervaded the wood. Many bats flitted to and fro in their airborne quest for food.

At 4.15 a.m. I found a white Ford, its engine still warm, parked in the Briarmead entrance. I thought it could possibly be that of a young man I had seen here twice before, very early. I checked the setts and met Missy's cubs before they went to earth, then returned up the lane to see if the car was still parked there, only to meet a patrol coming down. They told me the white Ford was still there and asked if I knew whose it was, I said I thought the owner was harmless and had wondered in the past if he was doing some research in Ashcroft Woods. If I saw him close to, I might ask him. We discussed the lamper and the chances of catching him and I explained that the other radio would be in our possession for another two weekends, so we would go on trying. The constable said they would be around and with luck we might catch him. I thanked them as they went on their way; I'm very lucky with the police here. At 5 a.m. the white car had left.

The next night, Sunday, was very mild with a heavy dew and some mist about. The badgers were busy on Cliffords Bank, digging out and bringing in cut grass from the hay field above their home. There had been no lampers, although I did see a light on and off for a brief time far over the scree slopes, but felt it was probably a couple of youths camping somewhere there. It was the warmest weekend that year.

I followed the animal trail round to the Cherry Sett to be greeted by Crisp with her ball. The badger had been digging out some of her entrances, so possibly re-discovered it for herself. Before badger watch I went down to the lake accompanied by the yearling. Together we explored its margin and the trees and wild flowers of the mudflat. Then I sat on the stump left from the fencing, Lesley's daughter on my lap, and watched the mallard and her fluffy ducklings, reflected on its still surface. There was peace for the soul here.

I knew now where the quail nested on this side of the wood. They had five creamy eggs mottled with brown, just off the grass verge and a short distance into Pete's barley. Sitting quietly there (with a near-sleeping badger on my lap), I saw the dumpy shapes of the adult birds searching for food along the wide grassy edging of the field.

Walking round the setts later, I found the small prints of the badger cubs clear in the muddy edge of Long Field. A bright orange sun climbed the misty sky. It was going to be another fine, warm day.

I had promised to take Clarissa, Stephen and their mother to the Old Cherry Sett later that morning. I had so often described the badgers there and they wanted to see the place for themselves. By the bridge in Holmoak Lane we stopped to speak to the farmer and his daughter on their horses. He told us that quite recently he discovered the chain on the padlocked gate had been partly sawn through and in the mud by the gate were the tracks of a large vehicle. Someone had reported a lorry, with tailboard let down, parked there before midnight. He told Oakley police who said they caught men tack-stealing in the area some months back. Horse rustling is popular in our county. The farmer felt their three horses wouldn't have been resold for riding, but gone as horse meat. He and his daughter never leave any tack in their stables, but bring it with them each time.

We continued over the sunlit fields to the sett. Clarissa asked me if I had named the five badger cubs yet and I admitted I still hadn't thought up suitable ones, so she and her brother sat on the Old Cherry's trunk and did so for me. Susie's cubs would be Topsy, Turvy (for the young boar), and Bluebell; Missy's were Gemma and Mick.

The days continued hot and sunny and the nights, warm and mild. I wore no jersey or anorak at night and the hours of darkness had never seemed so brief. The rising sun each morning was a child's painting in a hazy sky and every farm had fields sweet-smelling with newly mown grass. To my surprise, I found Little'un and Sis had moved to the sett on Colts Farm. The sisters were collecting new-mown hay from around their sett with such gusto, that I felt if Pete didn't hurry, he wouldn't find any to bale! I left them and wandered towards the lake, enjoying the tranquil beauty of the land at night, only marred by the occasional sound of the birdscarer from distant Newby. Then I spied movement and saw a man dressed in a knee-length coat and boots, game bag over shoulder and gun in hand, coming down the hillside towards me from the wood.

I moved away from the lettuce field to the cover of Pete's barley and crouched down out of sight round the corner of the standing crop to watch as he proceeded between the rows of lettuces nearby. Then he bent down, cut a lettuce and put it in the bag; walked a few paces further and repeated the action. I watched him slip the long knife back into one of the interior pockets of his lightweight 'poacher' coat, then pick up his gun and look round carefully. He moved over to an irrigation trolley and began to fiddle with the sprinkler head, twisting and turning it in an effort to find how it disconnected. A spell of warm summer nights will guarantee the appearance of night wanderers as surely as a spell of rain guarantees the appearance of fungi. Unfortunately, these wandering gentlemen tend to resort at the least to petty vandalism on farmland, and at the worst, well-organised theft. It is not uncommon, hereabouts, for a van to be loaded up with portable irrigation parts for re-sale elsewhere.

One enterprising greengrocer and his wife were discovered by a vigilant police patrol not far from here, filling their van with lettuces!

Interfering with the sprinkler head could be dangerous, for the water is forced out under great pressure. So I slipped behind the giant hose reel nearby and in a gruff voice demanded to know what he thought he was doing! He charged back into the wood, his coat ends flapping above his knee-length boots, rather faster than he came out of it. I checked the sprinkler head and walked slowly back to the badgers, who were still hay gathering, the sweet smell of cut grass lingering pleasantly on the warm air. I wondered if the Cliffords Bank chain gang were at it too, and walked through the wood to see. At the back of my mind I registered that the bird-scarer was sounding irregular, but with my thoughts on the poacher, I let it pass. There on the hay field above their sett, were my Crisp and big, burly Jude also taking in bedding. It was the boar who saw me first, sniffed the air, then came swaying over to musk my boots. Barry and Alfie had baled this field and the bales, three or four high, stood in curving rows all its width. Lesley's young daughter, emerging from the elmbrush cover of her sett, saw me and came over whickering, whereupon I, teasing her, disappeared round a stack of bales. Running along the row, I wound in and out as an excited pair of badgers tripped over one another in their efforts to reach me first! Little Crisp was nearly up to me when a shotgun blast deafened us and I stood stock still with the shock.

The sow gave a great cry and seemed to leap into the air and fall. I was sure she was hit. But next moment she was racing back to the safety of her home on the Bank. Jude had disappeared. There was no point in trying to hide since I had no idea of the direction from which the shot had come, but I knew it wasn't only the scarer I had been hearing for some time. Someone had been firing further down this land earlier on. With Charlie Foxtrot on holiday and Ross holding the other radio, the only point of contact was on the far side of High Ridge. I moved slowly along the bale row towards Cliffords Bank. Once under its concealing cover I would go its length, then on to the Ridge and make radio contact. Again a blast was fired just as I reached safety and looking up field briefly, I saw two figures coming along the row.

On the Ridge, I contacted Ross telling him to ask a patrol to check the perimeter of the land as it would soon be first light (by now it was 2.50 a.m. and these characters would surely be away by then. They must have not only telescopic sights but also image intensifiers. They wouldn't know I had radio, so probably wouldn't be in a hurry. The police might see them. I would radio Ross back later. I returned not as I had come, but

159

through the back of High Ridge, meaning to look out from the enclosed path on to the hay field to see if the poachers were still there. I never reached it however, for suddenly a lurcher appeared from the tree cover and another, on slip, with the two men. I couldn't have said for sure if one was the lettuce-cutting man, but certainly these two were dressed as he had been; both had shotguns, shoulder bags and one carried a small lamp. They turned and ran for the wood. It was easy enough to follow till one turned and shot at me, which made me keep my distance. Once inside the tree cover, shot tends to ricochet and come from any direction. I gave up and returned to tell Ross they had gone in the direction of Pete's land, Colts Farm. He said he would let the police know at once.

By now, it was quite light and time to do my usual vehicle check. I had no way of knowing whether Crisp had been hit, though I rather suspected not; I would have to wait until that night. All was quiet and empty at each possible parking place and at 4.30 a.m. I was walking through the wood almost to where Briarmead goes into it, when a figure ran in from the lane making for the main pond area. I had a fleeting glimpse of a white parked car through the foliage and thought it was last Saturday's Ford and the young man who sometimes came here early, so I called him back. He turned at the sound of my voice just as I came out on to the track. Long coat, boots, face running with sweat and straight hair wet and plastered to his forehead. Certainly not the young man, but almost certainly one of my night visitors. He glared in anger; his glance dropped to the radio hanging from my shoulder and then to my face. I asked him what he was doing at this time of the morning and he answered 'What business of yours is it anyway?' I said that it was my business and (since he had already seen the radio, but had no way of knowing it was useless to me here), would he tell me what he was doing, or the police? I could easily call them up if he preferred. No, he was only going for a walk (at 4.30 a.m.!), had never been here before and thought he would have a walk round. I told him to get on with his walk and when he had disappeared – rather unhappily – into the wood, I went down to his car and took the number. I wondered what he had returned for; there was nothing in the vehicle except a travel rug lying on the back seat. I continued down Brairmead, undecided about what to do. Soon afterwards he drove past me on the lane, in the white car. I stood by to let him pass and saw the back seats contained something bulky now, draped by the rug, and gun-carrying cases propped against the near-side window.

I continued down the lane, checked the Old Cherry Sett and was on the lane again at about 5 a.m. when a patrol car drew up. I explained that the man must have been one of my night visitors collecting equipment left in the wood. Had the poachers by daylight, decided it unsafe to take guns with them and merely returned home with the dogs? The sensible thing would have been to leave, returning well on into the morning when there were other cars about, but the equipment may have been poorly hidden, or the man may just have panicked. Certainly, he had been sweating and agitated. I was asked if I could definately recognise his face as one of the poachers that night on the fields and I had to shake my head. It seemed that the car was known to our police, but nothing had ever been proved against the owner and his friends. The constable said that his uniform apart, if those men thought they could beat him up at night on the land and get away with it, they wouldn't think twice about doing it! He said 'We are concerned for all life, but most especially for human life. We would patrol here sometimes in any case, but mostly we come up here because of you. I know and appreciate your commitment to the badgers, but please remember your commitment to your family and don't ever approach anyone like that again. Letting them see you patrolling this lane is fair enough, but don't approach'. I promised I wouldn't again. Actually, I had done so in error, but it seemed pointless explaining that as he was speaking in good faith and, of course, was right.

Saturday 21st was a cold, blustery night. I met a lamper just off the Sleet House Path as I was going to my area. He dazzled me for a moment with his light, then switched it off. I said 'Good evening' as I walked passed him standing there with his two dogs. He replied, then followed me along and one of the dogs, who turned out to be called Sam, snuffled my leg. I stopped to stroke it and the lamper asked where I came from. 'Oh, round about; and where do you come from?' He said from Oakley. By now we were walking together and he went on 'You're like a cat. I never know when you're around. You creep about like a cat'.

'Do I? I thought I just walked', I replied. 'You go to those woods at night, don't you?' he said. 'What do you do there? Woods are bad places at night. I'm not trying to be nosy', he added, and I laughed. 'You want to be careful. There's some that don't like you being around, or being in that wood of a morning. You'll have a knife between your shoulder blades if you're not careful!'

'You think so?' I asked. He nodded and we stopped at the row of balsam poplars, each to go his way, just as Sam thrust a cold nose into my palm. 'Good-bye' I said as I stroked the dog's head and turned to go down the path.

'Be careful love, I've warned you'.

'I will. Good-bye'.

'It's in the stars I tell you; it's in the stars' replied the gypsy and walked on, lamping as he went. Near the tunnel of Maddon Lane I stood watching his light in the distance and the dogs running the beam. I suppose I should have called Ross up once I reached High Ridge, for the patrol to come along and try to catch him, but somehow I couldn't. Soft-hearted? Not really. He doesn't touch badger, nor did he see the radio beneath my jacket, but undoubtedly he would connect me with any police activity that night. He knows the direction from which I come and what's to say it wouldn't be his knife between my shoulder blades in a few months' time?

There were no more lampers that night, which was just as well, for Watcher escorted me on my rounds and a bitter wind had sprung up. I felt very ill, had a return of the pleurisy pain and was coughing. I couldn't get warm. I went up to the hay field between the wood and Cliffords Bank and sat down, trying to get out of the wind. Every now and again I walked round to the hay field of Colts Farm, slowly and painfully, as the badgers were still interested in the cut grass and lampers could always turn up. But all was quiet and peaceful.

There had been quite heavy showers of rain, although it was still very mild. The elderflowers were in full bloom and the briar roses trailed through hedgerow and over bank in lovely profusion. The badgers were digging-out at all setts; not taking in any more bedding (except for Crisp and Jude) as I think at last their homes had reached saturation point. The sandy earth showed up very bright at the Old Cherry Sett. Earlier, I had found Missy and her cubs digging into one of Barry's grain dumps. These were all covered with well-sprouted corn, but the earth that had been turned up was rich and dark. Many nestlings were dug out and eaten and one adult vole leaped clear just in time to avoid becoming a meal.

The dogwood flowers bordering the Wildflower Path would soon be opening. The campions, white, red and bladder, were flowering every-where and the banks of Briarmead were a mass of bloom. There were many moths by night and already the bees and butterflies were busy although it was still only 5.30 a.m. The tiny green and yellow flowers of white bryony, with its five-lobed leaves, twined through the hedgerows.

At 7 a.m. it was already hot as the sun climbed the sky. These were lovely, summer days. Walking home across the field above Cliffords Bank I discovered a bundle of carefully selected hay that had been left in the middle of the path there. I had to smile recalling that earlier, young Crisp was helping Jude bring in bedding and clearly, he would have preferred to manage without her help. It wasn't even the part of the bank she occupied – hers was nearer the hives – but she's such a bossy little character. She reminded me so much of her mother with Sam, for Lesley was always in charge. After awhile she became bored, dropped the hay that she had so painstakingly collected, and chased me round and round the baler until we sat down to get our breath back, I on the ground, she on my lap.

But now the night was gone and the day was with us. On the horizon was Prossers Wood, a deep green massed against a vivid blue sky with white clouds; the pale green barley in front and here, the flaxen hay field with its bales and dried grass. Far above, a cascade of song, came from the tiny, pulsing skylark.

Saturday 28th June was a half moon in a cloudy sky with slight ground mist and strong wind. I was with Crisp when she dug out a wasp's nest in the bank of Briarmead. Unlike the young badger however, I'm not keen on angry wasps, but she wasn't bothered and continued eating as they buzzed furiously around her. Fleetingly at first light, I saw the hen quail with her chicks. I counted four, though there could have been another. They probably hatched out at the beginning of this week; by this time next week they should be capable of a little flight.

At 4.20 a.m. I looked out from the shelter of the wood over the mist shrouded land. The trees of the two-oak track and those round the soakaway of the land were distant shadowy shapes in a grey world. Then I came out onto Briarmead and looked at the remains of Crisp's work. She had dug down between thick tree roots and the nest was tucked near the tarmac surface below a root running horizontal with it. She had worked at it very quickly and powerfully. There were pieces of nest lying on the lane and along the bank with a few occupants crawling about amongst the ruins of their former home. Badgers don't heed discomfort if there's a sweet meal to be had. They're not called *Meles meles* for nothing!

The white flowers of the dogwood were all open now. We were still in our sunny spell of weather.

I watched the bees go into foxglove trumpets and back carefully out again coverd in pollen. The Cherry Sett had a host of these tall, stately spires lighting up the dark greenery of the slope. Missy and cubs with their main entrance, Susie and cubs with their two main entrances, had dug out but, no other badgers had been doing this. Though the fields had quickly become dry and the paths very dusty, beneath the heavy shade cast by the trees, the earth was still moist.

Walking back along Holmoak Lane, I met Philip's patrol car and was given a lift home. He asked how the badgers were and seemed particularly pleased that there were five healthy cubs. I told him about the rural patrol I had recently visited and how impressed I had been with the rapport built up between the landowners and farmers of that force and its police. A mobile unit concentrating on the poaching problem without being called away on other business, had a greater chance of success and a better chance of co-operation. We fell to discussing the need to get to know the community more and foot patrolling, which in fact, Philip was doing in my home area the following week. This was clearly something he felt strongly about, for he said if they don't do more footwork, then they end up having contact only at the bad times such as death, accident or a member of the family in trouble with the police; the emotionally charged occasions which aren't the best moments to foster good relations. Philip was good to talk to. I mentioned the lamper and his 'friendly' warning. The constable said quite rightly, it could be taken as a warning of others' bad intent, or as a warning from the lamper. Getting out of his car I was told to keep out of trouble.

It was the night of the bird; another mild, dry, overcast night. There were lapwings feeding on the newly prepared fields between the motorway and Maddon Lane. Their plaintive cries were all around. I sat on the fence watching the badgers up field under the irrigation sprays. In the valley to my left, the mist was creeping, but here on the hillside it was still quite clear. Crisp was sorting out the bickering cubs, only to be turned on by all five and given the treatment; serve her right! She ran down field, saw the fence looking different, scented the air and found me. I was tempted to stay on top, as she looked so wet and muddy, but she whined so much I felt mean. However, I shouldn't have got off that fence, for soon I was wet and muddy! At 2.40 a.m. as I started through the wood, all eleven badgers trailing behind, I heard a quail's wispy call. Once off the irrigated earth, everywhere was dusty, so wet feet, paws (and in the badger's case) tums, quickly had a powdering of dry earth. All the animals, except Jude and Crisp, left me in the wood and swayed off in the direction of the calling tawnies and the Old Cherry Sett. We three continued through and came out behind the Old Barn ruins, *en route* for Cliffords Bank.

A short distance along, with the badgers in front and myself, deep in thought, behind, a badger squealed as a dog ran up and went for the little sow. Jude, with a great snort, turned on the lurcher from behind. I ran up and tried to grasp it, but off slip and with its short fur, there was really nothing to grasp. It was massive. I had not seen a lurcher quite like this before. It had a large greyhound body, but the head, neck and shoulders of a bull terrier. I had never seen one with such a breadth of head and jaw. Someone was whistling and I looked along the field which rises up before dropping away, but of course, could see nothing.

But with two badgers one a very angry, fluffed-up boar, and me to contend with as well as its owner calling, it changed its mind and raced off. I had a feeling that lurcher was tired anyway. It would soon be first light and the lampers must have been packing up to leave. I reached the brow of the hill to see a large, dark van bouncing over the rough track and turn down the Poplar Row. It was a field distant already; no chance of seeing the number or telling how many occupants or dogs. A large transit-type van, I thought. It would be far away by the time I ran to the phone in the farmyard or ran to the far side of High Ridge to radio Ross.

I walked back to see Jude, still fluffed-up and stiff-legged, making a fuss of his shaken mate. Poor little Crisp, but at least she had us to protect her. I must watch this field now the hay had been cut. It could be seen clearly from Briarmead. I left the badgers and with the day becoming clearer every moment, back-tracked the bruise-trail left by the van's tyres on the dew laden grass of the path, to the little lane. They had come here via Briarmead and the two-oak track.

I doubted if these lampers even realised that the badgers or I were here. They were probably just about to leave before it became properly light and one of the dogs had wandered off. Since the shooting incident on this hay field, I had been inclined to see the badgers safely home and felt I must continue to do this. I found seven separate bits of rabbit strewn about on the field. Whatever the other dog or dogs were like, at least the bull-terrier type wasn't a rabbiter – good to put to deer or badger though, with such a powerful jaw and shoulders.

Walking home via Oakdell on the last Sunday in June, I met the terrierman/lurcherman from Maddon Lane. He said he'd heard I had had trouble recently and asked if I was all right. News travels fast in the lamping fraternity! I just nodded and changed the subject by admiring Honey, his new suluki/collie lurcher, whilst two of his terriers sniffed, growling, at my badger-musked boots. This man passed information and under his concerned veneer lay a thinly-veiled hate. I had spoilt lamping for him locally and had also spoilt his badger-digging. He cultivated a macho image and viewed himself as an authority on all country matters. He was also a compulsive liar and that was his downfall, since he lied over irrelevancies then forgot that he had lied. Nevertheless, his malevolence was dangerous and not to be underestimated. He was at great pains to tell me how he now had shooting and lamping rights near Helton, about 40 miles away.

At the start of July, I returned the plastic pail and scoop to my area to water the young trees, as everywhere was becoming so dry. I also carried some photocopying on local history which I hoped to deliver before dawn at the doctor's cottage in Warby. The badgers and Sandy were busy worming under the sprays of Colts Farm, so I took the opportunity to hide the pail and crept off unseen by the foragers.

The package safely delivered, I stood by the cottage in the village listening with delight to a barn owl calling between the river and the hotel over the way. Walking back up the dusty track of the farm, I came across a hedgehog intent on food in the grassy verge. It bit off pieces of shell round a snail's opening, until the occupant was extracted and the soft body chewed up with much smacking of lips. Absorbed, I didn't at first register the commotion, then in panic, left the hedgehog and ran in the direction of the noise.

It was the most extraordinary sight I've ever seen. My pail was bouncing down the steep hillside with the badgers in hot pursuit! It came to an abrupt halt against a water hydrant; an excited cub popped out just as Crisp came pounding up, grasped the plastic bucket in her jaws and continued down field, with the rest of the gang closing in! Lesley's daughter, probably hot and puffed by now, tripped over the handle somehow, sprawled her length and was overtaken by Sis just above the lake. There was a swirling confusion of badgers, and my pail seemed to take flight, to land with a splash, well out over the remaining water! The little scoop I haven't found to this day and it was a week before I recovered the pail. I tend to forget that badgers, and foxes, can pick up my scent trail and find anything I have hidden, unless I leave it well above ground level.

After a night of violent thunderstorms and heavy rain, it was a dull, misty morning. Pockets of mist were trapped like puffs of smoke where the curving wood meets the field edge and within the trees' shelter came a steady drip, drip, drip as if it were still raining. Beyond it, however, there were patches of ground already dry, for the air was becoming warmer with the daylight.

Earlier that night, at the first hint of distant thunder, the badgers under the sprinklers disappeared for home. I had stayed. Now it was 5 a.m. with an occasional flash of lightening far away in the distance and a rumble of thunder. The storm had reached someone else. I heard the geese call, but couldn't see them, then heard them calling as they passed overhead. By the sound, they had been feeding on Glebe Farm, but I couldn't be sure as it was too misty. There was a lovely smell of vegetation now with the damp warmth. My jeans were wet up to the thighs with walking after Watcher on the trail through Barry's barley. My fox, well into her moult, looked thin and dark; the wet fur clinging to her spare body.

Before the storm at about midnight, Missy dug out a wild bees' nest in the Briarmead bank. Looking at it now, I saw the remaining bees were dead in the hole she dug, which was almost the size of her sett entrance. The honeycombe had gone. What she left was washed away in the storm. This bank certainly held some surprises. Just then, the sudden leap of a squirrel, high in the ash overhanging the lane, sent a cascade of water droplets to leave me soaking, as it searched for young, tender shoots to eat.

At 6 a.m. I tested the radio with Charlie, who was back home after his holiday. Reception was clear with no static at all. As the rising sun climbed higher in the sky, it pierced the greyness and sparkled on the barley, still bejewelled with rain. There were many insects in flight over the standing crops with swallows and martins diving and skimming to catch them. Walking home each day, I checked the soakaway of Holmoak Lane. That morning the level had risen and there under the droop of willow, dappled with sunshine within its darkness, was the mallard duck. I did a quick count, then again . . . and again. When I passed last night, she had seven tiny ducklings, but now she had ten! Dark tan with yellow cheeks and chests, they bobbed gently up and down, keeping close to their mother.

By the end of the first week of July, the male cub Mick had forsaken his sister Gemma and Missy to dig out the small Dump Sett and was denning there. I must make sure I checked this place now for it was very vulnerable on the edge of the wood. All was quiet on the hay fields. The badgers were under the sprays again, with two of the young foxes worming near the badger cubs. I went to sleep on the meadow above Cliffords Bank, though I hadn't meant to, and was discoverd by Crisp and Jude on their way home. One moment I was fast asleep, the next Crisp was a purring in my face and Jude was musking my arm!

In spite of recent storms, the level of Pete's lake had dropped drastically by 6th July. My pail lay trapped in the reeds and I took a chance, running quickly across the exposed bed to retrieve it. I could feel the treacherous mud pulling at my boots, weighing them down. The drop in water level was strange.

The badgers dug out yet again at the Old Cherry Sett; little Mick at the Dump Sett and Crisp with Jude on Cliffords Bank. Fortunately, the latter was completely hidden with lush growth, but I thought both lampers and diggers knew they were there. Three young men, camping overnight in the log cabin, began shooting in Ashcroft Woods at 5.15 a.m.

I had a fox escort that morning as I did my vehicle check rounds.

Watcher appeared, her coat soaked from walking through the barley. In spite of her scraggy appearance, she was a lovely vixen. I squatted down to her level and as she rested her chin upon my knee, I stroked her long, delicate muzzle and marvelled at her beauty. Her eyes seemed to see deep into mine. What goes on in her brain, mine wondered; this vixen that I valued above any fox I had known, above any dog except Wendy? I might not see her for some nights, though she must often find my scent. Sometimes I would look up from where I was standing with the badgers, conscious of being watched . . . and there, perhaps at the tree edge some distance off, would be Watcher. She seemed to accept that I was often in their company; just looked and went away. Then as I walked on my own, she would suddenly be at my side. There had been no absence – she was here all the time. She was my mirror image, my other self.

Two mornings later I checked Mick's sett at the Dump to find fresh boot marks on the spoil heap and a faint tobacco smell. Just a few metres further on lay a smouldering cigarette end. I waited until 8 a.m. by now it was raining hard, but all was quiet, with no sign nor sound of anything except the pouring rain.

Missy was forsaken by her cubs, for not only was Mick denning at the Dump and had dug out yet another entrance there, but his sister Gemma had gone round to the Seam Path, dug out in the bank of Little Chantry Field and gone to earth there. I came upon her still busily engaged in good light and stood watching. Backing out with the umpteenth load, she paused for breath, turned and saw me. For a moment Gemma froze, till I spoke softly. Then with almost a chirruping sound, she bounded up and made a great fuss of me. I was very surprised, since she had always been the least interested in me of all the badgers. For the first time for a long while she musked me, so I went over and admired her work, that is, patted the earth with one hand and stroked her with the other as I knelt there, all the while talking to her softly. This was her first attempt at independence. Like Mick, she would race back to their mother at the slightest sign of trouble, but it was an important phase in their natural development and I was pleased for her.

I checked the radio with Charlie, in part of Ashcroft Woods we hadn't tried since before he went on holiday. I had found previously, with Ross, that reception altered once the foliage had grown. However, it hadn't affected reception with Charlie Foxtrot at Crosshampton. I stood in the middle of the Chantry at its darkest and most secluded spot with tall, soaring beeches all around and begun to speak, when I had competition from a nightingale at the trees' edge! I momentarily stopped, then told my radio what was happening. The bird continued singing beautifully, quite unbothered by my voice softly describing the scene. 'Hmmmm, some people have all the luck', remarked Charlie Foxtrot from the depths of his bed.

Later, standing on Briarmead, there was a faint rainbow in the sky. I hadn't realised it was raining since the sun was shining behind me, but I was soaked.

At the wood edge, viper's bugloss was a vivid splash of colour with bees busy amongst its blooms. As I was going home along the two-oak track, Watcher appeared from the wheat and walked at my side. It was interesting to notice how unbothered the rabbits were at our approach. On the grassy path above Cliffords Bank, they grazed until we draw near, then made a sudden dash for the warren within the Bank. Doubtless they felt secure with safety so close and Watcher so indifferent. She snuffled my leg, then thrust her cold nose into my hand.

Sunday 13th was mild, damp at first light, as mist swirled over the land and crept along the woodland paths. Mullein bloomed on the wood edge of Colts Farmland and the pinks, flowering further along, showed up with startling clarity in the poor light. The Wildflower Path was strewn about with cherries that Watcher and I shared. So many lay there that we were both very choosy.

On the hillside of Colts Farm, the barley stretched field after flaxen field from the motorway to wood. Next to these fields, the moist, fresh earth, awaiting the day's lettuce-planting, smelt wonderful. The badgers had thought so too for nothing misses a good badger nose. The equipment was out ready for the women, together with the hut on wheels they could sit sheltered from the sun or rain to eat their food. They would soon be here, for everyone, including Pete, was working from early until late and Sundays.

By the 14th July the lake had vanished as if it had never been, leaving a vast stretch of cracked, spongy mud. There were duck, fox and badger prints but the water was no more. My trees at the far end, especially the willows, were enormous. They had long over-topped me and stretched far above. The water lilies were dead. The white, fragrant flowers of *Nymphaea alba* and the smaller yellow 'brandy bottle' *Nuphar lutea*, lay withered and dried by the sun. All the other aquatic plants could survive periods of drought including the great clump of marsh marigold. Provided this place stayed damp, they would survive.

Later, Tony came to say that Barksham police had news of Don Francis who was holding his annual terrier show later in July. Sergeant Collins had suggested police cover, for it was thought a dogfight was held after the show last year. It appeared that some men went to an outhouse and others weren't allowed anywhere near. Tony would be away that weekend and couldn't be there, so the police interest was good. Recalling last year's show I said I definately wouldn't be attending since certain terriermen and I weren't on the best of terms!

There was a clear sky and half moon two nights later. The young foxes were increasingly independent and their mock fights were for real now. At the wood edge, about 1.50 a.m. I could hear a quarrel in progress and under cover of the noise, crossed the hay field and found the two contestants on the path by the Poplar Row. It wasn't so much a tooth and muscle dispute as a war of nerves. Each fox had its forepaws on the shoulders of the other in a bid to push it backwards and both were screaming and yelling open mouthed. They may do this in play, without the noise, as Josh used to do to me. Or they can do it for supremacy, as now, without biting. This time, one fox finally fell backwards with his brother standing over him. Then the vanquished was allowed to regain his feet and ran off with the other chasing behind. These were Sandy and vixen's litter; the parents no longer hunted for them.

At dawn on the Wildflower Path I watched tiny banded snails, on the black and white bryony leaves. The two bryony plants overlap just here and seven little snails were moving slowly over the surface of the leaves, back and forth, back and forth. All was still wet and as the snails didn't appear to be eating the leaves, I wondered if they were taking the moisture or were eating something too small to be seen with the naked eye. The most attractive of these snails (none more than ½ inch in diameter), was a bright orange with deep amber bands. Watcher, accompanying me, was absorbed in a movement in the nearby corn or the snails might have become a meal. I collected the ripest of the wild cherries and sat well out of sight at the corner of Long Field, sharing them with her. She could eat a great deal faster than I!

The following night I played with Susie's three cubs, Topsy, Turvey and Bluebell. They were lovely animals and getting quite big and strong. I left them at the Old Cherry Sett to play about for awhile before going to earth while I checked for vehicles before dawn. All was clear. About 4.25 a.m. I came to the Cherry Sett and stood there gradually feeling more uneasy and knowing I wasn't alone. I carefully checked each occupied entrance, but all were undisturbed. I stood against the chestnut standard, pushing the radio right to my back so that it was hidden between the trunk and my body with the strap on my shoulder covered by my open shirt collar. There was nothing to see. I was being ridiculous, but I didn't want anyone to know I had radio contact. No point in contacting Charlie Foxtrot over a feeling – but suddenly there was a movement at one side and two men stepped out from the thick undergrowth.

The light was still poor under the trees, so I couldn't tell the colour of what they were wearing – industrial type boots, trousers and jackets. One man was short, stocky with a podgy face and rather scruffy, the other was taller, more neatly dressed, with thinning hair. I had last seen them with a group from Ledwell at Don Francis' terrier show, but they had come here several times, so we knew one another quite well.

The short man put a knife against my thoat and told me they didn't want me around here any more. They seemed highly pleased with themselves. I was glad they hadn't seen the radio; they could so easily have taken it from me. They had no gear with them, no spades or dogs, so hadn't come to dig. I was sure, in retrospect, that it was these two who had been about here recently, though I hadn't actually seen anyone. I didn't say anything for I knew from past experience that such folks can turn nasty very quickly.

After a few moments, having made their point, they went off unhurriedly along the sett path, openly looking at the occupied entrances and making comments, still grinning. They shouted at me not to follow or it would be the last thing I ever did, and sauntered off along the bottom path in the direction of Pete's land. They must have come in that way somewhere as I had just checked Briarmead for vehicles.

I recalled that once I had found – too late – where that group had parked by the tyre marks in the mud, at the side of Capel Spring at the end of Warby Hill Road. I made contact with Charlie asking if a check could be made for a vehicle and giving a description of the two men which he relayed back. Some while later, we again made contact, I explaining at more length where and how I had met this couple before, and again he relayed it on. Then it was time for Charlie to go to work and I returned home. We both felt that nothing had been found – there are so many ways on and off this area.

PC Alan Matthews came later to say that no vehicle had been seen leaving and we discussed the details of the incident. I decided to mention that after this winter, I wouldn't have the stamina to go out regularly each night. I therefore wanted to help them secure as many convictions as they could before then. Otherwise, I knew only too well what would become of my badgers. This had been on my mind for some time and it was a relief to bring it out into the open, though I hoped he wouldn't think I was whining. However, he understood and said he would speak to Sergeant Collins.

I spoke to Barry after he returned from holiday and it appeared that during his absence, the bird scarer had been activated and the police received complaints. That explained the scarer sounding at night. Someone must have tampered with it several times as the times it had started and the periods between the sounds had varied considerably.

I mentioned that Mick, the young badger, was denning on his own in the field edge of the woods and asked Barry if he would keep an eye open for any human activity there, especially in view of the boot prints in the fresh spoil heap and the two terriermen.

Towards the end of July my hands were cold, for the first time that summer. It had been a cold night, for my breath and that of the playing badgers was vaporising; but the rest of me was hot, and sweat was running from my hair on to my face and neck. At 5 a.m. the owls were calling and I had found a vehicle well tucked away inside the wood; but it was holiday makers, staying overnight. I felt very cold by now and couldn't seem to get warm. At the Cherry Sett, Susie, Topsy and Bluebell were with me, though their brother had already gone to earth. I tried to persuade them to do likewise, but the three badger ladies were taking it in turns to musk me. I was sweating again and my scent must have been strong and interesting to them. I felt strangely weak sitting against the old trunk. At least I couldn't fall, as I was on the ground already. I hoped I would have no human company this morning.

I opened my eyes to find my vision blurred by fur. It was Watcher, curled up against me. We were bathed in sunlight and the time was 9.20 a.m.! I spoke to her softly; her eyes were mere slits that stared into mine. I stood up cautiously, with her watching me, but I was all right. Whatever was wrong had passed.

Common centaury, tufted vetch, wild marjoram, bugle and nettle-leaved bellflowers were all in bloom along the Wildflower Path and touched by the rising sun to send them all aglow. Squirrels had been eating the unripe cobnuts and left the remains scattered in the grass. Watcher carefully sorted them over, selecting a few to crunch up. I noticed lucerne was growing on part of the bank as we walked up the lane. A pair of partridge flew low across us and vanished into the wheat; there were plenty of partridge and pheasant this year, but very few quail. I was glad my quail survived the winter for his family was doing well; I had seen them several times during the last few mornings. The young birds were growing fast and Papa was very puffed-out and full of himself; rather comic for such a tiny bird!

By 5 a.m. it had been raining gently and steadily for several hours. The tawnies were calling one to the other and their fledglings, not very musically, joined in – young owls have a lot to learn. I recorded them

172

beautifully on tape. Approaching the Old Cherry Sett, I saw the male tawny adult; next moment he was on my shoulder. He didn't wait to be invited. The wren who had been feeding her young a moment ago as they were begging on the cherry trunk itself with one drinking from the pool in the fissured bark, was alarming. This started the blackbirds off and then a thrush. My tawny preened himself on my shoulder, quite unimpressed. I wondered if there was method in his madness; after all, he was not likely to be mobbed from that perch.

I walked along slowly and carefully with him there, to check the entrances of Susie and her cubs farther along the slope. All clear with no problems. I noticed the badgers here had again dug out that night. Her youngsters were also going independent, but still denning at this sett. It's such a long one, stretching the whole distance of the hill ridge. Then I sat on a fallen trunk with my beautiful friend on my knee. In truth he was looking a trifle untidy, partly since he was well into the moult and partly because his grooming had left him damp. I tried stroking his wing with a finger and he turned his head to watch it, then touched the finger with his curved back. He didn't peck, merely ran his beak softly against it. I spoke to him gently and he lifted his head to look into my face, doing the same action first to my lips and then chin and cheek. A shaft of light touched my face and then his, from the sun rising outside the wood. He blinked uneasily, his wings shifting as the beam transformed the feathers to a brilliant beauty, every shade of red, brown, white, black and tawny. Then off he flew to roost high in the chestnut standard and disappeared from sight. As I walked home across Colts Farm, one of Pete's men on a tractor drew alongside and asked me if I had any trouble early last Friday morning. I told him about the two terriermen with the knife who had threatened me. It seems that at approximately 4.50 a.m. a dark van containing two men came quickly out of the Oak Dell entrance of the wood, passed down the track leading to Maddon Lane and there turned left towards the motorway. Pete's man said the car park was empty as he approached it. On a tractor you sit high up and look down into that space; he always checks as he goes by as a matter of course. It was only after he had turned with his trailer that morning and progressed some way up the track by Oak Dell that he saw the van as it went towards the road. We both thought it must have been parked well up into the wood, which was quite possible, as the big wooden gate that was stolen from its hinges last autumn had never been replaced.

One night I stood surrounded by honeysuckle and briar rose, watching the nightjars feed on the insects and moths attracted by the fragrant blossoms. Their gape close-to is quite amazing. Sometimes, they brushed against the trailing plant, covered as it was in flowers, but not often. There was a never-ending food source here. It was raining slightly and this merely enhanced the heady scent. The white spots on the male bird's wings showed very clearly at night.

Later, I looked at this flower-bower in daylight. The honeysuckle was creamy-white and yellow and the rose, white with yellow stamens, the entwined plants so over-canopied with bloom as to render the green foliage well nigh invisible. There must have been many hundreds of individual flowers growing there.

Soon it was very warm and humid with clouds of insects including gnats. The water-laden chestnut catkins were dropping with soft sound. One fell on Watcher who twitched her body to dislodge it as we passed on our way. The sun pushed its light through a ragged triangle of dark cloud and the beams appeared to touch Barry's barley beyond the two-oak track; shafts of rainbow shimmered above the wet crop. The vixen yawned, looked up at me, then thrust her muzzle into my slack hand. She was quite right, I shouldn't be idly gazing when someone could easily be digging out a badger! I ran down the lane with Watcher pacing me just ahead. I liked her doing this. It kept me going, especially when I was very tired.

The late evening was cloudy with a half moon shining through and very mild. I was testing new equipment for the radio with Charlie and Crisp was being very irritating. In view of the surprise encounter at the Old Cherry Sett, I had been given a switch-lead and earpiece, the idea being that in similar circumstances I could switch on the radio hidden beneath my coat from the device in my pocket. Charlie Foxtrot would be able to hear anything I said without me speaking into the micro-phone, whilst I could hear him through the earpiece without anybody overhearing. I found it was not practical, however; my hair is very short and the earpiece and lead were far too obvious. Also, the places where we could contact one another were greatly reduced using this device.

On the last night of July I came down the slope of the Old Cherry Sett from the field above to see a solitary man kneeling at the very largest and lowest entrance, his head bent as he examined it. He had a stick or metal rod in one hand. I kept well away and was a distance above, so couldn't distinguish his features. I watched a while, then crept back onto the field and contacted Charlie, saying not to alert our police as so far, nothing wrong had occurred. I would go back and watch. Returning, I found him gone and though I walked round all the other setts, I didn't see him again. At the cub setts, however, I noticed boot prints partially obliter-ated. A handful of bracken lay nearby with sandy earth upon it. Walking back to the Old Cherry Sett again, I looked more carefully and saw the same boot prints roughly obscured and chestnut leaves, freshly pulled from a tree, used to sweep the area clean. If I didn't know the spoil heaps so well, I might not have noticed. At this sett too, there was a curving line of neat, round holes, not there before. They traced the badger tunnelling beneath, so it had been a metal rod the man was holding.

Before I left for home that morning I fixed two pieces of wire netting, that Ross had cut for me, round my wild service trees. Their bark was being nibbled, I suspected by rabbits. I hoped that would do the trick, for these trees were growing so well and I would hate anything to harm them now.

On the hay fields above Cliffords Bank, the swallows were wheeling and skimming in an air alive with insects. I checked this sett containing Crisp and Jude as I went by, with the mystery man very much in my thoughts. Everything was fine however, with no boot prints here. I was loth to leave Ashcroft Woods that morning and walked the length of them back once more to the Cherry Sett. This wood was searingly beautiful as the bright sun from outside sent its red beams into the dark depths to touch a trunk here, a patch of ground there and light up the sombre places. Many fields were now harvested and the year was creeping away. Soon the lampers would be back.

Chapter 9

As it happened, neither the RSPCA nor the police were able to attend Don Francis' terrier show and I despaired, for unless observers went, how were we going to get closer to the problem? Someone did go, however, who knew how sick and frustrated I felt – two men from the NFBG. They set about blending into the background and listening to conversations. They had only been there a few minutes, when one proud dog owner began boasting to others about a scar inflicted on his lurcher's throat by a badger. Later, another group discussed a recent badger-dig in which a terrier had its nose bitten off and the vet had to mould in two holes for it to breathe. I wondered what tale they had told the vet. Like myself last year, the NFBG members had intended to note down vehicle numbers, but with so many parked, it wasn't practicable. Well, at least they had seen for themselves the types I and others encountered in wood, copse and fields. I appreciated their going, more than I could say.

Some time afterwards, Tony had a badly bitten dog reported to him and on investigating was told by the owner, a Mr Ayres, that he had acquired it at the terrier show. He had bought it as a scarred 'game' dog, but not of course, with the open, untreated wounds it now displayed. Often, owners dare not take their injured dogs to a veterinary surgeon, but stitch the wounds themselves, though this Patterdale's owner hadn't even done that. The wounds were tears rather than bites, so Tony asked what had caused them, trying to appear naïve. The owner said contemptuously, 'Can't you see, he's been clamped?' (the term used for the badger's pincer and tear mark). In dogfighting, the bites are generally round the shoulders and front legs; with badgers, they tend to be on the ears, face and throat. This dog had been put to badger and the clamping was particularly evident on the throat. We wondered how many other game dogs had changed hands at Don Francis' show and where they were working for their new owners now. Both the police and the RSPCA had been alerted to Ayres before when he and his other terrier had been seen in suspicious circumstances, but nothing had ever been proved.

The roll bales on the Top Field had been gathered into piles to await collection. I seemed forever exhausted nowadays, but if I rested out in the open, one or other – or all – the cubs would find me and I just wasn't up to their rough-and-tumble. They were wild animals after all and I must expect this. They were healthy and full of energy and it was good to see their high spirits. This night, however, I climbed up the roll bales and made myself comfortable with my jacket over me, secure in the knowledge that I couldn't have a finer view point than up here.

Some time later there came plaintive badger sounds, then much scruffling and scrambling, till Little'un's face peered at me in triumph! I put my arm round her as together we looked over the edge at those who hadn't made it, down below. Viewed from above, they seemed rather comic; flat, swirly, whirly shapes, their striped faces gazing upwards, five little faces strongly protesting. Little'un pushed her snout against my cheek and I swear her expression was smug! I went down and helped them all up; all, that was, except Mick. He seemed to dig his claws in and heave himself up once he got the knack, as if he had climbed roll bales every night of his life! Even for a badger, Mick had an usually small head, which together with his lopsided mouth gave him a crafty, alert look; a look that wasn't entirely unjustified. Mick was a survivor. He took note of what the other badgers did and made the most of his opportunities. This didn't make him over popular, however.

Soon, the salmon sky warned us we should be going home. The young badgers had no difficulty descending as, with Mick leading, they slid down on their rumps. Only Little'un remained on top as I clambered down and walked along the Bank path. Happening to look back, I saw the little figure high up on the stack, her snout raised to catch any scent and the sky behind all diffused with streaks of light.

By 7.15 a.m. the sun shone warm on the straw of Long Field. At the Wildflower Path, I tupped earth gently over the dung pits containing many cherry stones. Before Crisp and Little'un had gone to earth yesterday, we had played 'hunt the cherry' under the spreading geans.

The badgers won; they were nearer the ground than I! Everyone liked the cherries – squirrels, foxes, birds, badgers and myself. Then the hawfinches moved in and cracked the stones that littered the ground. On the great trunk of the old cherry were many cracked stones empty of their kernals.

For 48 hours we had thunderstorms and rain. By 5th August, the sky was clear again; everything was sweet and fresh-scented and the Old Cherry Sett's lower entrances were dug out once again by their busy occupants. A pair of thrushes drunk from the pools on the great tree's trunk. All was quiet and peaceful.

Enjoying the morning, I was late going home and even later, on re-membering the wire netting I had fixed around the wild service trees. Had it really deterred the rabbits' bark nibbling? I left my gear well hidden and with just the radio ran quickly through the woods to see. My trees looked wonderful; strong, sturdy and refreshed from the recent rain with no more damage done. I ran down Briarmead in the sunshine, turned right by the hedge and so back into the wood by the Dump. It was shadowy, dark and colder beneath the cover of the trees; my steps made no sound on the wet, catkin-strewn path. Rounding the curve, I stopped short with a gasp at the sight of two men who turned and saw me too. They have often been in these woods, sometimes in the company of the knife-carrying terriermen of last month, sometimes with others. They know Don Francis, were at his show last year and I was sure they came from Laversley. As one raised his shotgun, I threw myself to one side, just in time. Even so, the explosion seemed to be in my head and for moments I felt stunned. I rolled over and on to my feet as they crashed through the undergrowth. The noise of their passing went in the direction of the Main Pond and probably out to Maddon Lane. Certainly, there had been no vehicle parked by the pond or Briarmead a few minutes earlier.

I contacted Charlie and queried whether he thought it worth asking a patrol to check the area. I wasn't hurt, only startled, but would dearly love to trace their vehicle as these were diggers and dogfighting men with a vengence! Shortly after, he radioed back for more details and I described the men. I would collect my gear and go home, keeping a good lookout, though I doubted they would still be around. I felt the terriermen were as startled as I and imagined they had thought me gone. They certainly hadn't expected me to run along behind them. I hadn't either! They may have intended checking the setts for fresh signs of badger after the recent rain, expecting me to have left by then, as I normally do during the week. At home I found a constable on my doorstep, asking if I was all right. No vehicle had been seen leaving and I explained how well I knew the men by sight – it was frustrating for us all.

Suddenly I found that against my will, I had come to a full stop. Physically, I had coped with the feeling of pain and illness, but what I found so oppressive was the eternal weariness and exhaustion that clouded my days and nights. I went away for a few days complete rest, first asking the police if they could patrol the lane for me.

I returned to my area on the 15th August. It was a mild, starry night with all the badgers worming under the irrigation, except Crisp. The woodland paths were wet and it had apparently rained locally in the last few days. The rowan berries were brilliant orange and the blackberries smelt sweet. But there was no Crisp to share them with and I wondered where she was. Susie's three cubs had moved right to the far end of the Old Cherry Sett and were denning within a few metres of each other.

I found a dead animal acrawl with maggots inside the wood at the Briarmead top and for a horrible moment thought it was Crisp, before commonsense told me it couldn't be. Once it had been a large black and white cat. This was one of four cats I was to find in the wood that summer, all killed by gunshot. This one could have been dumped here already dead, so near to the lane like this, but the others had been shot by someone deep in the wood.

At 6.45 a.m. a tractor moved slowly along the horizon from Newby farmyard. It was going to be a lovely morning. I hadn't seen Barry for ages, so thought I would wait for him on Briarmead. I told the farmer that Crisp seemed to be missing and he said that two nights earlier, he heard shooting on the land near his yard and realised it was a poacher. He saw no light so thought the gun must be equipped with night-sights. He decided not to interfere or contact the police as his barley or the stubble could so easily be set alight in retaliation. Once set on fire, the stubble and the old barn near the cottages, would burn like tinder and the family living there . . . I could appreciate this only too well. He also told me that he had recently seen the van owned by the lurcherman with the black dog whom he fell foul of earlier in the year. On the first occasion, Barry had told the man he was trespassing, to be nearly run down by the poacher a short while later. Only the farmer's quick thinking had saved him. Recently the lurcherman, in the company of two children, was walking across Newby as Barry came up the lane in his car one afternoon. The same van was again parked on his land, this time on his crop, which the farmer felt it best to ignore.

Going to my area the following night, I watched the railwaymen working on the track between Oakley and Warby stations. A machine was cutting down the trees each side of the line. The noise and bright lights were unbelievable though it couldn't be avoided of course, for the job had to be done.

Crisp found me examining dog prints in the fresh-rolled earth of the Top Field. It must have been coursing a rabbit earlier that night. I was so relieved to see the yearling that I temporarily forgot my concern over the lamping and played with the silly animal, chasing her in and out of the rosebay willow-herb on the bank, till we both were tired. Then I sat on the ground and she scrambled on to my lap and began to groom my hair. Later, we had a big blackberry share-out from those growing halfway up High Ridge. The crickets were very clamorous here; it seemed the most popular place for them in the whole 800 acres. Crisp went to earth at 4.55 a.m. and I was just moving away, when suddenly she returned and running up, musked my boots, once, twice, a quick check and a third time. Then up on hind legs she stretched, her front paws at my waist. I put my face against hers and stroked behind her ears.

After an evening and night the continuous rain finally ceased. The morning was mild with the sun trying to break through the lowering clouds. My badgers had been digging out, of course! I stood in a beam of light and held the rays in my hand, whilst watching my smoky breath travel up the light and through my outstretched fingers, all rainbow-hued. I could see my eyelashes darkly protecting my half-closed lids; the only light in a dim, wet woodland; the only sound, the drip, drip of the trees. I was still standing, my hand upheld with the beam warm upon my unturned face, when something soft touched my leg – Watcher, quietly watching. I looked down into her strange eyes and told her we were two of a kind, forever wandering, forever watching. She yawned, sneezed, and sitting back on her haunches, had a good scratch. So much for philosophising Chris, hurry along and check the next sett. Together we passed down the muddy path and left the ray of light like a beacon behind us in the gloom of the wood.

My vixen was with me as I stood watching the squirrels on the field above the Old Cherry Sett. Suddenly she darted forward; there was a high pitched squeal and Watcher had one in her mouth. She came back to me and I took hold of the tail gently as it dangled from her jaws. Whereupon she bit it though as they do a vole's and I was left holding the delicate, gossamer thing. Whilst she ate the owner, I stood looking at the tail freshly wet from her mouth. The squirrels too were moulting now, so some hair came away on the air. I left her to her meal and continued on my way to check Mick's small sett. All was quiet and untouched there. I stood in a beam of sunlight and held the fine, furry tail up to the light. The vertibrae hadn't yet stiffened, so I could wave it to make it float like the squirrel. Predominantly brown, the outer hairs brown at their base, turning to black and ending with grey at their tips, so giving an 'edging' effect; the whole so airy, it seemed no weight at all. I took it home with me for Stephen with some evidence of squirrel eating habits too. The boy would be interested. I also found him some cherry leaves turning a fiery red. By now, someone had started shooting in Ashcroft Woods and was going at it full blast as I left.

Along the Embankment Path towards Holmoak Lane, ribbons of bark and wood hung whitely from the living trees. I stood by the chainlink fencing and saw the badger sett entrances on the bank strewn with torn trunks and foliage. It must be a terrifying experience for the occupants, though hopefully, they were away foraging when it was actually carried out.

High winds and torrential rain caused by the tail end of Hurricane Charley, had kept both badgers and foxes well under cover on August Bank Holiday Monday. I saw Jude and Crisp briefly as they wormed at the sheltered field edge below Cliffords Bank, but no Watcher or the other foxes and badgers at all. I felt very tired at about 3 a.m. so curled up on the sheets of corrugated iron in John's barn and went to sleep for half an hour. I woke up to find Watcher sitting inside the heavy door looking out into the night. When she realised I was awake, she came bounding up to me.

Together we walked down to Newby farm and the old barn there. It was a wonderful place to explore, especially by the light of a full moon such as this. It shone through the narrow windows on to the wooden floors and showed the beams in startling relief. I wished I could take photos by moonlight, for this great barn would make a fabulous picture. I enjoyed my vixen's company. I had come to have an affinity with her only equalled to that which I had long ago with my old dog Wendy. Something inexplicable bound us together; I could not describe it in words.

By the first week of September, the nights had become cold and I was glad to wear gloves again. It was a time of heavy dews, misty first lights and leaves turning colour with the bracken. Autumn came early, with a rawness in the air. Each morning the squirrels were active in the tree tops and skirmishes amongst them were commonplace. All the badger cubs had returned to the Cherry Sett and were opening up long disused entrances in which to den. I was glad to have them back under one roof, as it were, feeling that this return home was partly due to the season's changing rhythm. We are conscious of the ageing year for all our civilized way of life and living. How much more must they be, creatures of element and earth.

One morning I watched a kestrel hunting over the fields where the barley had been gathered in and the wet straw lay in long lanes. The raptor was hovering above, intent on something within the broken stalks. Behind me from the wood, a young tawny was practising his calls as a blood-red sun rose fiercely from the distant horizon casting a mysterious glow over the land. Mist snaked along the valley. Soon it would be a lovely day. This straw was too wet to bale or burn and the dropped grain had re-sprouted pushing fresh green growth through the dead stalks lying over it.

That Friday evening was a clear, mild one with the stars seemingly painted in a velvet sky. I stayed a long while with the badgers under the trees in the orchard. By day, the pears were being picked and any dropped or damaged had to be left. It was a great pear bonanza and the badgers weren't wasting time. It was far from quiet. The snuffling, crunching, munching, and lip-smacking of numerous pairs of jaws had hidden the noise of the motorway traffic!

I tried to contact Charlie Foxtrot when a van drove up the Bank path, turned at the two-oak track and parked. It seemed to be a case of stolen goods again. Two men got out, opened the back doors and stood talking as they moved things about. But the radio was dead. Either the family were out visiting, or it hadn't yet been switched on. I crouched down on the harvested field and slowly crept nearer, hoping to get close enough to view the vehicle number through the monocular. I had gone a short distance when my left hand touched something and looking down, I saw a sloughed-off grass snake's skin caught up amongst the barley stalks. Snakes will use anything rough like this to scratch and pull away the old one. Very gently I eased it round, praying it wouldn't break, then laid its length over my shoulder for safety and continued down field. But by now the van doors were closed. A few moments more and it was driven back the way it had come, so I never did get that number! I hid the snake skin at the bank edge to collect on my return in the morning, for I knew at least one small boy who would like it.

I was near the edge of the trees, when a young hare came leisurely and noisily bounding through the undergrowth on the opposite side of the path. It came to the slight bank covered in deep moss, saw me on the path and reconnoitred – I kept still. It appeared to stare at me at about my chest level, its prominant eyes, black-tipped ears and quivering long-whiskered face, very close. Then, still upright it turned on one hind leg as we turn on our heel and went to bound back but changed its mind. Again it reconnoitred, then made to dash in front of me. Again it changed its mind and casually bounced past only to turn round, roconnoitre yet again and standing so, quite upright and staring straight at me, seemed to be lost in thought! Then casually it dropped down on all fours and walked as only a hare can, along the path and out on to the field. With long hind legs so out of proportion to their front, a hare turns its pelvis as it walks and saunters with a wiggle! Highly amused, I began to follow and that was my mistake. The eyes are set high on the head, so these creatures, like the woodcock, can see behind them whilst still facing forward. My leveret gave a great bound far out into the field, turned, looking back at me, but didn't rush off. Instead, he treated me to a frantic display of 'bouncing' round, up and down, twisting and turning. Then, still at no great speed, he went up field and moving parallel with Briarmead, high bouncing as if on springs, disappeared into the wood edge. What a performance!

Now flocks of lapwings were calling from the burnt-off stubble on which they were foraging and the stubble's arid smell seemed to carry a long way at night. Although it had turned so much colder after dark that month, the crickets stridulations still sounded harsh and sustained.

Sett-checking at 7.20 a.m. I stood in the Chantry where the beech mast was falling and the great trees' leaves fast turning to bronze.

On the way home in the sunshine, I searched for but couldn't, at first find, the snake-skin I had hidden. Finally I retrieved it and, examining more closely, saw it was probably the most perfect skin I had ever seen with the head clearly marked even to the eye holes.

It was later this fine and sunny Sunday morning that two terriermen chose to dig for badgers on the Taylor's property at Weldon. A car had been parked outside a neighbour's house and on walking along the road, the neighbour heard sounds of digging coming from beyond the hedge. The Taylors were alerted and Oakley police arrived to find the terriermen with two dogs underground and one above, all with locators fixed to their collars. One terrier was particularly striking with gross scarring to its nose and face. The poachers claimed they were after a fox, so at this stage, with no badger in their possession, details were taken and they were ordered off.

That afternoon when everyone had gone, Mr. Taylor and I took a look at the devastated sett. The crowning-down hole and infilled entrances were bright scars with fresh earth thrown about the site. Thanks to everyone's quick intervention, the badgers were unharmed, but after such disturbance, they might easily move to a place where they would feel less threatened. We knew badgers were present, but proof of their occupation would need to be photographed. This might take some days for the police Scenes-of-Crime Officer (SOCO) to do, as anything from an accident, break-in or murder, fell to his lot.

It was still a lovely, sunny day and the bright light only served to emphasise the battleground appearance of the little sett. I knew there had been dung-pits very near and standing on the raw earth, could smell the musky dung scent. It was concealed under the fresh earth. I asked Mr. Taylor if he could smell anything. 'That's funny', he replied. 'I was just about to say, that's a smell I've noticed here and at the other sett. What is it?' Together we began a systematic search of the undergrowth and there, hidden beneath the trees, were some more pits containing fresh dung. In theory, one should find the stiff, bi-coloured hairs of badger amongst old bedding turned out on their spoil heaps, but here all was covered with the diggers' soil.

I phoned Tony who came immediately as witness to the badger and human activity at the sett. By then I had taken photos of the fresh dung pits, the entrances, the deep badger trail through the thicket and general views of the sett. If these animals deserted and the SOCO officer couldn't come here for several days, at least these photos might do instead. None of us knew how many badgers occupied this sett and the Taylors were curious as to what cubs might be present. I promised to forsake my own animals for once and wait for theirs to return from foraging the next morning. I thought also that it might prove extra confirmation of badger occupation. I pointed out to them however, that not only might these badgers quit their sett, but also they could choose to go to earth at the far side of the thicket where there were entrances almost certainly connected by underground tunnelling. I would miss seeing them, though I would probably hear them. Before I left that afternoon, I laid sticks across a well-used entrance untouched by humans to see if they should be disturbed by an animal emerging.

I returned the next night to find that the sticks had been pushed outwards from the entrance. Strange badgers in a strange place! This was a novel and exciting experience for me and I settled down to wait. It was beginning to get light when I heard the familiar sounds of whickering and high-pitched chattering, interspearsed with short barks. Then four badgers appeared in single file, returning to their sett along the trail through the thicket. First the mother, followed by her two cubs and lastly another sow, possibly a yearling from her previous litter. The yearling stayed briefly with a cub, playing and butting it, then returned the way it had come. The mother groomed herself awhile, then begun half-heartedly to digout a blocked entrance to her home. Presently, she gave up and went to earth at the entrance where the previous day, I had placed the sticks. Her two cubs took over from where she had been digging and finally disappeared there. I waited perhaps ten minutes more while the birdsong increased with the light. Then I left my hiding place to see where the youngsters had gone. The re-opened hole was not very large, but big enough for them to squeeze through. Where the mother had washed herself, I picked up some fresh badger hairs and returned home feeling the neglect of my badgers had been well worth while.

The next night saw the first really hard frost that autumn, with mist in the distance. Lapwings called mounfully from the fields for there were great flocks now feeding on the ploughed earth. I was relieved to find all my badgers safe. Deep down I had feared something might have happened to them when I was at Weldon. There were boot marks on the fresh earth of three spoil heaps at the Old Cherry Sett. I must take care no terriermen dug out here. The Canadas flew over from a different direction, so they must have moved to feeding grounds elsewhere. The lingering calls of the young quails at first light were a sad reminder that my quail with his deformed wing was no more. His absence coincided with the lamper and black lurcher that Barry encountered and we had drawn our own conclusions. Never mind, he had fathered these to perpetuate his race so his brief life-span hadn't been in vain. Soon, they too must take their chance on their journey to warmer places. I recorded the quails, but unfortunately, their lisping, wispy calls never playback well on my mini-talk book which of course, is meant for just that – the human voice – not wildlife sounds. But a poor recording was better than nothing for I would miss my gentle birds when they were gone.

Returning through the wood I heard the tawny female calling, so stood under her oak tree calling back, whereupon she came to my hand. I walked with her along the Beech Path making the soft noises she makes that one only hears when close. We were both engrossed in our mutual interest when I fell flat over a tree root. The hen was quite unperturbed, merely flying up to the beech above my head. When I had dusted myself down she returned, this time to my shoulder, but I hadn't done my camera any good at all! I had been standing for a while with the tawny still on my shoulder, when her mate's muffled fluting sounded nearby. This tremulo is surely one of their loveliest calls. That morning, the owl seemed the very spirit of the trees, as he slipped softly through the branches, unhurried and eternal.

That Friday, I met the SOCO officer and showed him the badger sett at Weldon. The Taylors had reinforced the hedge separating their grounds from the road. In the process some elder branches had been sawn off and lay on the ground. The berries on them were nearly ripe, but not yet falling. This little badger family had made the most of its opportunity as their fresh, dark, pip-studded dung bore witness! Only the badger trail through the thicket was a problem to photograph with the officer's black and white film, so I stood along it to give an idea of its depth. In any case, I had photographed it in colour so we had an alternative. Driving home I asked the photographer about his work, some of which was extremely harrowing. He agreed that he had to be detached or would soon give up. His work was often routine, sometimes macabre, but never boring. That day for instance, was the first time he had photographed a badger sett!

It has stopped raining for a few hours one night, when I came across another glue-sniffers'/shooters' camp in Ashcroft Woods, apparently used in the daytime and made from sheets of plastic. It had been agreed to dismantle these when found, to discourage their use. Large sheets like this are not easy to handle alone (perhaps that was what Crisp thought too!) and I was struggling valiantly, when a little badger decided to help by hanging on an end. I finally gave up and walked off leaving her to 'worry' it like a dog.

I was glad to be alone, for I had a problem to mull over and wanted time and peace to think. Several times this year I had been asked if I could help in moving or translocating families of badgers. On each occasion the animals were blocking drains or undermining fields and tracks with their digging. The occupiers of the land were applying to the Ministry of Agriculture Fisheries and Food (MAFF) for a licence to cage-trap and cull them, but could they be moved elsewhere?

I sympathised deeply with the people who contacted me, knowing full well how I would feel in their place. It had been suggested on this occasion that I find a vacant sett and area in my county and heaven knows, we could do with more of these animals. With all the help I get, we still only managed to keep the badger numbers fairly constant – and low. Places around our large towns have very few badgers and many setts have been completely annihilated through a surfeit of lamping and digging. But would it be right to put them there? Rather like placing homeless lambs amongst hungry lions, then expecting the shepherds (police and conservationists) to be extra vigilant. It was surely better that these badgers be cage-trapped and painlessly shot.

Even in areas that have few badgers and few lamping/digging problems, translocating or relocating has its problems. Any badgers in the area are liable to react badly to the strangers and fighting, even to the death may take place. Relocated badgers are more likely to become road and possibly rail casualities than others. They are, after all, on strange ground.

Ideally, an empty sett and an empty area is chosen with special regard to food and bedding availability. It shoud be asked why the sett and site are empty. An area round the release site is fenced for 2/3 weeks as a means of getting the occupants accustomed to their new home, with people to feed them whilst they are confined. When the fencing is removed, the animals should be monitored to find the outcome of the translocation. Badgers must never be moved from December to May inclusive, for during this time implantation occurs, sows are particularly sensitive to disturbance and cubs may still be below ground. Such a movement of badgers is only truly successful if they have settled at the sett to which they were relocated and produce cubs there. Far more research needs to be done in this field to decide the 'best way' and indeed, whether it really is in the badgers best interests to be relocated at all. It is an offence to move badgers now without the MAFF licence and consent of the Nature Conservancy Council (NCC), and their relocation should never be regarded as the 'easy option' of landowners or building developers. Having said all this however, badgers have in the past been successfully relocated without all these precautions. There have also been tragic failures.

For the rest of that week we had days and nights of rain, then miraculously, a night of slight frost and mist in the hollows. With a full moon and stars bright, it was the perfect lunar landscape. Water had appeared again in the lake, though not a lot, and some of the badgers were with me, one drinking, the others snuffling about in the grassiness of the lakeside. Pete's farm looked a model of tidiness for the big event next day – the official opening of the nature reserve of Ashcroft Woods. The grass was cut and the verges neat. I preferred it as it usually was, but the badgers looked upon it as an extra 'bedding' event and were toiling up the sloping land backwards with their bundles of cut grass.

An elegant notice board and a large marquee stood on the meadow by the wood on Pete's land. Everything looked mysterious under the great white moon. However sunny the day proved to be, it would never appear more lovely than this. The badgers and myself were very interested in the marquee and whilst I opened the entrance flap, they went underneath! Inside was a disappointment; just a few trestles and lots of empty space. This was the field of the badger sett after all, so one could say they were having a sneak preview!

Crisp wanted a game so I played with her, running up and down inside the near-empty tent. She tripped me up, then jumped on me before chewing a loose flap nearby. 'Leave it Crisp' I ordered, 'Don't mess things up. You're being officially opened this afternoon'.

The noticeboard had been beautifully lettered with the crests and symbols of the organisations involved. I read what our woods were notable for and was very impressed. Next moment something hit me at the back of my knees and I lurched forward hitting my head on the newly painted surface; the noticeboard was hard as well as impressive. Crisp looked at the results of her head-butting with interest. She was bored with my inattention and wanted a game. So rubbing my head I chased after her and left the place in peace.

A cloudy first light found me counting tawny pairs that were territorially boundary-calling; five pairs in all. The pair sounding as I stood on Long Field were those I know best, although it's amazing just how curious these birds become if you imitate their calls.

The moon struggled over a darkening cloud, its silver radiance illuminating the hazy nebula below. After such a clear night it seemed a strangely overcast dawning, yet the perfect moon spilled clear, white light down on the land beneath. The leaves of my wild service trees were a vivid red and although someone had trodden a path through the bracken around them, my precious trees were unharmed. One sunbeam spread far across the field and a deep, red light crept into the wood beside me. Three hares were playing amongst the stubble – this year's leverets – boxing, chasing and leaping over each other. One 'walked tall' while another ran in circles. Then one spied me, reconnoitred on hind legs and went slowly away across the field, followed equally slowly by the others, and they disappeared into the bank.

I arrived home that morning as the phone rang and a farmer's wife asked if I would check their land for badgers if she came and collected me in her car. It was a long, but very beautiful ride through countryside quite unknown to me and I thought not for the first time, how little of my county I really knew. The farm contained one large, old sett – probably one of the oldest I have ever seen and decidedly occupied. The owners had recently moved here and knew nothing of badgers, but they and their three children were interested and together we quartered the farmland. There were plenty of badger and other signs to show them and soon the children in particular, were finding more themselves. There were hare and rabbit prints on a wet part and we picked up badger hairs from a spoil heap. Clive, the youngest of the family, who had seemed rather left out of things, said he had seen 'a big white bird' near the stables and the rest of the family laughed as they went indoors.

I spoke to Clive and together we searched under the tumbledown beams. He was only six, but he was describing a barn owl as we stood in the dust and litter. Could it be? I found two pellets, then Clive found three, just as a rat scuttled across the floor. I pushed the door to against the bright sunshine that made it difficult to see into the darkness and hand in hand we walked silently round inside the old stables. Something above stirred slightly, fluffed its feathers and settled its wings. A head turned smoothly to watch us, its face inclined. A heart-shaped face, a ghostly figure and a cruelly curved beak. All owls have much in common, yet all are different and each is unique. Who was the most excited – the boy or me? He had seen his first owl. I had been privy to his wonder, his vision. Our treasured memories are of the small things in life and these memories we carry to the grave.

I had four offers to 'mole' for me from The Horse and Hounds and other pubs farther away. Two of the men already owned lurchers and now all owned or loaned terriers. The pubs are the haunt of terrier/lurchermen and the moling soon yielded interesting results. The Ashcroft Woods shotgun incident last month, when Oakley police came out in force, hadn't gone unnoticed. Our area was now considered 'hot' as one terrierman put it. I was right in thinking that the men of this incident and the two in July were connected and that they came from Laversley. They were also deeply involved with Don Francis. This didn't surprise me, since I saw them talking and laughing with him at last year's terrier show. So things here were likely to be peaceful, at least for a time, though one couldn't rule out those that worked independently.

The warmth of the last few days had been like summer and now at 5.30 a.m. while it was still dark, a tractor was rolling one of the sloping fields above Warby. In the blaze of headlights, the dust rose in great swirling clouds. Everywhere was very dry. Standing just within the wood at the View, I found Watcher at my side. Since August, I had been very conscious of my own frailty and knew that my 'nighting' here was making this worse but I was determined to keep track of my badgers, their whereabouts and their well-being for as long as possible. I have had to choose what is more important and my badgers have won – at the cost

I'm afraid, of the foxes. This vixen is rather different. She finds me and, doglike, seems to sense when I'm unwell.

Last month a vixen with very young cubs appeared on Barry's land. Both of us had noticed them and were surprised at their obvious immaturity. Nevertheless, these cubs were living above ground and lay up in the bracken of the wood edge. I thought there were only three youngsters, but couldn't be sure. Barry probably knew as much about them as I. He would drive quietly up the boundary track during the day and watch them playing in the sun on his meadow. Although he used to ride to the hunt, he isn't anti-fox and is genuinely interested in *Vulpes vulpes*. Many people would think us odd. He should be very opposed to me and what I do; I should be very opposed to him and what he does. But we aren't. It's rather like politics or religion. You should be able to see another's viewpoint, without necessarily agreeing with it, and still have a good relationship. Barry has always enjoyed foxhunting and doesn't hide or excuse it as 'vermin control' like so many. I don't pretend to like fox hunting and I dislike even more the putting of terriers to a fox underground to be dug out and killed. To me there is something sickening in the man who enjoys putting terriers to earth to worry and tear a fox or badger in its lair. His dogs may end up mutilated, but that makes him the more proud of them. His argument is that they are eager and willing to go to earth and of course, they are. After all, they have generations of breeding behind them for that very purpose. A bullock is bred for its meat. A cow is bred for its milk. We do not decry either for what they produce; the more and better quality of meat and milk, the more we are pleased. But – and this is the point – they are not naturally like that. They are what man has made them. Likewise, the dog that is bred to fight fox, badger, or dog, is not naturally like that. They too, are what we have made them and the responsibility lies with us. We cannot use the excuse that they like it.

We had been having problems with the radios which in consequence had just returned from the makers for overhaul. The last evening in September, I came out early to test them and noticed a van parked in the shadow of the motorway tunnel as I started up High Ridge. Below me it was very misty, but a wall of thick fog from the top of the slope stretched out across the farmland beyond. Soon after 10 p.m. we begun testing the radios, but static and general interference made reception very bad. Charlie could hear me, but I could only hear his voice, not make out what he was saying. To crown everything, I had the uneasy feeling I wasn't alone on the land! After half an hour, I signed off in disgust, getting the three-stop signal from my co-radio that he understood.

With my giveaway radio safely switched off, I attempted to trace the cause of my unease in the swirling blanket of icy cold and twice thought I saw a light flicker in the railway direction. No traffic lights or those of the village visible of course, and my night vision was of no use to me at all under these conditions. Eventually I walked down to the yard of Glebe Farm and nearly came face to face with two men in anoraks (hoods understandably over their heads), examining the barns and outhouses there. Luckily they hadn't seen me. They began walking at the back of the cottages, but the alsatian started barking urgently which made them hasten off through the pear orchard. There, I think they lost their way. 45 minutes later I was at the top of High Ridge expecting them (rightly as it happened), to find their way back. I followed them as they went down the scree slope and drove off in the van. At John's office I passed the information and vehicle number on to the police.

Hours later, the fog lifted and it began to get light. The tawnies were calling and answering over Long Field which had recently been ploughed. The cloudy sky was speckled with pink and blue, and no other birds were singing yet, only the owls duetting one to another in the quietness. I joined in and the male perched on my shoulder. His mate flew round us and landed on a gean branch above our heads amid a gentle fall of dead leaves. It was still too dark to see colour, but I knew the leaves strewn about our path were a fiery red. They reminded me of my wild service trees and how I had found the finest of these pulled up yesterday, the wire netting thrown aside and a few deep red leaves amongst the bracken left to tell the tale. I had hoped to find the 5 foot sapling thrown somewhere in the undergrowth and perhaps replant it. But it was nowhere to be found. The other little tree a few metres away still stood splendid and straight – and most conspicious in its red, lobed leaves, but its twin was gone. The seeds of these wild service I originally found in Ashcroft Woods, grew at home and later, planted here and in the hedgerows. These seeds took two years to germinate and the trees are now four years old. Six years to become a 5 foot sapling and less than six minutes to destroy. I would like to think that the person (who also left the rubbish in the trampled bracken) took it home and planted it in their garden, but I doubt it.

That afternoon, Tony Gould told me Oakley police had charged the two terriermen found at Weldon with attempting to take a badger. Then he dropped his bombshell. 'Steve Hammond says you know one of them, Roger Smith'. It was the man, who with another and a child, lamped my first badger two years ago. In those days I was totally unprepared for lamping and although I took their van number before they drove off, Roger and Co. had disposed of the badger before the police caught up with them. At that time the police of other areas knew them as diggers, but not lampers. More recently, they had been stopped and questioned for lamping too. Though suspected of taking badgers several times, they had never been charged due to lack of evidence. When next I contacted Steve, I learned the RSPCA had also found this lurcher/terrierman in the company of another involved in dogfighting. Roger Smith had certainly got on in his world!

Everywhere the sound of falling and the ground strewn with colour; October in Ashcroft Woods. I had changed the time of my 'nighting' and now would come to my area for a few hours, then go home making sure I returned again well before first light. Alternatively, I might come here after midnight as I used to before the lamping troubles and stay till the morning. Hopefully, this compromise would enable me still to come here and get some rest. There was no point in trying to rest out here. One badger or another would be sure to find me.

The 1st of the month was a misty night with no first light or dawn as such. I like this kind of morning. All the badgers were in perfect condition, especially the cubs. I wasn't up to playing with young Crisp, who was very cheeky, pulling at my sleeve and chewing my boot tops. So I sat well out of reach on the old cherry and left them to play amongst themselves. When they had gone to earth, I did the rounds, accompanied by my vixen. Her thick coat matched the dying beech and cherry leaves.

Barry's car caught up with me on the Cliffords track and we discussed the pigeons eating his newly-sprouting rape. They were causing a great deal of damage. He mentioned that Rob and family had seen a lamper's light on Friday evening at about 9.45 p.m. as they were driving home. The poacher saw their car headlights and the beam went out. I told him of the green van with the two men in the mist. I had informed the police, but should I mention it to his neighbour? Barry thought a moment and shook his head. All the farmers hereabouts had equipment stolen and were well aware of the problem. Best to say nothing and not alarm them; wives and families were nervous enough already. The police had the number now and we had. It would be interesting to note whether this van turned up during the day with people walking their dogs, for these men had known the farmland well and only the fog had made them lose their way.

A great noise of rooting and grunting came from under the damson trees verging Briarmead. It was Little'un and Sis, searching in the grass there for fallen fruit. Damsons, like so many wild fruits, start off sour, but by the time they are falling, become very sweet. The last few were deep black and high up near the tops of the trees, but all the lower ones had been picked. During the recent sunny weather, the farm tracks had been crowded with the parked cars of people coming damson-picking round the field banks. Barry had wryly laughed as he told me 'You couldn't get my car past them, let alone a tractor', and remarked that he had nearly put a Pick-Your-Own notice nearby! Once upon a time, people used to ask. Now they took it as a right.

That morning I 'helped' the two badgers by searching the tarmac and opposite bank, knowing that blackbirds often try to spear a damson, only to send it flying off the tree across the lane. Sure enough, I found nine and gave them each four, keeping one for myself. Their moist snouts crossed and re-crossed my hands, one held out to each sow, just to check they really had eaten them all. Then I quickly popped mine into my mouth and indignantly Little'un let out a grunt and stood on hind legs against me, staring upwards into my face! I started to laugh, swallowing stone and all, which made them both begin to play, running around me and bumping my legs in between bouts of jumping up.

At first light, the sound of hooves approached as I walked down the lane, and a horseman came into view. He was local and would ride here regularly for a time sometimes accompanied by a black dog, then come no more for months. I sometimes hear the quiet clip-clop though we rarely met. He had never asked me why I was here and until this morning, we had exchanged only the barest greetings. Today, however, he reined in and asked me how the badgers were, which startled me a lot. Was he someone Barry knew? Seeing how disturbed I was, he apoligised, saying 'We wonder sometimes how you are here. It's a lonely place to be in trouble', then trotted on.

By 7.30 a.m. a brilliant orange sun was breaking through the misty sky. It was high up and flooded the undergrowth of the wood with burning light. Watcher, sitting on the old cherry trunk with me, heard a sound on the slope below and went in search. She walked into a pool of light and stood transfigured, all unknowing. No photo, painting or film could have done her justice, my fiery, fey and flaming fox, engulfed yet not consumed. Then she turned, listened and high-pounced into the gloom. Moment and vixen were gone.

That night, thick swirling mist shrouded the farmland, but inside the wood it was clear. All the badgers were together with me in the Chantry, either grooming or rooting for mast, fungi and insects beneath the beeches and on Great Chantry headland just outside. I walked down to Old Joe's Sett, now taken over by rabbits.

At daybreak I watched a dominant rabbit 'chinning' on a moss-covered log to mark its territory, using the scent gland beneath its chin. Their territories are also marked out by the scent contained in deliberately deposited urine and droppings. I noticed many very young rabbits about. If the weather is mild and there is an abundance of food, they may breed nearly all the year round and certainly in the winter months. The doe however, has the ability to re-absorb her unborn kittens if conditions later become unfavourable or she is disturbed. Seeing how many rabbits inhabit this area, it's hard to credit that they aren't indigenous to Britain, but were introduced (probably by the Normans) and considered a rare delicacy. Even harder to credit, looking at all the burrows here, is that artificial burrows or 'pillow mounds' were built in the Middle Ages to encourage them to breed and a warrener was employed to look after their welfare and guard against poachers. That has a familiar ring! Obviously, rabbits have come a long way since then.

We were having radio problems so Charlie and I decided to do a check at about 10.15 p.m. one evening. Crisp found me almost as soon as I reached Top Field above Prossers Wood, so together we began testing. It was a lovely mild, clear night with heavy dew and crickets sounding. My little badger had come to accept me talking to the radio by now, though she liked it down at her level where she could home in to the microphone. Charlie's voice, like mine, is very quiet. The radio is housed in a black, soft, leather case and has even to me, a distinctive smell. If she wasn't allowed to have a sneaky chew on the end of the aerial (it had a rubber top in its early days), then she would thrust her snout hard at the mike and breathe in gustily. She had twice managed to scent mark the radio, with devastating results, for her musk remained for days in the leather.

That night however, I was busy and strode off checking each place for good reception. Calling up Charlie I was suddenly butted hard in the legs by a bored young sow looking for some action. Why wasn't I shaking the damson trees for her as I had been doing those past few nights? The smell of the last fruit high up in the branches was delicious. All those in the tall grass had been foraged for and found long since. Apologising to Charlie, I shook a tree and two protesting wood pigeons flew out with the damsons. A very amused voice queried whether I had anyone else with me. Was I sure it was just a badger? Hearing the laughter, Crisp ran round me in circles, then bumped me again, so I informed my radio that I was moving away from the Damson Bank for safety.

Walking home after midnight, through rain falling softly from a cloudy sky, I thought I saw a lamper's light near the bridge at Holmoak Lane as I came along the fields before the Embankment Path. Then I heard terriers barking and men's laughter. Now I was running, but as I reached the bridge, the beam disappeared and everything was silent. On the bridge, I noticed two things. An extraordinarily strong smell of musk, as if a badger had been terribly frightened or excited there shortly before and vehicle headlights coming along the lane. Standing aside to let the car pass, I saw its lights were visible here from a good distance with the leaves off the trees. The lampers had been disturbed from their occupation by the approaching headlights and had merely disappeared into the darkness over the farmland. This little bridge could become a trap. The Embankment badgers regularly crossed it in their foragings. Vehicles were rare on Holmoak at this time of night and no motorist would have an inkling of what was happening. I searched all round, but found nothing and walked on home feeling very disquieted.

I returned at 4 a.m. to my area. The rain was steady, the first for some time. By 6.45 a.m. it was still hardly light and my owls were calling from the holly tree in whose shelter I sat. I was wet, but only through walking round sett-checking; here I was protected. The damp leaves and undergrowth smelt wonderful with everywhere refreshed.

Watcher dug for something almost under me as I sat there. She pushed her nose into the hole she had made, breathed in deeply, then sneezed. The owls fell silent for a moment, one peering through the foliage at us. Then they continued duetting. The rain pattered outside. No other sounds, nor birds; it was still too dark. Time passed and I returned from sett-checking once more and leaned against my holly's smooth, grey trunk, to enjoy the quiet of the morning. Something moved on the inner branch of the old tree. It was a squirrel, descending head first as usual. It regarded me a moment, then began a fast churr, churr with tail undulating to the sound. I recorded it with the mini tape in my hand as the churring slowed to a steady rhymn, then played back the sound out of curiosity. The squirrel clearly didn't approve of the competition, giving his tail a last flick and turning stamped his foot once, twice and three times before shooting back up the hanging branch! Then there was peace once more and from the wood outside came the sounds of birds beginning their day.

I began to dismantle the log cabin after badger watch, as people were still using it and rubbish, beer cans and bottles were building up. Soon there would be just too much litter to cope with. The roof of long, slender saplings was awkward, but not impossible for me to remove and stack. The cabin's walls were a different matter. Stakes had been hammered into the ground to support the logs which were nailed or lashed stoutly together. Ross had offered his services and walked over to meet me that morning, armed with the necessary equipment from his toolbox. He not only dismantled it, but also stacked the heavy logs ready to be removed. Dr Howard was arranging this with the county trust who managed Ashcroft Woods, for as long as the logs remained, there was a good chance the cabin would be rebuilt. He had also agreed with Oakley's police inspector that a patrol should be radioed in via Charlie Foxtrot to deal with any future campers.

The last days of October were sunny, though there were mists and even dense fogs by night. I found Tossy's Sett at the wood edge had been disturbed and all the pruned pieces of trees, that Barry had so painstakingly pushed into the trench made by the terriermen years ago, had been removed. There were small dogs' paw prints everywhere in the soft earth. Terriermen again? The prunings had allowed for animal access, but would hinder human work and take time to clear. Time was vital to us if we were to catch these people. As it happened, no badger, or fox come to that, was living there at the moment, though Crisp had dug out an entrance recently, only to abandon it. All the badgers here were busy foraging and digging out with heaps of soft, sandy earth outside many of their entrances. They also will reopen disused setts at this time of year, though not necessarily den in them. This, fortunately, can prove confusing for the terriermen.

Everywhere there was plenty of food to be found, from insects and larvae turned up by the plough, to autumn fruits and berries. By day, the hedgerows and verges were alive with the movements and twitterings of birds feeding on the seedheads and I lost count of the greenfinches and linnets flocking the little lane. It seemed to be a plentiful fungi season too. The green barley shoots were growing quickly. The cycle repeats itself so soon that the farming year seemed scarcely finished before the next began. The damson leaves were a pale gold and lined Briarmead with delicate colour. Those left on the trees gave them an airy grace. The damson is a pretty tree in all its seasons.

For nearly twelve months I had been interested in the ferrets here that must have escaped at some time from their owners. There appeared to be two colours. The white albino and what I term the 'pole-cat' variety, brown or dark brown with white markings on the face and throat. I was certain there was now a wild breed of ferret here, and one would imagine the albinos to be less successful than their less conspicuous brothers. I have no proof of this however, and seeing a white one successfully pursue and kill a squirrel on the ground one morning just before dawn, I could be wrong. Ferrets can climb trees with ease too.

How many ferrets are now breeding in the wild and what kind of threat may this pose before long to our wildlife?

The last day of October dawned clear, with light streaming across the land. To the east, a soft blush of pink and gold, while behind me in the west, the moon stood high above the wood. The tawny hen had elected to perch on my shoulder unsolicited, and sat preening her wings, first one, then the other. Her mate was boundary-calling over Long Field on the far bank. There were no vehicles parked anywhere and the damp lane was clear of tyre marks. All was quiet, but for the owl kewicking.

Walking down the hillside towards Warby a little later I heard, then saw, skeins of Canada geese flying overhead up valley. On impulse I called and stood out in the field as they wheeled round, descending closeby. Now I knew that winter would soon be upon us. Imitating calls, known as luring, is done by wildfowlers to bring geese within range of their guns. Lampers do this also, to entice foxes into the range of their beams to shoot. Moving from area to area, one lamper recorded that twice the previous winter, he called and shot ten foxes in a night.

Chapter 10

Early one November morning, two men appeared coming up the Old Cherry slope, with three terriers apiece coupled together with chains and a lurcher running loose. I disappeared, well out of the way. Just as well, for the men carefully walked round the area before meeting at the secluded entrances near the chestnut standard. These holes are much used by the badgers and were the most recently dug out by them. I had no way of seeing the men or their dogs clearly if I wished to remain undiscovered and decided to give them time to settle down before contacting Charlie by radio. Moments later the horseman cantered into the wood from the Briarmead direction, turned right and rode up the slope. Here he stood in the stirrups, looked all round and remained so for a time. Then, apparently satisfied, he continued up the slope and out of sight. The terriermen obviously didn't like the situation, for they left their hiding place behind the chestnut and went back the way they had come. Two of their terriers were black Patterdales and the rest were brown, probably lakeland/fell. Then they were gone. I ran along the winding sett path parallel with the Wildflower one, in time to see a white van drive down Briarmead; I noted part of its number. Back at the sett, two entrances had been filled in and there were bootprints and dog pawprints clear in the soft, damp earth. It appeared the men hadn't reached the stage of sending a terrier down. The horseman must have seen the van and come to investigate; the terriermen were probably afraid he had taken their van number.

198

I walked round to keep warm, for it was far colder of late. By 7 a.m. a clear sky had dawned, after days and nights of heavy rain and winds which had brought down trees and many branches, also a great amount of leaves, so that light had crept into the dark places once again. Everything was quiet with the Wildflower Path at its glorious best; hazel trees with leaves still green and others yellow, geans and bracken all aflame, and the track below them strewn with every colour and shade, hiding the mud beneath. Now the rising sun struck the cherry trees' trunks. Spindles' coral and orange berries showed through trails of old man's beard.

The following night was a clear one with frost after hours of torrential rain. Foxes everywhere were very vocal. A fox called from the Rendcombe direction and another answered from the grounds of the old house near Holmoak. I saw one of the Embankment badgers rooting in the hedgebank of that lane; I wished I could watch over these animals too. Lampers in my area appeared non-existent at present, but what was happening here?

Tree-shapes barred the moonlight ground and water glinted from every upturned leaf and hollow. The old cherry's trunk was used as an eating place by squirrels and the fissures there were filled with brown, broken cases of the chestnuts. They, like the birds, drank from the pool in the bark here. Everywhere the water lay and many roads were flooded; if there was much more rain, the Bourne would burst its banks.

At the Dump Sett, now empty, I found large boot prints round the side of Sand Pit Field and leading in and on to the spoil heaps. The boot owners had crushed all but one specimen of that strange fungus, the earth star, growing under the trees at the entrance to the dump. There were no entrances fill in, but probably they had merely checked here and found the sett empty.

Leaving for home at 8 a.m. I met Barry on Briarmead and told him about the terriermen, only to find that he had had an encounter with the same men the previous Sunday morning. Their white van, whose number agreed with part of the number I had recorded, was parked at the top of the lane. Two men with seven dogs, one a lurcher and the rest terriers, were working along Cliffords Bank and the terriers' description seemed the same as those of yesterday. The field track was dangerously muddy and Barry couldn't get his car very near – he had no intention of getting out of it and accosting them. He shouted to them to get off his land or else ... and with some reluctance, they did. Barry too had noticed that Tossy's Sett had been disturbed and suspected that these men were responsible. We agreed it seemed all quiet here, lamping wise. Were they creeping back as diggers? The farmer asked how our badgers were and I was able to say they were fine. Their coats had thickened out and they were noticeably weightier in preparation for the oncoming winter. At a glance, this year's cubs looked almost the size of their mothers.

At home I contacted PC Mark Craig and gave him details of the van. He said that a colleague about 40 miles away was having badger-digging problems and he would check the van out with him. We talked about the badgers here and I said how marvellously quiet it was lampingwise compared with last season. Mark thought that the publicity then, after the poachers were caught, plus the fact that they were still patrolling and making it apparent that they were, probably accounted for this. I felt sure he was right and mentioned the Holmoak area; not that I could say much, as I hadn't actually seen anything. Now that I was going backwards and forwards at irregular times during the night, I would keep a careful eye on this area just outside my home town. I had frightened off the evening lampers from the housing estate there, who set their dogs on the tiny foal and on sheep, for fun, many months ago. Had I really frightened them off, or were they coming out later to avoid me? Only time would tell.

The next Friday I arrived on High Ridge by 7.45 p.m. that evening, as Rob had warned lampers off the Cliffords Bank area before 9 p.m. the previous night. All was quiet and I tested the radio with Charlie. There were no badgers to be seen, so they were probably rooting in Ashcroft Woods. It rained for a while but by midnight it was becoming cold and frosty. The atmosphere was very still, with a half moon showing through drifting clouds. I watched Jude snuffling noisily about the decaying stumps on Cliffords Bank. He stopped and looked at me a few moments trying to get my scent as he peered between the elm brush. I spoke softly and he came up, blowing hard as they always do after rooting, to clear their snouts. He musked my boot, then stood up against me on his hindlegs. I didn't recall him doing that before. I stroked his head and neck but soon had to move backwards to dislodge him, for he was very heavy. I left him digging out at his sett in Cliffords Bank. Later I found that the Crater and Cherry Setts were also dug out by their badger occupants that night.

On Friday 28th November there was thick fog over the land and in the wood came the constant drip, drip of moisture from above. A very wet Watcher found me listening and calling the tawnies in the Chantry. I called and one answered, then the other. If I was an owl, they would doubtless attack me, but of course, they knew full well I was not. They still had one of their fledged brood with them. He called a little, but was very wary of his parents. He was late finding a territory of his own.

Before it was light, I tested the radio with Charlie. My vixen, like young Crisp, was not frightened; she was curious.

The last night of November was cold and frosty. I enjoyed watching Jude play with the cubs. He was a very amiable, good natured young boar who merely ambled off if the five hoodlums over-reached themselves. Susie's offspring (Topsy, Turvey and Bluebell), with Missy's (Gemma and Mike) were full of mischief, headbutting Jude and running off, then returning to tweak his tail, almost asking him to chase them.

I was happier about Crisp now. There was a time when I couldn't imagine her as a mother herself or if she was to become so, she would have made a highly nervous and unstable one. Watching her now, relaxed and playing with the others on the Wildflower Path before first light, it was difficult to recall that this same young sow stood and squealed at the sight of a lurcher back in June. Time and events have been kind since then and only time will tell if, in adulthood, she can cope with 'stress' situations and fight for herself and her own.

As I leaned against a tree here, watching and thinking, Jude came and jumped up at me and the claws of his forepaw caught my cheek and eye. Inattentive as always, I had forgotten that stretched up on hindlegs this big boar can reach my face. When my eye finally ceased watering, I saw a very subdued Jude standing at the field-edge. My cry had alarmed him and he regarded me uneasily. I knelt down and spoke gently. A cautious approach, then my ear was snuffled, next the blood on my cheek was cleaned away. We were friends again and if I didn't stand up, I would be killed with kindness as the others surged around!

At 7 a.m., with the badgers gone, the mist over Long Field was lifting and the first birds tentatively began to sing. A sparkling crescent moon hung high over the Bank Sett and another day had begun.

December started badly with two of Susie's cubs, Turvy and Bluebell, missing. I searched Briarmead and Maddon Lane as well as the main road for casualties but there was no sign of either. When I had come on to the land at 11.10 p.m. the previous evening, there were fresh marks of a wide-tyred vehicle in the dew of the Cliffords Bank track. Two hours later, more dew had obliterated them. No courting couple would come that far on to the fields. It all pointed to a lampers' vehicle. Susie's three cubs tended to stick together and would come each evening to find Jude their big friend at his sett in Cliffords Bank. This time, their playfulness had cost them dear. Susie's remaining cub, whom the children had named Topsy, looked at me, then came up, when I knelt down speaking softly to her. I would never know for certain what happened that night, but she did.

That Sunday night there was deep frost in the exposed places; cold and damp elsewhere. The stars glittered in a clear-cut sky. Foxes are very vocal at this time of year and in these conditions. Watcher had three young males interested in her. As she came up to me, one was trailing her, which she set upon and routed. I had lost track of this years' foxcubs for the first time in some years; I just hadn't the stamina any more.

Barry had placed straw bales for shooting hides on his rape field, so Crisp and I investigated one. Then I happened to see her pulling wisps from one bale (bedding again!) and decided to disown her.

Pete's lake had at last filled with water and was living up to its name. Walking uphill from it to the wood edge at 6.30 a.m. that morning, while it was quite dark, I saw one of the men busy ploughing with headlights blazing. This week, too, saw the chestnut coppicing advancing well in Ashcroft Woods. Some trunks were already cut to length and stacked ready for transporting. Shooting started in the Chantry at 7.30 a.m. Several people were using shotguns, but I stayed well clear.

That evening, I discussed the badger cubs' disappearance – presumed lamped – with PC Craig and mentioned I was too predictable and, in any case, couldn't be out 'guarding' from dusk to dawn, through the long nights at this time of year. He mentioned some local lurchermen, whom we all knew, that he had 'warned off'. They had been lamping amongst sheep due to lamb and the shepherd had enlisted his help. Mark discovered an occupied badger sett not far from his house in the village and, by the signs, it would seem very active. Perhaps in the New Year there could be cubs?

One night I watched Susie and her remaining cub Topsy searching for and eating yew berries. There were many lying amongst the dead needles that surround this old grove, but several trees have trunks so sloping, or branches so near the ground, that it was almost easier to 'Pick-your-Own'. Badgers aren't the best adapted to climbing, but the yew bark's flaky surface gave a good claw-hold and even the branches of these ancient trees were wide and firm. Wrinkling back their moist snouts, the badgers delicately picked off each scarlet berry. The berry's bright aril is harmless and though the seed is poisonous, it passes through birds and badgers undigested, so they are not affected. One branch spread close to the ground, and Susie pulled it even closer by reaching up and clambering on to it. All was quiet in the frosty night, but for a tawny distantly calling and the rustle of greenery as a berry was carefully selected and snuffled over. Susie finally jumped down and as the branch swung back with a sudden whoosh, a rush of small birds, startled from their roost, rose upwards into the clear moonlight.

I left them to walk Barry's land and was greeted by Crisp. A skylark flew startled from the frozen furrow between the rape but, fortunately for the torpid bird, my badger was preoccupied with me. Crisp was determined on straw for her sett and since Jude and she were denning together on Cliffords Bank, both badgers 'carried back' for nearly two hours. I couldn't help thinking that the two Oakley police constables who had the shooting rights on this land had better hurry up and use that hide before it disappeared for good.

There followed nights of deep frost and clear skies as the moon neared the full. Temperatures dropped to $-2°$ centrigrade, freezing puddles lying on the land.

Crisp had been with me all night. Now it was 6.55 a.m. and still dark, though the sky was lightening to the east and Venus rode high in the sky to my right. On my left, the moon seemed to sit on top of the damson trees bordering the lane. Over the farmland at Rob's cottage, the lights of the Royal Mail van appeared, delivering the morning's post. Young Crisp was still at my side. She should have gone to earth by now. I dusted the dried mud pawmarks off my jeans and, glancing down, saw that a vehicle had gone up the lane and down again. Why hadn't I noticed that before? I was really growing careless. I followed the tyremarks that led into the woods and so to the side clearing before the turn-off to the ponds. By the depth of the marks here, it appeared to have stayed awhile. It could have been a patrol, but that was unlikely now I had the radio. The marks looked very recent and I was uneasy. I ran round to the Cherry Sett; everything was fine there and Crisp, the silly creature, was still above ground all 'eager-beaver' and jumping up, putting fresh dirty pawmarks all over my jeans! I spoke sternly to my little companion. It was 7.30 a.m. and getting quite light – high time badgers were underground.

The Saturday before Christmas was a frosty night with the Main Pond quite frozen. The three remaining badger cubs, Topsy, Mick and Gemma, had been playing together. Gemma had been bouncing up and down on the spot as if she was on springs! Another favourite of hers was chasing her tail. Usually she ended up giddy and would fall into another cub, setting off a mad twirling, whirling game with no holds barred and open to anyone, adult or cub. Chasing other people's tails was a popular game with all the cubs. The waning moon glittered on the frosted leaves lying on the lane and on the old-man's-beard hanging from the hedgerows.

I left home at 7 p.m. on the evening of Saturday 20th as I was anxious about lampers. It was the last weekend before Christmas after all, but everything was peaceful and quiet. Jude stood on hindlegs leaning against me, as I watched a deep orange, broken moon appear above the horizon of Crosshampton. Both sun and moon always seem to look larger when they first rise. The colour of both tends to alter, too, in their journey across the sky.

It was a bitterly cold night. Everywhere the water was deeply frozen and a bleak north wind sent snow flurries across the exposed farmland. I went to follow the badgers into the warmth of the wood, then remembered the shooter's hide. It was a wonderful place – snug, well out of the wind with the spare bale placed inside making a marvellous seat off the damp earth. Unfortunately, however, my absence had not gone unnoticed. You may dodge out of sight of a badger but, of course, they don't rely on their sight. First Topsy, then Gemma, came and shared my lap. A few minutes more and Mick with Crisp also tried to do likewise. Jude looked in, clearly decided that four was a crowd in that small space and disappeared. At first I imagined he had wandered off to forage. He had, but not for food. A snuffling, pulling, grunting from the other side of the straw wall and someone was collecting bedding! Using me as a ladder, Crisp scrambled onto the top of the bales and, looking down at the boar, 'rattled' to attract his attention. Jude, still busy pulling and tearing at the straw with teeth and claws, looked up startled, then tried to climb up his side! By now, I was feeling rather guilty. This was a shooter's hide, not a badger-hider's hide! So I stood up, shooing them off my lap and went into the wood after all.

The snow didn't lie, though occasional flurries were still descending by the 22nd. I fell over on the cherry slope, for the frozen grass was very slippery underfoot. Only the cubs and Crisp were out foraging that night and they kept to the wood where many places were not frozen. First light came reluctantly with the tawnies calling through the restless trees. The silvery sheen of birch bark is most striking in the gloom of winter, with the bramble leaves of the undergrowth, a vivid green set against the sombre dead leaves on the ground. A few gaudy spindle berries remained on the trees of the Bank Sett which was badger-occupied once more. There were now four setts in all being used.

Cliffords Bank	Jude and Crisp
Old Cherry	Susie, Topsy and Little'un
Crater	Mick, Gemma and Missy
Bank	Sis

That afternoon, Steve Hammond dropped by with his family, doing the Christmas rounds. It was good to see him again; I was glad he still kept in touch.

The night of Christmas Eve was bitterly cold and frosty, with clear skies and a crescent moon. Again, many parts of the wood were merely very wet. On the slope above the Old Cherry Sett, the badgers were busy digging up and eating bluebell corms, larvae and chestnuts. One of the cubs (I think it was Mick) found a hedgehog when he was digging with his long claws under a rotting birch trunk that had fallen many years ago. The urchin had gone there to hibernate in a leaf nest it had made for its deep sleep. The young badger was undecided what to do with his prickly find, but I saw Crisp and Little'un stiffen, then appear to continue with their foraging amongst the leaf litter. All the badgers gradually moved up the slope as they searched, the cubs eventually disappearing onto Sand Pit Field above. Then Crisp casually approached the hedgehog ball by the birch and batted it slowly over. At that moment her elder sister appeared, growling. The two badgers faced each other and Little'un 'fluffed-up', the raised fur of her neck and shoulders giving her a menacing look. Crisp stood hesitating a moment, then went off down the slope. Uncurling hedgehogs, I have discovered, is something learnt, not an inherent trait and many badgers never acquire the necessary knowledge. Little'un, too, batted the ball over, her long snout quivering. Then one forepaw dug deep into the 'join' where tail and head were tucked out of sight. Squatting back on her haunches, the badger's other paw did likewise and unrolled the hedgehog, spines downwards into the leaves. Sounds of snuffling then, as the snout curled back from her jaws, a tearing and a crunching as all but the skin with its prickles was left (and a tiny piece of flesh, I noticed when she had gone). One urchin that would not see another spring. From October onwards, gradually these hibernators' sleeping hours increase as their periods of activity lessen, till by December and the onslaught of thick frosts, the sleep deepens into true hibernation.

A few days earlier Rob made four magnificent scarecrows, each fixed to a pole, and set them irregularly on the rape of Top Field. The woodpigeons must have thought them as realistic as I did, for I had seen no woodies feeding there since. Yet on Barry's Briarmead fields, the birds took no notice now of the birdscarer's boom, nor the string and cloth 'scarers' blowing in the wind. Whether it was that the scarecrows were realistic or merely strange, I didn't know. Each was dressed differently from the others and had a head made from a plastic bag. It might be necessary to move them occasionally. It would be interesting to see if they did the trick for long.

The early morning of Boxing Day was dull and mild. Watcher kept me company as I did the rounds, checking particularly carefully for any parked vehicles well tucked away. All was peaceful, however, until shooting started at 8 a.m. Soon Ashcroft Woods were resounding to gunfire and I urged my vixen to ground. It was the traditional day for this, of course, but here it was contravening the bye-laws. Alfie came up on the tractor from Glebe farmyard to start the birdscarers. I noticed he did the rounds, going the length of Cliffords Bank as far as the sett and back. He stopped the tractor and remained for some time unobtrusively behind the soakaway opposite the beehives. Later we waved to one another as he went back down the lane. We all knew it was the traditional day for digging-out badgers too!

By 9 a.m. it was a bright, cold morning with frost sparkling on the growing corn. Barry's car caught up with me on the top meadow above Cliffords Bank. He asked if my cubs ever turned up and I told him no. We agreed they must have been lamped and said how quiet it was at present in that respect. It would seem PC Craig's warning-off the lurchermen had probably got about. I confessed to the badgers (and myself) being responsible for the damaged shooter's hide, but Barry seemed more amused than anything else. I told him I had hoped to try and come here later today, in case of terriermen digging-out on this Bank, but felt I must do an early evening shift and couldn't do both. The farmer told me not to worry as he would have a look round later in the day and drive right up as now. People or vehicles could not be seen on the Bank unless you were really close. By now there was firing galore coming from Ashcroft Woods and motorbikes roaring up Briarmead. Even as we stood there, the shooting and 'bike sounds increased until we could hardly hear one another! Barry commented that he wouldn't care to go for a walk with the family in there today; you'd be lucky to get out in one piece!

That evening I was out by 7 p.m. in case of lampers, for although many would know that Oakley police were clamping down on poaching, I felt that some with new Christmas presents to try out, might be tempted to go a-lamping early evening. However, I need not have worried for all was peaceful with the badgers scampering round me and foraging in the many wet places. There was no moon as its thin crescent wouldn't rise till early next morning. It was wonderfully warm with a fine white cloud blanket giving a near-day visibility.

I returned for a welcome cup of tea, then left home again at 4 a.m. as I wanted to intercept the gypsy lamper from the council estate on the edge of my town. I had seen him working the fields round Holmoak on several occasions in the last few weeks, but up to now I had avoided him. It was he who had warned me of the terriermen in the summer and time had proved him right. This man disliked and feared them. I wanted to find out how well he really knew their movements.

Sure enough, there was his beam on what had been the little bullocks' field by Holmoak Lane and I came close whilst he was busy. Using his normal greeting I said, 'Cushty bok. Noticed you had changed your shift to early morning. Find it quieter?'

'Don't know what you mean. Why d'yer creep about like that for, giving honest folks a fright? You're like a cat.'

'Haven't seen many terriermen about the woods since the summer,' I remarked, bending to stroke Sam and Queenie.

'Huh. Not surprising is it? Don't say I didn't warn you.'

'What do you mean?'

'Them terriermen – didn't I say they were sick of you around? Lucky you didn't get done. But you got friends in the right places, ain't you?'

'Oh, the police.'

'Yuh. They were leaping into the woods like fleas off a dog's carcase. Those giorgios won't be back in a hurry.'

'You know those terriermen well then?'

'What d'yer mean? I keep away from their sort. Can't stand them.'

'Not seen many lampers about either.'

'There you go again; lumping us lampers with the terriermen. You know missus, it's people like you wot gives us lampers a bad name!'

The male tawny came to sit on my shoulder before first light. I was talking softly while he preened, when there was a sudden movement and Watcher sprung up at him, growing. The owl's talons dug into my shoulder as he raised his wings, cloaking, and hissed. Surprisingly, he had no intention of flying off; it was the fox who turned back into the wood. I stroked the tawny's ruffled feathers with one finger and he walked down my arm to my thumb. The feet of these birds are fascinating, though perhaps I should call them hands. Each foot has four toes and though three face frontwards and one back, the outer toe can face either way. When they first perch on my hand or shoulder, they stand upright, but this cannot, I think, be a comfortable position for them as very soon they sit back on the thick pads of their feet and lower their bodies so that their dark, hooked claws disappear beneath the soft feathers. You only really see a tawny owl's length of leg when it is about to strike its prey.

It had been a fine, dry and mild night with very little wind. I had noticed earlier that Watcher had a companion. When she came up to me after midnight, he kept well away, watching while she fussed about me. I thought they would mate before long. It was the last Sunday morning of the year and at 7.50 a.m., as I stood in the shadow of the boundary hornbeam at the edge of Sand Pit Field, I saw a patrol car pass up Briarmead, stay awhile, then slowly go down again. I hadn't seen the police here for a long time, but now I had the radio, I tended to keep out of sight and well clear of the lane, so I wasn't likely to. Barry had said on Boxing Day that a patrol car quite often came up and into the wood during the day.

Rain clouds raced across the sky. Ashcroft Woods had a mighty voice, for the wind was a torrent of sound, tossing and bowing the upper branches. The trees standing together moved as one, as the gale, rising to a roar, hurled the frailer trunks back and forth. This rushing tumult in their heights was akin to the waves of the sea. It was an awe-inspiring sight, these stalwart monarchs shuddering and shaking in the wind's rage.

The amber lights of the road shone out brightly as the traffic passed along that and the motorway, quite unheard above the storm. I reached Little Chantry Field and stopped a moment to tuck the end of my jeans into my boots. A deafening crack above and ahead of me and the air was full of a rushing. As I straightened up, my mouth, nose and eyes were filled with dust and a branch torn from its parent hornbeam hit the path ahead. I couldn't get over or under it; it was massive as a trunk. The smaller branches and twigs radiating along its length were like a giant hand splayed across the way. After some searching, I found a route into the underbrush and so round the obstacle. Reaching Great Chantry Field and the leaward side, I was almost deafened by the quietness. Far below, the village lights twinkled; the layered clouds were all shades of grey and black. It was 4.30 a.m. as I relaxed under a beech, its branches swinging gracefully outwards over the field and framing my picture landscape. When I come into this wood at night, I have the feeling of returning home. Whether in storm, calm, stars, rain or moonlight, I belong here. The living trees seem to reach out and beckon.

Gemma and Topsy, the two young sows, passed in front of me quite unaware and whickered together over the wet field. The freshness of the moist earth was indescribable for the rain had heightened each fragrance. There was a noise behind me of something pushing through the cover and Watcher stepped out to my left. She had found me, whereas the badgers swayed unsuspecting by. The rain by now was penetrating and as she shook herself vigorously; I was showered. Watcher stayed awhile then, seeing I had no intention of moving, went along the wood edge, looked back once at me still there, and continued down-field.

208

Time passed as a mist crept up the valley. The twinkling lights vanished; wind and rain eased. It was time I shook myself and went off too. At 7.30 a.m. it would soon be light and the last day of the dying year.

Late on New Year's Eve and throughout the 1st January, it rained steadily. The earth, already soaked from earlier downpours, could absorb no more. Parts of Briarmead were well flooded, but the strangest thing happened on Sand Pit Field. There, a month earlier, water had washed away the topsoil and eroded a deep chasm through the barley. Now there was a dull roar above the sound of lashing rain, as the flood rushed along this earth-split to meet the field side of Briarmead, then burst through the bank to join that already surging down the lane. Earth, leaves, ashkeys, sticks and pieces of flint spun madly in the spate and were swept violently away.

I had the curious feeling all was not well around Oakley and the Holmoak Lane area. I was concerned and felt rather guilty about it, but physically could not patrol two large areas at once. I hadn't really seen anything much either. Once I encountered a man on the bridge apparently alone. Intuitively, I knew he hadn't been alone, but he was at the time. Once a Fell terrier and a bull terrier with long, lurcher-like legs had met me crossing Ingrims Fields. I was conscious, too, that someone was luring foxes. His vixen calls at night would attract not only dogfoxes within his beam, but other vixens too. Somehow, I must try to spend more time around Holmoak Lane. It was all quiet in my area thanks to Mark Craig and the patrols, but dare I leave my own? Then I thought of the last badgers left of Lesley's family and knew I couldn't risk it. Besides, the radio didn't operate this side of the motorway and Charlie was too far away. So I pushed the worry to the back of my mind, but the sense of guilt remained.

Someone had ridden a motorbike up and down the slope of the Old Cherry Sett and I hoped this wasn't going to be a regular occupation, or the badgers there would move. The stress this could cause might well inhibit implantation and therefore the birth of cubs. I found the Chantry's male green woodpecker, its body all shot away after the Boxing Day shooting, and in anger had walked round Ashcroft Woods collecting spent cartridge cases, determined that this time something had to be done to curb the shooting as well as the 'bike riding there. The bye-laws were a mockery. The new ones were not yet in force and even when they were, would they really make any difference? I remembered how, years ago, the man who helped me so much with my tawny work had exclaimed in horror at the continual killing of these 'protected' birds, and remembered, too, the badger sow so carelessly shot. I was unsure just what I was going to do, but collecting these shiny new cases was proof of what went on and at least it was a start. I also discovered what appeared to be rifle cases, apparently a little different from the usual .22 found here. PC Craig helped in identifying them and, in spite of the slight variation, they were .22. He happened to say in passing that fox pelts were fetching £30 in Brockton market. That made me think!

My badgers were sluggish and above ground for shorter periods, partly because it was winter and partly because they could get adequate food requirements in the soft, wet earth within a couple of hours. Crisp (often with Jude in tow) regularly came above ground if I called at Cliffords Bank. I really did this to check they were there, as this Bank is so vulnerable. If I didn't, I might not see them for nights at a time, as now Crisp was an adult she was becoming more fixed in her ways. The cubs, however, or rather yearlings now, loved playing, exploring and generally upsetting things, including me. So, unless the weather was really dreadful, they were guaranteed to be about sometime during the night. The trouble was, if I called Topsy, Gemma and Mick above ground, I couldn't get rid of them again till first light! One good thing was that I would certainly know quick enough if these youngsters came to harm, just as I did when Turvy and Bluebell were taken.

The 4th January was a freezing night with sleet showers in the north-east wind. I was so cold and wet by 2 a.m. (after being out since 8 p.m. the previous evening), that I returned home. I went out again at 5.40 a.m. in good time for first light. Walking along the Gully part of Briarmead just off Maddon Lane, I was greeted by Mick who completely flattened me! I must be getting weak. He wasn't that strong. As the Gully at present was liquid mud, I ended up more wet than when I returned home!

As late as 7.40 a.m. the tawnies were fluting beautifully in their roosting tree by the Crater Sett, as each bird allowing the other a few moments solo before coming in 'penillion'. Their harmonising gave me a feeling of tremendous joy. Even the little birds had the grace not to alarm, though this was probably due to the icy morning and very poor light.

Just afterwards I came out of the wood and, glancing over the width of Sand Pit Field, saw a blue car with a black top come up the lane and park in the layby there – an odd place to stop, especially in this weather. The people in the car were watching me, so I walked back into the wood just as the car turned and went away. It could have been an unmarked police car, but this was very unlikely. I left the area by 9 a.m., when the heavy sleet showers were turning to rain.

At the Embankment Path towards Holmoak Lane I met Philip, who asked me if I had passed any shooters across Roger Johnson's farmland with shotguns. He had found a white van parked at the far side of the railway bridge with a guncase inside. I told him of the Ashcroft shooting on Boxing Day and how I had passed some of the cases onto the chairman of Warby parish council in the hope that something might be done. I asked if a police patrol in an unmarked vehicle had been up Briarmead that morning, Philip shook his head. It would seem likely, therefore, that as I was rarely in view on the lane now, the owner of the car was expecting or hoping I was no longer around in the mornings. I wished I hadn't let myself be seen.

There followed some nights of deep frost and temperatures of $-7°C$. One such night, Gemma came with me over Pete's land when I went to look at the lake, now full and deeply frozen. She ventured out to the middle of the ice, then lost her footing, panicked and came scampering back to my side. Perhaps it was as well. She was the smallest of the yearlings, but very compact. These mornings it wasn't first light till 7.30 a.m. and no birds called, except the owls. The cold bit deep. The frost and wind had, as usual, caused cracks to form at the corners of my eyes, mouth and nose. The eyes in particular I find are very vulnerable and as they water in the extreme cold, so these cracks deepen and widen. A friend who has lived some years in Canada, tells me that there one wears a parka hood as it comes past the face, shading and protecting it. I never wear a hood, of course, unless it snows or rains heavily, as it badly restricts hearing as well as sight and I depend on both.

Saturday night of the 11th brought snow which by Sunday first light was a blizzard as the north-west wind swept across the land. The weathermen told us these Arctic conditions were coming from Russia. Certainly it was not difficult to believe as the temperature steadily dropped. Everywhere was incredibly lovely in the wood. The wind had stopped a build-up of snow on twigs and branches, but had frozen that which lay, so each surface had a delicate tracery of white. Perhaps the finest of all was the old fallen cherry tree that glinted and reflected like crystal as I gazed up from the path below.

At 8.15 a.m. I tested the radio with Charlie and found that reception in the sheltering wood was marvellous, with no static. Outside on the lane and fields there was considerable interference. Watcher, my dainty lady, appeared at some point and accompanied me till I reached the Main Pond, my last contact point, where she mysteriously disappeared. The snow continued till Tuesday 13th. The day before had been the coldest on record with a strengthening north-east wind. I had left home at 11 p.m. and, wary of drifts, made slow but careful progress, knowing that once wet, I would have to stay that way till I reached home again. There was no sound, no traffic, train or human voice until, crossing Roger Johnson's land, I heard a fox scream twice from the direction of Rendcombe. There was no sound or sign of my own foxes or badgers. The temperature was steady at −14°C.

Sometime before first light of that Tuesday the snow had ceased. All around me was a wonderful world of radiant white, for snow gives a visibility that is searingly clear. I knew approximately where Briarmead was although the little posts and lowest banks had gone. I decided not to chance the lane, however, when I noticed a short distance down it a steep bank that shouldn't have been there. I wondered how deep that drift was and chose the wood instead. There, each twig and branch was bent low with its burden, distorting the true shape of once-familiar paths. White upon white; all without substance but for the sky that seemed hard and near enough to touch. The frozen ponds had disappeared. One fluffy flake moved slowly down to join the mass below – another, another and it was snowing again. Something ahead barred the way; a fallen tree, its shape shrouded and mysterious. A movement from on high sent soft sounds dropping in a fantasy world. I couldn't stay too long, for the return journey would be more difficult. I reached home at 3.40 a.m. to find the front door frozen shut.

By the evening of that Tuesday, another two feet of snow had fallen and, apart from Scotland, we were probably the worst affected area. The schools and the motorway were closed, and there were no trains or buses. The snow continued throughout Wednesday, the strengthening wind causing extensive drifting in exposed places, with all our villages cut off from the outside world. I had no way of returning to my area, but was secure in the knowledge that if I couldn't get through deep snow and drifts, then neither could the lurchermen and terriermen.

For the next week we had the coldest day temperatures in living memory, with more snow. The north-east wind continued to cause extensive drifting. Icicles several feet long hung from our eaves and only twice in five days was I able to reach my area. The old cherry tree disappeared under a white cover and I could not reach the sett. That side of Ashcroft Woods had enormous drifts and twice I found myself up to my waist in snow. However, my badgers were safe. No one could harm them and they would survive as they had put on a great deal of weight the previous autumn.

Here and there in these woods I found fox prints, especially around the frozen ponds now well hidden beneath the snow. Ben's scarecrows looked like drowning snowmen and Barry's shooting hides were just humps. The effort of struggling through such snow was physically exhausting, besides being unwise. Once in a deep drift, I would probably remain there till it thawed. I would have to stop coming here again till conditions improved. It was a very beautiful and desolate landscape with no footprints except my own. Sadly, many trees had broken under their burden of frozen snow.

On Tuesday 20th the sun appeared briefly just after noon and, on impulse, I downed tools, donned boots, anorak and gloves and, with the Olympus over my shoulder, went in search of photos. Ashcroft Woods was not too difficult to walk in; it was getting there that was the mammoth task. I went by Colts Farm and Pete's land, aiming for the Cherry Sett from that direction. In Oakley there had been no pavement clearance; it was a problem what to do with the snow cleared from the roads and that problem had mostly been solved by piling it on the pavements! We weren't really geared for several feet of snow. Likewise, only the immediate area round Colts farmyard had been cleared. The farm tracks had gone. Only the tops of the hydrant marker tyres showed at intervals, indicating the route. With interest, I noted that rabbits, like the fox and badger, tend to keep to certain paths though these were only visible from their prints now. My progress across Colts Farm was slow – and musical! As I paced forward, my boot crunched into snow. As I lifted each foot, tiny particles of frozen snow dropped on top of that still untouched and untrodden, with a fine bell-like tinkling. I would raise a foot, watch and listen as the ice skidded and tinkled away. I knew the temperature with the sun shining was just above freezing, but so compacted was the deep snow that a far stronger sun would be needed to soften it.

Nearing the sheltering edge of the woods, I saw badger prints. The snow had been dug away to a depth of two feet, exposing unfrozen earth. Later I was to find fresh mole hills thrown above the snow at the foot of High Ridge and in one or two more sheltered places of Ashcroft Woods, though nowhere else. I followed the badger tracks into the wood and saw they were joined by those of another badger. Their path meandered round the holly trees and through the undergrowth and with great pleasure I read the signs. Here they had played together, with snow scuffed up and also knocked off a little beach tree, its brown leaves so revealed, bright in the surrounding whiteness. There, one had dug down to some fibrous roots. Then together they had passed through the 'log-cabin' clearing and so out to the path above the Old Cherry Sett slope. Everywhere were strewn the empty cases of the ashkeys. The squirrels had been hungry and the very last of these seeds were off the trees. The badgers' trail met with another coming in from Sand Pit Field and down they went to join the main route to the sett.

Arriving on the slope, I had a shock. Very recently, probably earlier that morning, someone had walked round the entrances accompanied by a small dog. They had taken particular interest in those most used by the badgers. I did rather wistfully, hope it was Charlie keeping an eye on things in my absence, but this was to prove a forlorn hope. I followed the human tracks out of the wood and discovered that their owner had struggled up Briarmead Lane, come along the winding sett trail, checked these entrances, then returned to Briarmead and continued up the lane. He and his dog had great difficulty, as I did, negotiating the snow drifts and like me they had to struggle along on top of the bank to make any progress at all.

I began to follow the footprints across the fields and saw a green tractor making slow but steady progress from Glebe farmyard. The distant driver got down from the cab when he reached the Cliffords Bank end of the two-oak track, stood looking at the ground and waited for me to come up to him. We stood discussing the weather, a popular topic at present with everyone, and then Alfie asked me what some prints in the snow were. I explained they were badger, but the sun had distorted them so that they appeared three times normal size. The very fresh human prints continued some distance away and it was evident that the owner and his dog had hoped to examine the sett on Cliffords Bank. Drifts had entirely covered this and the track above. Surprisingly, perhaps, the dog had floundered into a deep drift at this point and been hauled out by its owner. They had then returned the way they had come. Alfie had wondered about these prints, too, so I told him what I had seen. 'He must have wanted to look at the setts pretty badly, then. It's one hell of a job on foot,' he commented.

I said goodbye and continued on my homeward route. The badger tracks Alfie had asked about appeared to have come from the Bank, but fortunately, only such an animal could have travelled in that manner. A hole through the snow disappeared in this direction and I imagined that under the vast length of drift was a hedge path leading to the sett. Neither man nor dog seemed to have noticed and, indeed, like Alfie, they might not have recognised the spore if they had. After its fright in the drift, I hoped the dog and its owner had had enough. Certainly, they appeared to have given up and gone home.

By now the sun had gone, leaving in its place a wonderfully mottled sky that quickly became overcast. Holmoak Lane was the easiest part of my journey and I stroked the farmer's horses that laboured through the snow to greet me at their fence. They brought to mind the ponies abandoned by their gypsy owners that our RSPCA Inspector tried to reach with fodder through the deep snow. Oakley police had helped Tony with the loan of men and a vehicle. Even so, they had to struggle over the fields with the bales. The police had called out the army to help them with supplies to the isolated villages and everyone who owned a landrover had been working round the clock too.

That night saw me returning to my area, and to a great welcome from the badgers that were above ground – Missy, Jude, Susie, Topsy, Mick, Gemma and, of course, the terrible Crisp! What a reunion! Crisp managed to knock me over three times, which was a record even for her. I didn't see Little'un and Sis but had no reason to be worried for them. When it should thaw, allowing vehicular access, then I would have to be checking individual animals again.

I stayed until Wednesday 21st in a thick, clinging mist which was to remain for 24 hours. When the badgers were safely underground, I left some of our Christmas nuts (all rough-cracked except the hazelnuts) for the squirrels on the old cherry tree, then struggled home once more. It might be rough-going through deep snow but at least the effort kept me warm!

A slow but steady thaw began that afternoon. In the early hours of Saturday morning, I even saw some moths flying and found they were the mottled umber males on the lookout for their wingless females with which to mate. I found several dead birds, including a hen tawny owl, grey-partridge, three wrens and a dunnock, but didn't have time to examine them closely as either Watcher or her mate got there first. They had probably succumbed to the cold and then lay buried under the snow until it thawed. I saw other grey partridge that night, however, alive and well. Some villagers were feeding herons on the Bourne. A kingfisher, and many ducks of course, all seemed healthy enough; but there was no sign of the Canadas. I wondered where they had gone. Charlie at Crosshampton hadn't seen them either.

All my badgers were well, including Little'un and Sis, although very hungry. The earth was exposed now in many places, wet and very soft, so foraging was no problem. Crisp was digging up the fat, white cockchafer larvae that feed on plant roots and live up to four years underground before metamorphosing into adults. The adult cockchafers feed on leaves and fly in search of this food in the late evening or night, so there are always some of these grubs to be dug for at any time of year.

Water gurgled under the ice drifts of Briarmead. I struggled to the lower part of the lane where the houses end and found that the snow plough had cleared up to the last dwelling, leaving a high wall of snow some ten feet tall blocking the lane. I was pleased about this for it would be some while before the lane was open again to vehicles.

On the way home I checked the Yew Sett at Crawfords. It was unoccupied and, surprisingly, thick mist still lingered here. There was no sign of Uglybug and all seemed deserted. Remembering the bootprints and dogprints round the setts last Tuesday, I returned in the afternoon to check Cliffords Bank and the old cherry's slope. Although the thaw had made it possible for terriermen to dig out badgers now and it was Saturday afternoon, all was quiet.

By late January the snowplough had opened Briarmead Lane so that any vehicle could use it. It was a dull, overcast night with much of the snow melted but the drifts still lay heavy on the fields. They were particularly deep on the Top Field, Prossers Wood, so I found it easier to walk in the tracks of Rob's tractor at the field edge. I didn't know how he managed to bring the tractor round every day, but he did. Rob's scarecrows still stood and were keeping the woodpigeons off. They looked good; I liked them.

Earlier, I had brought more nuts from Christmas with me. The squirrels could cope with the hazelnuts unaided; the others I had rough-cracked, but didn't shell. I meant to leave them after badgerwatch that morning, but the badgers smelt them on me and made such a fuss that I left all the nuts on the old cherry's trunk and stood back to see how they would cope with them. They merely chewed them up – crunch, crunch, crunch – and that was that. Badgers undoubtedly have tough stomachs. The next day there were pieces of shell in their dung, not surprisingly! This made me realise something that I had never thought at out before. I have never fed the badgers here, except to share blackberries when picking them for myself or the rare time when an animal has been too ill to forage for itself. If I did carry food on me, I would probably get well and truly bitten and cause friction and fighting amongst them. They are not tame animals and sometimes if their boisterous games include me, I find it wiser to disappear.

On Thursday 29th there was a deep, deep frost with everywhere sparkling under a waning moon. In the coppiced clearing where the white mullein grows, I saw Watcher mate. She produced no cubs last year after her mate died and would permit no other male near her. This spring would be different.

It was on such a frosty January night as this many years ago and far from here, I saw a fox eating a cow's afterbirth. It was the only time I have seen this, but it has always remained vividly in my memory. The cow was facing her newborn calf, watched with interest by other cows. She nuzzled and licked it and the afterbirth began to come away in a long stream. A fox came under the fence, crept close and began to eat that part which was by now on the ground. The warmth of the placenta caused the surrounding air to vaporise and it must have been a warm, welcome meal to the hungry fox. After a while it became bold, reaching up and pulling at some, so that the cow turned round. However, she wasn't interested, for her preoccupation was with her newborn, and she turned back to the tiny calf, leaving Vulpes vulpes to finish its meal.

That night I couldn't find Mick and wondered where he was. Later in the morning, Charlie brought me a badger he had found run over as he went to work. I was saddened to find it was young Mick. He was just a year old. Of all the seven badger cubs born the previous year, Little'un's two were stillborn, Susie's Turvy and Bluebell were lamped and now Missy's Mick was killed on the road. Two out of seven wasn't a very good showing and I wondered how many would be born to survive a year in 1987. Charlie suggested that I have Mick stuffed to show to the schoolchildren to whom I gave talks on badgers and the countryside. At first I was revolted. Then, looking at his body, I tried to rationalise my feelings and remembered my very first talk on badgers at a primary school. The curator of a local museum had loaned me a stuffed badger. I sat on a stool with the children all around me cross-legged on the hall floor and talked for awhile, then brought the badger out and set it down amongst them. I will never forget the faces of those eight and nine year olds, the look of awe and wonder. 'Is he real? Can we stroke him? Isn't he lovely! Isn't he big!' Charlie was right. Mick was dead and nothing could bring him alive again; but dead, he could bring the badger to life in a way no pictures, talks or stories ever could.

The last day of January was a Saturday with the snow still slowly melting, but freezing again in the deep night frosts, making tracks and roads treacherous. The woodland ponds, the soakaways and Pete's lake had frozen to a great depth. The spring just inside the wood had overflowed and by day ran down Briarmead. This became a solid sheet of glass at night and in the early morning, which had certain advantages for me. In spite of the snow prints I had seen no lampers or potential badger-diggers but nevertheless would come out again in the afternoon today and Sunday. By day it had been sunny with a sharp wind and could tempt out the terriermen who had been cooped up indoors so long through the snow.

The rising sun gave a blue tint to the great snow drifts along my route as I walked. It sparkled diamond-like on the frozen crystals of the surface. I had no fear of falling through these great mounds; they were frozen solid after the night's deep frost and a −11°C temperature.

It was a beautifully sunny day when I returned that afternoon. I need not have worried for all was peaceful on these fields and in the woods. I walked about very tired − I seemed to be getting flu like the rest of my family − but enjoying the day and the relief of knowing all was well. I thought I should come here the next afternoon as it was a Sunday, though I wondered if I would be able to make it, if I still felt like this.

I was standing watching the blue sky reflected in the frozen surface of the Main Pond and was trying to summon up the energy for the journey home when someone said, 'Hello, Chris!' and there was Philip, off duty and walking his dog. I was very pleased to see him and stroked Emma as we talked. Philip doesn't normally walk her here now, but had been given a tip-off about a badger-digger living in Maddon Lane, who might be thinking of taking an interest in our badgers here. So whilst he was on night duty for the next few nights, he and Emma would take a daytime walk in Ashcroft Woods. He asked me why I was here that afternoon and I told him of the boot prints and dog prints in the snow. I also told him of my lamper from Maddon Lane and privately wondered if it was the same man. With boots, yellow sweater and his camera slung round his neck, Philip certainly didn't look like police! He told me not to worry about Sunday afternoon. 'We'll have a walkabout here, won't we Emma?'

Friday 5th February was my first night or early morning out that month, owing to flu. My daughter Karen brought me to Briarmead in her car the previous Wednesday afternoon and parked as near the Old Cherry Sett as she could for me to see that everything there was all right. We saw Alfie on the tractor just ahead of us on the lane and, whilst Karen waited, Barry Haines passed in his car. It was comforting to know they were about in the daytime, the sort of people who would query anything untoward.

The early hours of darkness that Friday were very mild with a gusty, south-westerly tossing the tree tops. All eight badgers were hale and hearty. One would think I had left them for a month instead of a few nights. I was so musked, I smelt strong even to myself! The slow thaw still continued with the moist air helping them to forage. It seemed strange without Mick and now Jude was the only male in the area again. Topsy and Gemma were playing together on Sand Pit Field. Their paws, like my boots, made a soft crunch, crunch on the snow still lying at the wood edge, but its surface remain unflawed. Gemma liked the sound and looked down at her feet. Pat, pat, as she plonked her front paws on the whiteness. Then up and down she bounced as if on springs. Topsy watched a moment, then bounced too. One little sow collided with the other and the bouncing was forgotten as they played mock fights in the snow. I wondered what made Mick go off that night on his own. Yearling males often do when their area becomes crowded or if there is an excess of boars but neither was the case here. He may have had an urge to find pastures new; instead, he found death awaiting him.

On Friday I left home at 8 p.m. It was a beautifully mild evening, still damp from the earlier rain, and visibility was wonderful. I saw two lampers with four big lurchers tormenting a young pony off Holmoak Lane. I knew from past encounters with one of the men that I would only get hurt myself if I interfered, so ran to High Ridge and tried to radio Charlie Foxtrot to tell the police. I couldn't hear him and wasn't sure whether he could hear me. In this sort of situation, he usually flashes the red light three times to indicate he has received the message, but the light was flashing anyway due, I think, to taxi use on a nearby frequency. Nevertheless, I gave the message hoping he had heard and understood.

All was peaceful in my area with Crisp, Topsy and Gemma frisky and affectionate towards me and one another. They had a game of Chase-and-hold-onto-your-friend's-tail on Barry's meadow and Let's-bundle-Chris on the path, which I wasn't prepared for until too late, so ended up very muddy.

By 11.20 p.m. the moon was rising above the trees and stealing into the wood. I left my companions worming along the wet field-edge and went for a walk by myself in Ashcroft Woods, an enchanted place with light touching each raindrop on the bare branches and reflecting in the surface of the ponds. Watcher and her mate were hunting in the most recently-coppiced area. She stood on hindlegs ready to pounce, her head turning to catch the rustling or squeakings of a mouse amongst the stools. A fox like this reminds me of a dancer pirouetting. Their sight is keen and their hearing phenomenal. Then down she struck and even I heard the shrill cry as the prey was caught. After a time first the dogfox, then Watcher herself became aware of me. He stood gazing as his dainty lady bounded up to touch noses and be stroked.

At 7 a.m. on Saturday, I checked with Charlie to discover he had come home late from work the previous evening and fallen asleep, his radio still re-charging in the cellar, so I just hoped that pony was all right. Charlie was very good as the radio must have been a nuisance both to himself and his wife at times, but they never seemed to mind the inconvenience.

The sunlight was turning the tree trunks a fiery red and glittering on the water that still gurgled on its way down the lane as I went home. A cock pheasant appeared above me on the bank, then jumped down close by to drink. It was a glorious creature, its brilliant feathers taking on a metallic sheen. In Maddon Lane I spoke to a patrol, telling him about the pony and also the general feeling I had about lamping in the Holmoak area. He said he would pass the information on to the night patrols and asked if I knew who the pony's owner was. I only knew his christian name, but I described the small-holding he owned some miles away. The constable promised to let him know.

By the 9th February, Sis was lactating! She emerged from the sett to wash herself while I was talking to Crisp, she nuzzled me briefly and returned to earth.

It was a beautiful dawn sky all streaked through with red and yellow. The weather was mild and damp with bluebell shoots, wild arum and primrose greenery showing a vivid green. At last the water had ceased its flow down Briarmead. The hazel catkins that had hung like lambs' tails throughout the winter were now opening to reveal their yellow pollen. Goat willow or great sallow were showing their silvery-white buds. Their familiar name of 'pussy' willow alludes to this soft whiteness and the term 'palm' comes from the traditional church decoration on Palm Sunday.

The following night I discovered that Little'un too was lactating. It seemed to be a race between the sisters. Last year this sow's two offspring were still-born but the badgers were under a lot of stress from lampers that winter. I fervently hoped everything would be all right this time.

I met Pete as I walked home. He told me that the lake was to be drained and the accumulation of silt removed down to the paving stones to drain somewhere far beneath. Contracts were being tendered, so it would be a few weeks yet. They would bring in an excavator; he thought the trees would go too. I felt sad but, of course, I knew this could happen one day, though I hadn't realised that the trees growing to one side would be affected. Later, I discussed the lake with Dr. Howard. It appeared that a date some weeks ahead had been given for the commencement of the work there and the cementation would continue for 25 weeks! It was difficult to imagine concrete involving half a year's work in so small and lovely a space and I wistfully hoped that a letter, and photographs extolling its beauties, might save some of the site. The chairman raised his eyebrows and shook his head as he found me the address to send to, and my heart sank, for he had an uncanny knack of being right. However, I wrote the letter asking whether, as the lake had been left for so many years undrained and had done no harm, might it not stay so? It was a haven for wildlife and I listed the birds and animals I had watched there. If not, could the trees possibly remain and might we discuss this please – either by phone or by meeting? Looking back, it was a pathetically naïve letter and, undoubtedly, the County Surveyor had thought so too. I was practical enough, however, to know that the lake's survival was unlikely. If the answer was no, then the aquatic plants would go to the chairman's wife who loved her riverside garden and the rest to another gardener friend who owned extensive grounds in Crosshampton. All I could do now was enjoy the lake while I still had it, and wait.

I didn't leave home till the early hours of Friday 13th, a still night with the full moon hidden by cloud. Crossing Ingrim's fields, I heard snarling and a man's voice in the direction of the farmer's horses by the bridge. Running towards the sounds, I could see the horses huddled against the fence nearest me. They were not the object of the growling and laughter, squealing and snorting. Those last sounds were a badger, I knew only too well. A man stood on the wide wall of the bridge with his back to me, on the lookout for any vehicles that might come along the lane. They had trapped one of the Embankment badgers in the confines of the little bridge and set their dogs upon it. Even as I approached, it was dazzled by a lamper. Had it been getting the better of the dogs? I could not contact Charlie and the police, and I had to stop this quickly. Turning up the radio's volume, I prayed for static and, for once, fortune was on the badger's side. This side of Oakley the reception is dreadful and I spoke loudly through the interference as if summoning the police, keeping well against the horses' fence as I did so. There were shouts and sounds of running feet, fast receeding, and just one dog still sparring with the badger. A distant whistle made the lurcher look round; he saw he was alone, jumped easily over his opponent and headed for home. I switched the radio off and knelt down on the bridge near a small sow that was probably a yearling. A strong smell of musk hung heavily on the air, thick and cloying. I remembered the same smell last October. Something was running from her nose. Was it blood? Colour doesn't show at night and any other smell was cloaked in musk. She stayed a moment then, raising her dripping snout, tried to get my scent before heading, at a steady trot, for home.

221

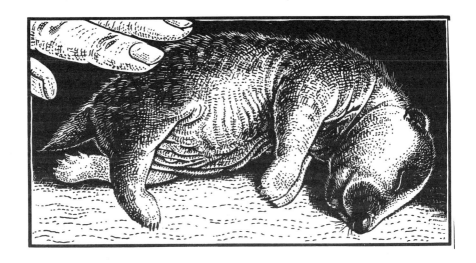

Chapter 11

Crisp, accompanying me on Glebe farmland, ran off with the radio when I put it down for a moment. I chased her, shouting, and she dropped it – right in the pool of water left by the thawed snow alongside Cliffords Bank. I took it out of its case and dried it, with an interested badger looking on.

First light came at 6.20 a.m. and half an hour later, three shotguns were being used. I walked up to the Chantry as during the night, I had seen jew's ear fungus growing there and I wanted to photograph the best specimens. The female green woodpecker was searching for insects amongst the fallen leaves and a lesser spotted woodpecker drumming territorially, high on an old beech trunk. I stood watching it through the monocular, such a tiny bird scarcely bigger than a sparrow, its head a blur at each session of hammering. Just then a shotgun was fired very close. Its owner hadn't seen me quietly standing there and I had been too absorbed in the bird. He was very abusive, mainly because he was startled, I think. When I pointed out he shouldn't be shooting here and this moreover was a nature reserve, he promptly reloaded and fired again. I checked for vehicles though I suspected that he, his son and the other man together here were locals. There was no vehicles anywhere. This reminded me to try and contact Charlie to see if the radio still worked. It didn't.

Walking home along the Embankment Path off Holmoak Lane, I saw that the trees the railway men had cut down were being burnt directly below the occupied badger sett. The sow had been digging out and carrying in bedding last week (I was sure she had cubs now), and the big spoil heap that forms a platform, had been used as a fireplace. I couldn't blame the workmen for how could they know? The spoil heap to them would be an obviously safe place to make a fire. Would the sow be smoked out? The thick smoke was billowing up the bank and covering the entrances. What must it be like inside the sett? If she did have cubs and tried to move them tonight, they might easily die from exposure. The yearling sow denned, like the others, farther along the bank so was safe. At home I phoned Oakley railway station, but could get no reply.

It was a lovely sunny day – too lovely. The first sunny Sunday for a long time. I decided to cook a quick roast dinner and come straight out again, recalling the boot and paw prints in the snow. At 1.15 p.m. there were two workmen tending the fire on the spoil heap by the railway. I called, but was too far away to make myself understood.

The woodland setts slumbered peacefully in the sun, so I walked across to Cliffords Bank and Tossy's Sett. All was quiet there too. Walking on, I turned and saw a police car going up the lane. By now the sky had darkened and it began to snow. As I went home I saw that the British Rail workmen had gone.

Indoors, I had a quick cup of tea and tried phoning British Rail again, but there was no answer. It was 5 p.m. and still snowing as I reached Oakley railway station. In the forecourt were the big yellow lorries with men loading equipment for this night's work along the track. I went into the station and called out to one of a team already busy on the line there. He directed me to his boss. In a room under the stone flight of steps leading down to the platforms, I found Mr Stock the supervisor and his foreman collecting up lanterns for the night's work. I had fully expected to be regarded as an animal nutter and looked at in exasperation, but nothing could have been further from the truth. Both men were concerned, with the foreman promising he would tell the men. Mr Stock had worked on the Hastings electrification and turning to the other said 'These badgers are extraordinary, you know. They follow scent trails, always the same, and don't deviate from them. It was dreadful. We were picking up dead badgers all over the section. Must have wiped out whole colonies – awful. And then to be told many were sows wtih cubs still dependent on them and left underground to starve!' I said it was just for the want of knowing and mentioned I belonged to the National Federation of Badger Groups. Its chairman had been promised by British Rail to be warned of future electrification well in advance so that sections could be left out where the badgers could safely pass through. This would involve the monitoring of local badgers' movements however, so reasonable notice had been agreed.

'Don't worry', said Mr Stock. 'I'll see the men burn elsewhere in future. If you have a problem again, you know where to find us, don't you?

That night the snow turned to sleet, then deep frost with only Gemma and Topsy above ground. There were men working all along the railway line and the three of us crept on to the high bank in Prossers Wood and watched some of them far below. A brilliant light showed us the scene in the cutting. There was a mobile canteen and workshop with men going back and forth and the noise of the work echoing from the steep sides. The scene had an unreality as the sleet caught the light reflecting back and dark shapes loomed and receded. If it hadn't been for the smells of food and coffee wafting up to us in the darkness high above, my companions might well have forsaken me. Though the badgers' fur was raised, their snouts were also, catching each tasty scent. It was a practical assessment of how easy it is for people to draw wild animals close with titbits. I looked at my duo as we trotted off, the voices shouted above the noise, receding into the distance. I was glad I had never enticed mine with food, or they might have gone to anybody.

By first light on Monday 16th the frost was treacherous on Briarmead's glassy surface. The snow hadn't lain, but looking over the fields where patches of January's snow still lay here and there, I recalled the country saying that 'lying snow waits for more'.

On a cold night with snow showers and fox scent very strong I saw no badgers, but spent a happy two hours watching the tawnies' courtship. Together on the branch, the male postured, raising his wings and fluffing out his plumage as he clicked his beak, all the while watched by the hen. Then her movements were echoing his as she responded with soft calls. Several times he mounted her and after each pairing they preened themselves and each other. During two of their five matings that night, the loud and startling 'cackle' was made, but by which bird, I was unsure. Much later, well after first light, I saw the tawny pair on a branch-end softly parleying together. They seemed oblivious to the birds all around, sounding their alarm calls. I felt I shouldn't be watching, so engrossed were they, beaks touching, each owl listening to the other, then a murmured answering. She touched and preened the feathers of his facial disc; her mate breathed a soft sound as he returned the gesture. Then she opened her broad wings and gliding silently between the trees, returned to the nest site in the old beech they had both chosen.

Snow borne on the wind was drifting over the land. It whispered into every crevice, seeking out the weak and the sick and shrouding the granite ground. Somewhere far over the open fields, came the high, thin 'child' scream of the hare.

On the night of Friday 20th there was a deep frost and temperatures of $-6°C$, but it didn't feel very cold as there was no wind. Passing along the Embankment Path just after midnight, I saw the badger sow rooting about on the sett slope opposite. So she hadn't been smoked out. The workmen did stop in time. I watched her for perhaps ten minutes till she disappeared into the entrance above the fire site and felt very glad.

That night too, I saw Crisp with Jude. The boar was walking round her with short, shuffling steps all the while accompanied by his penetrating purr, but a purring with a difference; a deep, whinnying, resounding purr. His stiff-legged gait made him look taller than usual. Crisp had at first, seemed indifferent and then began to purr too, which made him even more excited! He pawed, then dug the ground energetically for a few moments, only to return to her again with his white tail raised vertically. Then coming behind her, he mounted dog-fashion, gripping the fur below her neck to keep balanced. The whinnying purr was louder than ever and a strong smell of musk pervaded the surrounding air. This mating lasted nearly 20 minutes and was to be followed by another that night and the next two nights.

I had spent several hours exploring the areas as they were coppiced that winter. These woods were being opened up and I wondered what wild flowers would be growing here later, now that the light was penetrating. Foxes, owls, weasels, stoats and badgers find these new conditions have great hunting potential as more and more small creatures discover their privacy gone and their homes open to 'public viewing'. It was good to see the old trees coppiced again. Centuries ago, these sweet chestnuts and hazel had been planted for strictly commercial use, long before the advent of coal and plastics. It was divided up by boundary banks and pollards, each wood having its own name so that even today, it is still known as Ashcroft Woods. Each part was rented out for its timber, to a city miller and a captain among others. The latter, Captain Ashcroft, left his name to posterity on his wood. In the old deeds, I found that lopwood, topwood and underwood could be taken freely, coppicing was done in rotation, but pollarded trees couldn't be repollarded more often than every seven years and only those already pollarded. If a tree was found to be newly pollarded without the landowner's permission, the agreement immediately terminated. Most pollards here were boundary markers, so you were altering your boundaries by creating new pollards. Oak, holly, hornbeam and beech were left to grow to their full maturity and these are known as standards. Charcoal burning was also carried on here, which one local man feelingly described as 'a very dirty and uncomfortable business'.

The haulage firm came to tow the great trailer of logs away at 5.30 a.m. that morning, thus avoiding the rush hour traffic in narrow Maddon Lane and on the motorway – one problem they didn't have a hundred years ago. An hour later, there was a vivid sky just before dawn, all shades of pale blue, yellow, red and orange. It lit the frosted grass on the Briarmead banks. Mist hung over the villages in the far distance as orange flames fanned out in the dawn sky. They rippled outwards in a continous stream; a wonderful skyscape casting strange colours onto the land below. A few more minutes and a great orange sun rose over the Bank Sett. Birdsong was everywhere. In spite of the iron-hard ground and cold atmosphere, it was the loveliest of mornings.

For years I had known a local man by sight and as I returned home some mornings, we would talk briefly. He walked to work over the fields and, unlike myself, had been born and bred in the neighbourhood as had his father and grandfather before him. Now he had been retired several years, but still loved walking and most days he would pass on his way for an early morning walk, sometimes with a friend. 'It's the best time of the day' he would say and he was right. I never knew his name or thought to ask; if we stood talking, it was about animals and birds generally, the land and farming. I never mentioned badgers to him or anyone else and over the years have kept my badger involvement very much to myself, firmly believing that the less people knew about these animals here, the better for the badgers. After he asked me for help in releasing a fox from a snare in Holmoak Lane and more recently, told me of the fox caught in a gin trap, I privately dubbed him 'my friendly foxman' for want of a better name. Then one morning in late February, he mentioned that the railway workmen had been burning ten days ago on the embankment and was rather concerned that they might do so again. The large holes over there in the bank he thought were at least fox and might possibly be badger. He didn't quite know what to do about it and asked what I thought. I explained that they were badger and that the workmen wouldn't again be burning nearby, as I had spoken to the supervisor about it.

For the first time in all those years, we suddenly were on christian name terms and I found that quiet, easy-going Frank was the most forceful of men on the subject of badgers. It was the badger-diggers in these parts that really made him sick and no one, least of all the police at Oakley, wanted to know. 'Me and Dick just chase them off', he said 'Like what happened last Sunday morning in Ashcroft Woods!' It seemed that when Frank and his friend went for their usual walk (which they do about five mornings out of seven), they encountered men with terriers and a lurcher at the Old Cherry Sett. Frank knows quite a lot about rabbiting and he said they certainly weren't after rabbits. 'I'm convinced they were putting down the terriers to badger'. I had to tell him of course, that whatever was going on, with two sows plus their cubs there and two yearlings, they would certainly have encountered a badger before long!

He then went on to tell me about an incident on Cliffords Bank some weeks earlier. Again, there were men with terriers and one man, as he ran away, threw something into the elmbrush which turned out to be a bag containing 'One of those little folding shovel things, you know, with a screw that you tighten. They weren't after rabbits. They were after the badgers there, but no one cares so you just have to frighten them off!'

How ironic that we had all thought it so quiet digging-wise and I had never confided in Frank. I told him a little about myself; that I studied badgers and Oakley police were concerned, so please in future not to scare them off, but to go down to Rob's cottage and ask to use the phone there. He was uncertain about contacting the police, so I promised to give his name, address and phone number to Mark Craig, the wildlife officer for Oakley and Crosshampton's village constable who, I stressed was particularly interested. My foxman could then say, when he phoned, that the constable knew about him. I also tried to make him understand that with the Amendment to the Act, terriermen now have to prove they were not after badger if they dig or put a dog to earth in a badger-occupied sett. Thus a member of the public should always contact the police if there were terriermen at a sett and leave them to decide what they were doing. As Cliffords Bank now contained the area's only boar and two sows, one of which had cubs, it was certainly occupied! Frank seemed upset that I had never confided in him. 'Don't you trust me after all these years?' he exclaimed.

At home, I phoned Mark, who promised to make a note of it in his 'Badger File'. I had visions of an enormous wad of material! It was encouraging that he was so interested. Discussing whether I should confide more in people like Frank however, the constable was inclined to think that on the whole, it was best that as few people knew as possible and I was relieved. For every 'friendly foxman' there were many who would be too garrulous for such a confidence and problems could well arise. We talked of the shooting and it appeared he had patrolled several times recently in Ashcroft Woods, but had heard nothing. It was a difficult problem to tackle, but again, someone was trying to help the situation so perhaps things were looking up. We talked about the badger cubs and the possibility of Mark seeing some at the sett he knew. A few weeks earlier, he had noticed the animals had been digging-out, which was a promising sign. Only time would tell.

On the last night of February it had rained for 24 hours, but somewhere in the darkness over Glebe's fields, the skylarks were singing. The tawny hen was incubating her eggs. Incubation starts with the laying of the first egg. These are laid at two-day intervals so that the chicks hatch similarly and are therefore of different sizes. The largest chick is always fed first, thus insuring in lean times that at least the largest will survive. Her mate would hunt now for all their requirements, until the chicks had sufficient downy covering to be left uncloaked in the nest by their mother. So if any accident befell the male bird now (should he be shot) then the hen must leave her brood to find food and the family would die.

All the sows had been foraging for a part of the night in the warm, wet conditions. Musk clung to the sett part of Cliffords Bank and a line of dung pits marked the site. The musking of the sett could have been that of the lactating mother, but that along the railway bank and the dung pits there had been made by the boar. Jude, with all his badger ladies and cubs to protect, was very pre-occupied with scent and dung marking his area. Many of his dung-pits now were boundary markers and a visual, as well as scent warning to any interlopers thinking of encroaching on his territory.

On the way home I met Jane checking a burnt-out, stolen car off Holmoak and we stood talking.

The first day of March was a mild, wet Sunday with signs of spring everywhere. The delicate leaves of lesser celandine and the longer greenery of the bluebells, competed with wild arum to carpet the earth. Squirrels had strewn the ground with great sallow buds and dug many small holes beneath the Scots pines at the Felled Logs Sett in their search for last autum's caches. There were still chestnuts to be found if you turned over the leaf mould carefully.

I was having a rubbish clearance; the first for some weeks. There had been people here in spite of the recent wet weather, so there were plenty of empty bottles, tins and shotgun cases to be collected. I had found from experience that green plastic garden sacks were better than black ones to hide when full in the wood. Should they be discovered by walkers here before they were collected, I could be sure to find them ripped open and the contents scattered again! For once, young Crisp wasn't helping me, but instead was foraging beneath the beeches at the top of the Cherry Sett slope. It was grubs more than anything that she was finding there. When Susie went to earth that morning, I heard her cubs' anxious calls to their mother, then, magically, her soft, reasurring purr to them, which has a different quality from the adults' purring one to another.

On Tuesday evening, Jane came to say that the police had just had a phone call from an Oakley resident who had found a baby badger and asked if I would check it out. I phoned the number she had given, to find a very terse man on the other end. The cub was bleeding badly from the stomach and they wanted me to take it from them at once. I readily agreed, but something in Mr. Clements' voice, plus the fact that the police had not been informed of any injury, prompted me to ask the RSPCA inspector to accompany me. Tony Gould had just come off duty, having struggled against the symptoms of flu all day, but would be with me directly. The cub, we found, was about two week's old with its ears still plugged as at birth and eyes still closed. It had marks on its back and abdomen consistent with being carried by a dog. One tooth had entered the belly deeply, blood was seeping out and the tiny creature was convulsing as it kept up a continuous, high-pitched trilling – the distress cry of the very young badger for its mother. The man explained he walked every day passed Littlebeck Wood and on through the farm orchard. He picked the cub up from the ground under the trees at 1.30 p.m. attracted to it by its continuous cries, and brought it home.

In situations like this, one has to be careful. Tony queried the time lapse; 1.30 p.m. on finding it and contacting the police at 6 p.m. The man explained they had a new baby in the house and he had applied baby-lotion on cotton wool, holding it against the punctured abdomen to stop the bleeding. He was sitting doing this when we entered the room. He was surprised to find badgers lived around that area as there was no sett to his knowledge there. We thanked him. I took the cub, putting my gloved hand round it inside my anorak. It had been a bitterly cold day with light snow showers and now was a bitter night.

As we drove off, Tony said 'Now what?'

'Put it down', I replied 'It has little chance of survival. If a vet does decide it's unharmed internally and stitches it up, what then? If we locate the sett, the mother will never accept it back. It's doomed to a life in captivity – perhaps 15 years, if well fed and cared for'.

'Good', said a relieved inspector, 'I hoped you'd say that,' and he drove us home. All the while, the tiny creature kept up its piteous cry till Tony injected into the belly, whereupon a sream of blood shot out. It had been bleeding internally. Moments later there was one badger cub less around Oakley.

Looking at the body, Ross was angry that the man hadn't contacted the RSPCA or a vet earlier. It was ironic, especially when considering they had a baby too. If his newborn had been crying like this, Mr. Clements would have rushed to alleviate its pain. But it didn't occur to the three adults in that house, that the badger *could feel pain*. It reminded me of a little girl when I was talking at a primary school, who asked me 'If a badger sprained its ankle, would it hurt it?' It was the 8-year-old's first moment of awareness of pain in an animal. Some people go through their entire lives with no such moment.

After Tony had gone (looking even greyer and more ill than when he came), I contacted Jane and told her what had happened. Ross had offered to go with me the next day as I wanted to try and trace the sett to see if that, too, had been interfered with, for my own peace of mind. Most likely, a small terrier had gone into the sett and brought up the tiny cub, ran along with it awhile, then dropped it. But I wanted to make sure. Jane said if the sett had been dug we were to let the police know. Mr. Clements, I thought was O.K., though I wondered if he knew a little more than he was prepared to say. He 'walked that way every day'. Out of the council estate, past a wood and on to farmland in that sort of weather? Then probably he walked a dog. Was it his dog that had retrieved the cub? We would never know.

The following day however, it continued to snow and was bitterly cold. There was no point in searching the area in this weather but I contacted the owner of Littlebeck Farm who gave his permission for us to go on to his land. He had never seen badgers in the area I described, but thought there could be a sett much farther over his fields. The sett we would be looking for however, should be nearer. We would have to see.

That Thursday was a frosty start to a lovely morning. Ross and I went out early and once there, split up. I would search Littlebeck Wood and the immediate farmland including the orchard. Ross would check the area nearest the council estate and the motorway banks. We would meet up later at home. It was to prove one of the most sobering mornings of my life.

Twenty-seven years ago, when I had first come to live in Oakley, Littlebeck had been a beautiful old wood on the far side of our town, quite as lovely as the woods I had grown so much to love. The once clear, flowing stream from which this wood derived its name, had meadowsweet in masses growing along its banks, the delicately chequered fritillary's bell-shaped flowers nodding from the damp places, with primroses and dog-violets spreading from under the trees, on to the railway bank nearby. I had been here perhaps half a dozen times since those early days and been conscious of its deterioration, but pre-occupied with a growing family and my interest in Ashcroft Woods, hadn't really given it more than a passing thought. Sergeant Collins told me months ago, the police had complaints of illegal motorbike 'trials' here. The people doing the damage were mainly from Oakley and the nearby estate, but the wood and land belonged to the city council and another police force. In effect, therefore, it fell between two stools.

It was from this same estate that the log cabin men had come to camp in Ashcroft Woods and now, I could see why. People had camped here over the years and the havoc left behind them had simply remained. Old shelters and camps littered what had once been the undergrowth. Trees were hacked down and the ground beneath the remaining great oaks was liquid mud created by the tyres of countless motorbikes. No-one would want to camp here now. There was a home-made clay pigeon tower just outside the area and shotgun enthusiasts used the wood itself. A deep, muddy track ran through the trees, obviously made by large vehicles. Where this was very waterlogged, thousands of spent shotgun cases had been used as 'rubble' to make a more stable surface. These cases lay everywhere. I had never seen so many at one time, or known so many different sizes and colours existed. An attempt had been made to gather some into great heaps that had been partly burnt. Rustied oil drums stood full of them with whisky and other bottles, many broken, strewn about. House refuse and rubble lay everywhere, but what struck so forcibly that bright, sunny morning was the absence of birdsong. As with Ashcroft Woods, the motorway and railway weren't far distant, but where were the birds that of an early morning in March, should be calling and nest building now?

Near the beck, I found two dung pits and many snuffle holes, then a small, undistrubed sett in the steep, railway bank. A very freshly dead, young, male badger (approximately three years old), lay shot in a clear area near the bank. The shotgun enthusiast had scored a hit to the body, either yesterday or Tuesday. The sub-zero conditions on Wednesday would have preserved it. There was still a great deal more to explore, but I had been out all night and now it was mid-day. The rest would have to be left for another time.

Ross had found no badger evidence, but had come to the conclusion from prints of coursing dogs across the farmers' field, that lamping was carried on there. The farmer hadn't seen any beams that season. Last year he had a lamping problem that the city police had been slow to deal with until spotlight beams had dazzled drivers on the motorway. This had reached the local papers and effectively stopped the lamping. It had not occurred to him that his lampers, like ours, might have taken to using smaller beams and being more discreet. He took my name and phone number and we agreed to keep in touch. There was still a lot of land to explore for setts, though I didn't know if I would have the time that week. We were welcome on his land whenever we felt inclined and I would keep him up to date on incidents there. I would also tell Oakley police about the dead boar badger and I thanked him for his co-operation. At least we had another farmer who was concerned.

The terrible state of Littlebeck Wood – the broken trees, ground raised by motorbikes, shotgun cases, dumped rubbish, shelters and human excreta, together with its badger deaths, left me very depressed. There was no way I could look after it or even keep an eye on it. Local people had done what they wanted there for too long so it had become, for them, a right. I felt, too, that there was far more badger abuse just below the surface.

It did make me view my own actions in a different light though. It bothers me sometimes that I worry our police, Dr. Howard and the county trust with the shooting, litter, badger and other problems in our woods, often feeling that people must curse me for my insistence. I know I am a dreadful nuisance, but I do care. Littlebeck Wood is unloved and unlovely; a terrible object lesson. There but for the grace of God go Ashcroft Woods.

By 2 a.m. the following night, it was sleeting with a penetrating wind which I tolerated for two hours, then returned home to dry my clothes, get warm and go out again. By first light the sleet had eased and the tawny male was calling his boundaries. At the Crater Sett there were primroses in bloom and I wandered off the path and through the trees to look at their pale yellow flowers. Tucked against one primrose clump, I saw a small folded plastic bag and out of habit, picked it up to put in the rubbish 'collection' I keep until there is enough to ask Dr. Howard to take it away in his car. It emanated a strong, decaying smell and looking inside the bag I found a tiny dead badger cub. It might have been a duplicate of that found near Littlebeck Wood, but this cub had been gripped by the head and must have died immediately.

Tony Gould came at 10 that Sunday to ask if I would go on site with him to Brockton golf course where he had been called out by their police the previous evening. Two terriermen, Roger Smith and friend, claimed they had been digging out a fox, when a member of the public spotted them and gave the alarm. By the time the police came on the scene, Roger had a dog underground. Had it been entered for fox, or could it be badger? That was the question. Tony had waited whilst Roger tried to get to his dog, then at 9 p.m. in the falling snow, understandably decided he had other calls to make and phoned the fire brigade to get the dog out. Roger would clearly have liked to be left to get to the terrier in his own time, especially as he would have to pay for the service. By then it was very cold and very dark. The dog was rescued, apparently none the worse, and Tony particularly asked everyone present that the holes be left open. When we arrived that morning however, all were filled in. Either Brockton police had short memories and tidy minds (and enjoyed filling up holes in the dark on golf courses), or Roger, true to form, had come back complete with his shovel earlier that morning. There was still a little snow lying and with the evidence well concealed under bright, wet earth it was difficult to say, but I felt it was probably fox. But why fill it in, Roger? Did you just want to be on the safe side? We agreed that this terrierman, whose case regarding his attempted badger-dig at the Taylors was soon to be heard in court didn't seem to be curtailing his activities. Perhaps he was trying to earn a bit extra to pay for a possible fine.

That morning whilst I was still in Tony's van, there was another call-out to the scene of a suspected badger-dig off a footpath between two country lanes. We had some difficulty finding it and when we did, it was to discover that although it was very badger-occupied, the crowning-down hole had been made a long time ago. Obviously our informant had only just noticed but that didn't matter. We now knew of another badger occupied sett that could be added to the ordnance map.

The inspector said that the case of the 'clamped' patterdale belonging to Ayres, had been heard the previous week. This was the man who bought his dog at Don Francis' terrier show last August. He had been convicted not of having put it to badger (which would have been difficult to prove in court), but of causing unnecessary suffering by failing to provide veterinary treatment for it. He was fined and banned from keeping a dog for two years. His other terrier had been confiscated until the case was heard, so Ayres demanded it back from the inspector saying quite rightly, that his mother could have it in her name. 'O.K.', said Tony, 'but you'll have to pay its board kennel fees which amount now to £350'. The badger-digger changed his mind. We discussed the ban. Two years is such a short time. I said how frustrated I felt and the RSPCA inspector replied he had never brought an actual badger-digging case to court (Roger Smith and Co. were being prosecuted by the Crown), and at times felt very frustrated about the whole business. I remarked that at least he had achieved the removal of the dogs in Ayres' case even if technically, it wasn't for badger-digging. A terrierman won't stop taking badgers just because of a conviction (there's a possibilty he'll take more to pay for his fine) but the confiscation of his dogs is a crushing loss. Pups take time to train and need an older, experienced dog with them. If you want an adult dog that has proved its badger-worth and will save you time, that costs even more. Nothing is of more value to the dedicated lurcher-terrierman than his dogs. He can buy another secondhand vehicle and any amount of equipment for the job. The wording of the Badger Act 1973, doesn't really help either when it states '. . . the court can order the forfeiture of any weapon or article in respect of, or by means of which the offence was committed'. Vehicles have been confiscated as 'weapon or article' but a dog scarcely comes under this heading. Ironically, the most vital weapon or article that the badger-digger cannot do without is his terrier.

One afternoon a few days later, Ross and I thoroughly checked the railway bank at the side of Littlebeck Wood till it reached the far lane. A very large area of this embankment contained an extensive badger sett with some digging-out on the animals' part suggesting that at this time of year, there were cubs present. We followed the lane till it joined another and re-entered the wood. Then splitting up, each of us searched the rest of Littlebeck thoroughly for setts. There were four, with only a possible one still housing a badger. There was no fresh animal digging-out at this, but dung pits nearby and two entrances smooth with use. The three other setts had long since been dug out by men with crowning-down holes galore. In one instance, the sett was totally destroyed.

This ancient wood was a mess, yet still held a certain beauty. Its pollen laden pussy-willow and surviving primroses were a breathtaking reminder of spring, the eternal promise. I longed to care for this place and its remaining badgers. Their vulnerability distressed me.

There were more frosty nights, with my badgers snuffling for grubs and larvae under the hedgerow trees round the fields and deep in the boundary ditches within Ashcroft Woods. These animals were at their lowest bodyweight now and the sows, with young cubs to feed, were particularly hungry.

I watched Jude use a dung pit then doglike, scrape his hind feet before going off to forage. This was the third time I had seen him do that recently. Sometimes the action was more of a shuffle. Not for the first time, I wondered if badgers' paws have inter-digital glands? No one seems to know, but it is a possibility. Earth wasn't thrown backwards and badgers don't cover their dung or latrine pits. Old Joe sometimes did this scraping, and looking back in my journals, I found with him too, it occurred in early spring. I had not observed the sows doing this at any time, so feel it could be connected with male territorial activity. Other writers have also noted this, but they don't give the sex or time of year.

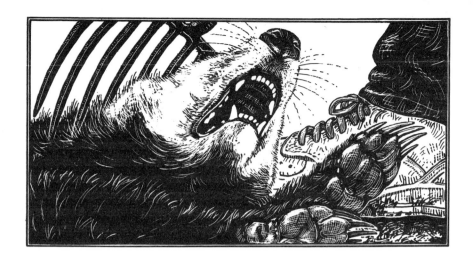

Chapter 12

I had a phone call from Jane to say she had seen men with 'little dogs' on the railway bank beyond Ferndale Avenue, just outside Oakley, when she was patrolling the previous afternoon. Three ran away when she called to them and escaped by running up the steep bank and crossing the railway line in front of a passing train. The other two she ordered back and though they said they were rabbiting, she asked if I knew of any badgers there. Since the terriermen were actually on railway property, permission to examine the area would have to come from British Rail. Jane said the bank was fenced off with high chainlink so she didn't know how I would get over. However, if the terriermen could get over, I was sure I could. I suggested I would look where she described off Ferndale Avenue that day, whilst waiting for permission to go on to the bank. She agreed, saying that with binoculars I should have a good view, and asked me to let her know what I found.

Next I contacted Oakley railway station and was told I must request permission from the area manager at the mainline junction. I spoke to his secretary who said that this week, her boss was at the terminus station in the city. This way it could take weeks, so in desperation I mentioned Mr. Stock at Oakley and all his help over the badgers.

Then I set out in glorious sunshine and walked down Ferndale Avenue, a not-too-salubrious part of our town. Although I was casually dressed for that very casually dressed neighbourhood, I was conscious of causing some interest. This is the sort of area where people stand on doorsteps calling over to others and litter, months old, blows about in front gardens. At the end of the road, I walked through to the field next to the high railway bank. A short distance on, there was a portion of chainlink cut and bent back which puzzled me, recalling Jane's words. Had it been like this when she was here yesterday, or had she not noticed? A little way above on the bank, there were three holes with sandy earth in front and quite large spoil heaps showed clear. High above these through the trees, and almost directly below the railway lines themselves, were two far larger excavations. What they were I couldn't have said from the ground, even with the monocular, though they were old and not recently used like those below. The lower ones I thought were probably badger, but until I was allowed on the bank I couldn't be completely sure.

I continued on to the railway crossing and so to the other side, where I walked back along the railway. Now I was on Ingrims fields that I crossed every night and morning to get to my own area. Here local lampers plied their trade with Holmoak Lane in the distance. Two men propping up the chainlink stopped talking to look as I passed and some youths on motorbikes were roaring over the wheat a short way off. (It was here that the barley was set alight at harvest time, nearly engulfing the combine and driver). The path dipped round a heap of old rubbish, plus some fresh, high piles of earth and ballast; it was a popular dumping ground for the council estate nearby. Then I passed a row of garages with a man lying under a van, whilst another fixed (or unfixed) its front number plate. Walking by, I saw the back plate was a different number; and the man at the front of the vehicle had noticed I had noticed! I strolled on, telling myself I was supposed to be looking at the railway bank for evidence of badgers.

That night was probably one of the frostiest so far for 1987 and the sun rose as a deep orange disc in a ghostly white sky. No badgers or foxes to be seen, but the latter would doubtless be out hunting soon in the morning. Walking home I met Frank who had been watching a vixen with one cub on Roger Johnson's land. My Watcher hadn't yet had her cubs, but I felt she would very soon.

That morning Mr. Stock phoned from Oakley railway station to say, 'I have only been given a telephone number, but are you our badger lady who came about the trees?' He gave me permission to go on the bank, provided I wear one of their regulation orange jackets. At the railway station I explained about the terriermen and asked whether, this week's incident apart, I could borrow the jacket another time to map setts on railway property in the area. He told me to keep the jacket for use whenever I had reason to search the banks. 'But please', said the straight-faced supervisor, 'be careful and whatever you do, don't play with the conductor rail!' We both laughed. I really felt the badgers had found another friend.

I phoned Jane at 10 a.m. when she came back to the station for breakfast and told her I had permission to explore the bank and would let her know what happened. The police were too tied up to come that morning, but perhaps that was as well; I really prefered exploring on my own and didn't want to waste their time.

As I walked down the avenue, I had the most curious feeling I was being watched. This was nothing to do with the man and boy washing a car. They watched alright, but the feeling was different. It was a lovely morning however, after the frost. The first shock I had was the chainlink. I walked by it at first and puzzled, retraced my steps to discover it had been carefully pulled back in place and fixed with short lengths of wire. No wonder Jane had seen nothing amiss with the fence! I noted where I would need to come down the bank to the holes and walking on to the crossing, donned my bright orange jacket (too bright for my peace of mind), and walked along at the side of the line. The climb down wasn't difficult, merely uncomfortable. I had brought no gloves and the bank was not only covered with brambles, but also old bramble cuttings chopped from above by the workmen and thrown down. I think I knew in my heart of hearts what I was going to find. It wasn't difficult to guess. The three lower holes had been carefully filled in; they might never have been. I wished I had come on to the bank yesterday, with or without permission. Even so my word against theirs would never have stood up in court. I climbed carefully up to the highest excavations and saw a great, old crowning-down hole and farther along, a huge dug out portion large enough for a child to stand upright with a badger tunnel disappearing under the line itself. Pieces of corrugated iron and part of an old sleeper lay to one side and a long-pronged fork with a short, broken off handle bound with plastic, the type that was used, I thought, for spreading the clinker. A harmless enough object on a railway bank but just here? The prongs were long and curved, reminding me of badger claws, but much longer. There was something infinitely sickening about the scene. Something had been enacted just below the passenger view of anyone travelling above; something cruel and long ago. Someone had returned to boast proudly in pub or home and show his game dogs' scars. I scrambled down to the infilled holes where the sun struck warm on the bank and smelt the musky smell of badger dung, just as we had at the Taylors' dig. But there were no dung pits, only a sandy, fresh patch to

238

one side. I began to dig with a piece of stick and in moments had turned up the hidden dung with bright earth clinging. Someone had covered their tracks well.

Carefully checking the few unstopped entrances, I could find no evidence of rabbit or fox. Surely the droppings of either should be very distinctive at this time of year and on a railway bank. There were no pungent foxy smell, nor tufts of soft rabbit fur from their territorial skirmishes. My search led me back to the top of the embankment again and the gaping holes below rail level. On the right, by the triple bole of a small tree was a large, abandoned badger entrance and leaning against, yet partly concealed by the thin trunks – something shiny like new steel. I picked it gingerly up and stared at it in my hand, not quite crediting what I was seeing. A flail, a metal flail, the wiry ends teased out rigid from the woven handle, all facing one way. Cruel and long ago? The holes had been dug long ago, but at this, they must still be in use! I was tempted to take it home with me, but how? I had nothing in which to put it and the sharp ends caught and tore at everything in passing. I ran my finger along one silver length and drew blood. I would injure someone on the busy pavements and attract attention. Carefully wrapped up, it could be carried safely home, but not like this. Where could I hide it? I laid the flail on the bank with rubbish covering it.

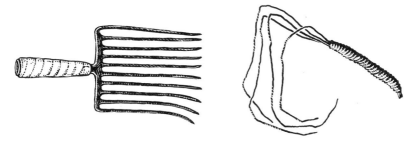

I picked up the heavy long-pronged fork (there was nowhere to hide that here), and retraced my steps till a passing train broke in on my thoughts. I looked at what I carried and realised there was really no point in walking home with that. In any case, I supposed it was British Rail property. I laid it under some dead branches and continued to the crossing in the sunshine. There, sitting on the steps leading down, were three men; a thickset, middle-aged one with a dirty red and white bobble-hat minus the bobble; a thin man with steel-rimmed glasses and tatooed arms and a young man (another ferret-face, my home town seems full of them), with lank hair and a smirk who called 'Been for a walk missus? Like yer coat!'

'We got coats like that for when we go for walks, ain't we?' laughed another.

'Find anything love?' guffawed the third. 'Where yer going now, back to report?'

Further along, I folded the jacket and pushed it out of sight into my pocket. The sun still shone; it was a lovely day, but I was walking out of the darkness and leaving the darkness behind. Halfway along Ferndale Avenue, a young man was approaching on the far side. He was in his mid-twenties, thickset, flashily dressed and walked with a swagger. I looked and saw him looking, the swagger gone. He held the slips of a tall, light-coloured lurcher and another with a linty coat, while an old jack russell bitch ran on in front. It was the lamper whose dog injured Susie last May – and I thought he came from Rendcombe village!

At home, I phoned Jane, but she was out patrolling and would be back after 12 noon, so collecting some heavy duty polythene and a thick sack, I returned to the bank. It would be good to have included my camera, but I was frightened of damaging it scrambling about the embankment with all that I had to carry. Once there, I spent an hour carefully and thoroughly checking the whole site, but the flail had gone. I did find a latrine/dung pit tucked to one side and freshly used however. I pushed away some earth from a recently stopped-up entrance and in it I found several badger hairs. I bitterly regretted the flail being taken. I looked at the crowning-down and baiting-pits again in the forlorn hope of finding something more, jumped down into the pit and picked up a rusty curve of metal. If it hadn't been so old and brown it could have been a length of flail. Were there any more amongst the dead leaves lining the pit? Scooping away the debris, I found another length and an old, rusty flail that except for its age was a companion to the other. Undoubtedly, badger-baiting and worse had gone on here. There was something dreadful about the place.

Carefully, I wrapped the old flail up and carried it back then returned for the fork still hidden where I had left it. It seemed to have been a very long day and night when I finally returned home. Two weeks earlier, I had damaged the cartilege of my right knee playing with Crisp and scrambling about on railway embankments was not improving it! By now, Jane had gone off duty so I left a message for her asking if the DC SOCO officer would take photos of the site.

That night was one of deep frost and dawn found me bagging up litter in Ashcroft Woods. After badger-watch, I walked down to the village to enlist the aid of my friendly rubbish-collector. Over a welcome mug of coffee, we discussed my frustration with the shooting. He told me I didn't go about things in the right way. I had a sneaking suspicion he was right. I was not to worry, but to leave it with the chairman. The new byelaws were at last coming into force. He would speak to Oakley's police inspector; some sort of plan was needed. He would also collect the rubbish tomorrow morning. Philip's car drove alongside as I was walking home along the steep track above the motorway and he gave me a lift home. Suddenly, I found myself speaking of the baiting-pit on the railway bank. It was on my mind and an enormous relief to tell him how I felt. For years I had walked back and forth across the fields on the far side of that railway. The same line that further on became the home of the Embankment badgers and further still, passed through my own area. It was scarcely a ten minute walk from my own home. Yet I had never realised and somehow that made it worse. But if one young woman had seen and wondered, so must many other people walking their dogs from the estate or taking the short cut across the fields . . . and for how many years? It had waited for Jane to query the men on the banks and take it a step further.

As I walked indoors the phone was ringing and I spoke to Sergeant Collins. He had been given my message and promised that the SOCO officer would come to photograph the site and would be contacting me. The next move then was to find out about the clinker fork. At Oakley railway station I described it and was taken to their supply stores. It was indeed a 'stone fork' for spreading the clinker with the handle cut down to use in the close confines of the pit. Standing in the long room under the steps, I described the open sett, corrugated sheeting that had been used to block the badgers' re-entry leaving a trench in which to place the dogs. The stone fork would be ideal either to jab at the baited creature if a terrier was down and injured, or to skewer it whilst the dogs finished it off. But there was nothing in the store that remotely resembled the flail. It must have been bench-made and brought there from outside. Intent on explaining, I hadn't noticed the quietness, till I looked up and saw the men's faces under the electric light. 'What do they get out of it – kicks?' said one and the silence hung. I asked if I could unfasten the chainlink that the terriermen had cut and secured, provided that I fasten it again before we left. It would be easier for the SOCO officer to get on the embankment with his tripod and camera. I was told that would be fine and one man even hunted round for a pair of pliers, but I assured him we had a pair at home.

As we walked back along the platform together someone said 'We know pretty nasty things with animals go on along these banks'. His companion agreed. It was nothing to find freshly killed and mutilated foxes with 'things stuck in them or up them and you can see it was done when they were alive, by their faces! But what can you do about it? We never see it going on'. It occurred to me, walking home that day, that if ever these workmen did see anything going on, it would bode ill for the terriermen.

That afternoon the DC phoned. He would be at court all day tomorrow and Saturday was his rest day, but on Sunday he was on duty and would phone at about 9 a.m. that day to say when he could come. He was sorry he couldn't come sooner than that, but they were inundated with work and often worked their rest days. I knew it wasn't his fault, but just hoped there would be something left to photograph.

That Friday night all my badgers were in fine fettle, especially the lactating sows Little'un, Sis, Susie and Missy. Crisp was a tearaway, head-butting my legs when she appeared with her ball. Snow showers blown on the breeze, rustled the dead ashkeys above our heads. It was a selfish thought, but at least my badgers were thriving.

Before leaving that morning, I took my camera from its hiding place and walked over Pete's land to photograph the lake. I had never heard from the county surveyor and time was creeping away. I knew now I would lose the lake. No letter of mine would stop the machines moving in ten days time, but the plants were going to good owners and were to be collected this weekend. The sun came out as I walked down the hillside and shone on the flakes of snow still lying from the night; diamonds sparkling till the warmth melted them and they vanished. I came to the crest of the hill where it drops to the water and stood disbelieving. Where the lake had been was a gaping maw; a great, open mouth like a scream. Something obscene had crunched through the trees leaving white, teeth-stumps. Heaps of black silt torn from its bed, hid the plants. Only the motorway remained with its traffic and overhead gantry. Strange to notice them now of all days, when they never intruded before.

At home was a neat, white envelope with the county crest and the words: 'I am not able to comment in respect of the proposed works at this site, but I have today referred the letter and photographs to the engineer responsible with a request that he makes a more detailed reply to you in the near future'. It was too late and he must have known it.

That same morning, I decided to look in at the Ferndale Avenue sett as I dreaded taking the SOCO officer there on Sunday, only to find the dung pit covered up. In theory, my photos would be no good in court, but perhaps they would be better than no photos. There were two dung pits now side by side with very fresh dung in the second. I photographed them in closeup then, moving away, took more pictures in order to have the surrounding area recognisable. (Later, I found that this would be acceptable to a court, provided I could take an officer to the site to confirm them).

However, the dung pits were there to be photographed that Sunday. Perhaps having cleared the area twice the terriermen hadn't thought to check again. We didn't reopen the chainlink either, as the photographer's new equipment was housed in two neat cases. Instead, we walked to the crossing and so approached the sett as I always had, from above. The SOCO officer was better than I at clambering about on the steep slope, but seemed very wary of walking next to the passing trains. Then all was explained; he only has occasion to do this when photographing suicides. There had been two within the last year on this little stretch alone, both of which he had attended. He remarked that photographing badger items on railway property made a welcome change. As we walked back to his van I thought how people look at the same thing in a different light. For instance, this railway line and bank for many, just means trains; for some it means maintenance, their job; for me it means badger setts and for the SOCO officer it means suicides. Yet it's all the same place.

As things turned out, no case could be brought against the terriermen as Jane hadn't actually seen them holding spades. Whether they had put them down on the bank or the other men took them, one couldn't say, but just being on the bank with the dogs, didn't prove anything. The CID would send cautioning letters to those whose names she had taken. I thanked her for her concern and alertness. It was the badger still living there that bothered me. It foraged in the field below and the farther farmland. Where it pushed out beneath the chainlink, its regular trails were clearly defined through the rank grass. Next time the terriermen came to its sett, there would be no Jane to care. Badgers are creatures of habit. They cannot reason. The ability to reason is given only to man and separates him from the lesser animals. He can contemplate his own end – and that of the lesser animals.

It was a beautiful mild night with no mist and a half moon. I decided to return home for an hour's rest, but was out again at about 4 a.m. Crossing Ingrim's fields, I heard mens' voices and the barking of a terrier to my right. The field between footpath and Holmoak Lane rises in a sudden hump there, so I could see nothing.

Then a fox raced down towards me, hotly pursued by a lurcher. It saw me, swerved round and returned at an angle towards the lane. Renewed yapping, mens' voices and laughter, then the fox crying and yowling. I ran up the hill, shouted, and on reaching the top, saw three men racing off towards the Ferndale estate. I had nearly caught up with the last man when he turned and holding up a knife, dared me to come closer. I walked up to him and he shouted for the others to come back which they did. With the terriers and lurcher milling round and two men at my back making comments, I demanded of my man what had he been doing to that fox. At first he denied doing anything, then said what did it matter, it wasn't a brockie, only a fox. I was a 'divi'; foxes didn't matter. Still I demanded to know what he had done. Suddenly, he began laughing and stretched out his other hand towards my face. He was holding the fox's ear!

In that moment, everything seemed to come together. My private agony of the baiting-pit and the badger still living there; the desolation of Littlebeck Wood and the dead badgers, but most of all these fields, with their lampers and mindless cruelty. Suddenly, stupidly, I was taunting him, jeering and calling him trash. Oh, wasn't he brave, knife in hand, to maim and kill in the darkness and creep back home again! I have heard of living foxes being seen without brush and ears and knew that some men get pleasure from mutilating and releasing them but, thank God, had never witnessed this before. I tried to remonstrate with him, more calmly, but it was useless and the others began jostling me from behind. He and his friends were lampers; more than once, we had met on this land. He didn't deny or confirm this, merely laughing and saying I couldn't prove anything and it didn't matter anyway – foxes were only vermin, as he moved off. No way could I radio from there and to return home to phone the police would have taken 15 minutes, by which time they would be safely tucked away indoors. It was all so hopeless.

Before I continued to my area, I searched around but the fox had clearly made its getaway. Well at least, I suppose I should be glad that there was only time for it to have one ear cut off, but the whole affair disgusted and sickened me. I had told the man he was trash and he was.

I didn't reach the Old Cherry Sett till well after first light, but everything was peaceful with the birds singing. Forgetful, I walked down to Pete's lake deep in thought, all unconscious of my surroundings . . . I wouldn't go down to the lake-site anymore. It hurt and didn't help me to look at its destruction. It was my own fault. I helped to create something and loved it too much. Everything has a price – I had paid the price and seen it destroyed.

Tony and I discussed the fox maiming and technically, the man who cut off the fox's ear was almost certainly not committing an offence. The 1911 Protection of Animals Act only covers domestic or captive wild animals. The definition of 'captive' at present reads: 'which is in captivity, or confinement, or which is maimed, pinioned, or subjected to any appliance or contrivance for the purpose of hindering or preventing the escape from captivity or confinement'. The RSPCA lost a case of a man using a live hedgehog as a football. In theory at least, it could have unrolled and run away, therefore the accused was cleared though his ill-treatment had killed it. I recalled another RSPCA inspector finding a hedgehog speared through with a pointed stick where someone had nailed it to the ground alive. Again, it wasn't an offence. If the fox had been caged and then had its ear severed, the man would be guilty. We discussed the possibility of finding exactly where the man lived for the RSPCA to take the case, even knowing they would probably lose it. They were trying to get the law amended and any publicity of this sort would highlight and strengthen their position. Tony also felt that the technical definition of 'captive' would be better aired. Would the holding of the fox for instance, be defined as captive? However, I hadn't actually seen it done, we had no maimed fox and it would be the word of three men against mine. It had stressed for me once again, the inadequacy of the law, though in this case the wording is to protect the legal animal sports such as foxhunting or hare-coursing. Our wild birds are much better protected.

We stopped off at some horses outside Oakley. A caller had reported them as being in poor condition and 'scabby' but they looked fit and healthy enough. Tony had a suspicion when he received it that this was a malicious phone call. The RSPCA get a lot of these time wasters, but all have to be checked.

Then we went on to view the baiting and crowning-down pits off Ferndale Avenue. He had never come across anything quite like the stone fork and flail before. I had read reports of badgers being found flayed and had wondered, with what? Are the flails I discovered, merely stereotypes common to badger-baiters, or isolated weapons peculiar to the more perverted? Every morning now I diverted my homeward route to check this railway bank. The badger was still there. But for how long?

The badgers were busy in the wood, leaving many snuffle holes amongst the undergrowth and under the hedges. The meadow had been partly rolled and the roller left near Cliffords Bank soakaway till it was finished. It was a mild, damp night and I wandered along with Crisp as she wormed, first at the wood edge of the meadow where the spring seeps into the ditch, then to the spring itself. She lapped the water, then came to stand on hind legs against me, her jaws still dripping. She turned as she got down and suddenly squealed twisting and pulling. Her left foreleg was caught in a snare. In moments she was beside herself with terror and pain. Pulling off my anorak, I threw it over the badger, pressing it around her with all my strength till she calmed. The so-called 'humane' snare (that runs free and doesn't lock), was anchored to a nearby tree stump and once I had relieved the tension on the wire, she wasn't difficult to release. If she had been left to struggle for long however, it would have been a different story. Wire cuts through flesh and muscle very quickly and soon becomes embedded in the bone. As the wire noose eased, I gently slipped the leg out before she could pull back again. Crisp licked the released forelimb while I undid the anchored wire with the help of my penknife, then hunted round the area for more snares. I spent nearly an hour there, but could only find two more. I was very lucky not to have been bitten. An injured badger is a dangerous one; its bite can easily sever a finger. Crisp is a fully-grown sow and her jaws are formidable. She is a wild animal after all and would have attacked anyone in her fear. I wandered about other parts of the wood where I have found snares placed in previous years, but discovered no more. Three seemed an odd number to set. I suspected, from their placing, that they were intended for fox but snares cannot distinguish between species. Whatever the poacher was after in Ashcroft Woods, the bye-laws state that no animal or bird may be taken or killed from this nature reserve.

At home, Karen and I discussed covering a badger to calm it. The ideal way of transporting a live badger in a vehicle for instance, is still the old way – in a sack. For some reason, perhaps because it is dark, sheltered and confining like the inside of its home the sett, a badger will remain quiet and unmoving like this. Nowadays however, if terriermen are caught with a sack in their possession it immediately incriminates them, since sacks are synonymous with badgers. A fox net can be taken along and cause little comment, in fact it tends to strengthen the impression they were only after fox. (The breaking strength of such a net is considerable; after all, one doesn't see badger nets advertised). But a netted badger in the back of the vehicle, covered with a jacket or anorak, serves the same purpose.

I couldn't get Sergeant Collins or Mark Craig, so after some hesitation, asked to speak to their inspector about the snaring. I suggested that if his men should see vehicles parked near the wood containing any type of poaching equipment or owned by known poachers, they could make a point of stopping them.

I dreaded the prospect of another animal caught in a snare. Its frantic struggles could disembowel it if the wire passed over the head onto the body. As for badger sows with cubs . . . I was not going to be in Oakley on the coming Saturday as I was attending the Westonbirt Meeting of the NFBG. Karen had promised to come up the lane in her car, morning and afternoon (though I was not too happy about this for Ross was also away that weekend so she would be on her own). The inspector was very concerned and promised to step up patrols for the next few days and especially over the weekend.

That Wednesday night and Thursday morning found me still searching for snares. Just three seemed so strange. Crisp was little the worse for her mishap and made much of me. Jude did too. He wondered what all the fuss was about and felt left out! A very fine rain was falling at first light and the birdsong was wonderful. The trees had a faint haze to clothe their bareness; a haze made of tiny leaves, buds and catkins. I was longing to see the badger cubs. They would be 8 weeks old and hopefully above ground, about the second week in April. More and more toads were on the move; the great migration would soon be with us.

I was looking forward to the NFBG Meeting and seeing other people involved in badgers. That afternoon I phoned West Yorkshire's wildlife officer who said the vigilance of his Badger Monitoring Group was proving itself. After a long period of peace, the badger-diggers had returned and several were caught; some as recently as that Sunday. He couldn't make it to Westonbirt, but one of his Group would be representing them.

Friday brought rain and gale force winds for 24 hours. I searched and searched, but reluctantly concluded that either I was getting bad at finding things, or only three snares were set. Maybe, someone new to the area was testing to see if he could snare unnoticed.

The badgers were foraging in the more sheltered part of the wood. I was with Missy and Crisp when there was a cracking sound from on high and looking up I saw the top of a silver birch break off from the rest of the trunk. Incredibly, it seemed to stay suspended, defying gravity, then slowly, quicker, quicker, it dropped down through the smaller trees. A tearing rushing and the earth below our feet seemed to jump as the birch's crown hit it with tremendous force. A great cloud of dust, twigs and debris covered us. After a moment, I walked up to the stricken tree, to find I was on my own; the badger ladies had made a quick exit. The tree was quite rotten; woodpecker holes and fungus adorned its length. It had fallen across the footpath and was too high off the ground to clamber over. Walking round to view the far side, I spied my timid sows appearing out of the hanging foliage of a holly, farther up the hill. Moments later, they too were exploring the trunk, walking along its length as they did so. Their appreciation, however was not aesthetic, but gastronomic.

I found the Meeting of the National Federation of Badger Groups that Saturday very rewarding, with many matters discussed. The NFBG had representation on the MAFF Consultative Panel on Badgers and Tuberculosis. What we now knew of the disease was that we were not dealing with an instance of high risk, but rather, a random risk. Therefore, the continued gassing of badgers in some areas was not acceptable.

It is known that there is a relationship between blocked setts and non-productive sows, so this is a practice which is detrimental to the welfare of badgers. Therefore regarding foxhunts, there is a basic objection to disturbing setts either by putting down terriers to fox, digging for fox in an occupied sett, or earth stopping. To stop an entrance with straw bundles or bundles of sticks (as advocated by one of the doyens of the hunt) is acceptable. That is sufficient to prevent a fox dashing in, yet is easy for the badger to dig its way out. Flints, cans and old barbed wire that so often are jammed into an entrance, or earth trodden down hard and preventing the flow of air, all cause great stress to the badger.

A standard system for recording badger data had been adopted. Incidents of known persecution were being monitored and badger road casualties recorded; neither had been done on a national scale before. Thousands of badgers are killed each year on their regular runs, crossing roads to feeding areas or to neighbouring setts, and knowing the exact circumstances and places where badgers are regularly run over may help to prevent this.

The care and rehabilitation of orphaned or injured animals, methods of deterring and/or translocating badgers, dealing with local authorities on badger issues and other matters were aired fully.

During 1986, the NFBG had been deluged with letters from members of the public, badger groups and other animal welfare or conservation bodies seeking information or advice on a wide range of badger-related issues. The Chairman remarked that 'The volume of correspondence received had sometimes resulted in delays in replying for which we apologise. However, we are not perturbed by the demands created. The time to start worrying is when the correspondence stops coming in'.

The federation had kept a close record on the monitoring of prosecution cases since the 1985 Amendment to the Wildlife & Countryside Act. In none had terriers been successfully confiscated, even though in some instances, dogs had been severely injured. This was a matter of serious concern, since the prospect of forfeiture of dogs was no doubt a more effective deterrent than the imposition of a fine. The brutalisation of the animals involved, badger and dog, justified stronger legal powers to confiscate and ban ownership. Really the only alternative was to try to change the wording of the Amendment to 'weapon, article or dog'. It was agreed that the federation would lobby their MPs and make representations to the Government on this issue.

I was very impressed with the badger patrols in operation. These were separate from badger groups and were working very well in close co-operation with their local police to carry out patrols on a rota basis. Several of my friends in different parts of the country, keenly interested in badgers, had come across such patrols and spoken to them. It was a waiting game needing infinite patience; and it was paying off.

Sitting with others at lunchtime, the conversation turned to court cases. One badger group member was soon to act as an expert witness for the police. This led to discussing the recent spate of badger-digging in their area and suddenly, his companion was describing a metal flail recently found at the scene of a baiting pit. It would seem from that, my Ferndale find was far from unique and I wondered how commonly these flails were used.

I returned home to find all peaceful in my area. Karen had seen nothing to alarm her and my badgers were great! The day of the Meeting had been a warm and sunny breath of spring, but now it was a dull, cool morning with a breeze and occasional rain. Coming here that night, I watched and counted the Embankment badgers off Holmoak Lane. There were nine animals all told. Two sows had cubs; one had two and the other three. There was a yearling sow and a mature boar. They were digging-out and re-opening old, disused entrances along the steep bank.

In Ashcroft Woods the bluebells were opening with many primroses still in bloom. Yesterday's sun had unfurled the cherry blossom, so these geans would soon be clothed in white. The blackthorn (damson) blossom always opens a little later. Some Canadas flew calling overhead as we stood by Long Field. I say 'we' for Watcher did the rounds with me that morning. She was very much in milk and had bald patches on her chest and belly where her pups were kneading as they suckled.

Before I left, I walked round for half-an-hour, searching for one of my gloves. It puzzled me that I had managed to lose it as when not wearing them, I tucked a glove down each boot. I came home very annoyed with myself, until Ross suggested that Crisp probably took it! He was almost certainly right for she had been snouting in my boots earlier.

It had been agreed with Dr. Howard and Oakley's police inspector, that I would give Sergeant Collins a monthly report on events in Ashcroft

Woods, so that a picture might be built up of the situation there. Where possible, shooting incidents were to be dealt with by the police whom I would radio in via Charlie. The sergeant and inspector came on site with me to Holmoak Lane. We discussed the lamping problem there and how best to deal with it. I pointed out the poachers' quick escape route from the little bridge along the path by the railway line, straight into the estate. They also saw the badgers' sett in the embankment with their up-and-over path from the lane on to the field. We all agreed it was much more satisfactory to see the place as we talked. I asked if Oakley police would help the NFBG by recording badger road casualties. I was doing this locally on foot, but they patrolled a far greater area. The inspector readily agreed. He queried whether I thought the lamping problem had worsened and I replied that four years ago it was virtually unknown here, apart from the odd, often middle-aged man, lamping for rabbit. Now it was all stations go; the 'in' sport, with everyone lamping anything. Discussing the different dogs bred for terrierwork and lamping, I was told the police would definitely be sending a plainclothes officer to mingle with the crowds at Don Francis' next show.

At last the tide was turning. It has been so many years, so many hunters and so many badgers. But with all of us working together, the wildlife round Oakley, and most especially its badgers, would at least have a sporting chance.

It was well into April now and the days were lengthening. There were eight badger cubs in my area. Susie at the Crater Sett had one, with Little'un and Sis having two each. Missy at the Old Cherry Sett had three and all sixteen badgers seemed active and healthy.

Sometime after midnight, I began a rubbish clearing session and soon had three sacks full and placed ready for Dr. Howard to collect in the morning. I was happily staggering along with the fourth half-full, when Crisp suddenly appeared and decided to hang on to the end of the plastic sack. Next moment her ladyship was swaying off with the bottom of the bag and the carefully collected contents were strewn about my feet! I decided to lose her.

My thoughts went back to the courtroom of the previous day. Roger Smith and his friend had been convicted of badger-digging, though only their nets and spades were confiscated. Never mind. It was our first case. We had all gained in knowledge and would build on that knowledge. Mark Craig from Oakley station, who had co-ordinated the case, was appealing to the public for help in starting a register of local badger setts. For me this was wonderful news, more important in the long term than any conviction. The more setts we knew that were verified as active and the more information we had on them, would mean more protection; if only people were willing to contact the police when they saw anything suspicious, even if it turned out to be harmless, then more cases would be brought to court and more badgers saved. It would encourage the public to be involved. 'All that is needed for evil to triumph, is that good men do nothing'.

Missy chose that night to dig out two entrances of the Old Cherry Sett and take in fresh grass for nursery bedding. I sat on the slope awhile, listening to the sounds of suckling below and watching the rabbits grazing nearby. There was a rustle at my side and there was Missy, who pushed under my arm with her snout. She could scramble into my lap more easily that way. I must have slept for I opened my eyes to see the sow eating a very young rabbit, skinning it deftly as she did so. She may have caught it when it first came above ground to graze, as nestlings tend to crouch down when danger threatens, rather than run away.

There was a clear sky at first light and a magnificent sunrise an hour later. Pheasant and grey partridge called in unison from the fields, against a background of the skylarks' cascading song. These mornings vibrated with birds and the urgency of life. There was a warmth within me and comfort in the thought that however cruel the winter, however harsh the night, the sun would always rise. As the dead make room for the living, so spring returns to the land once more and the seasons fulfil themselves.

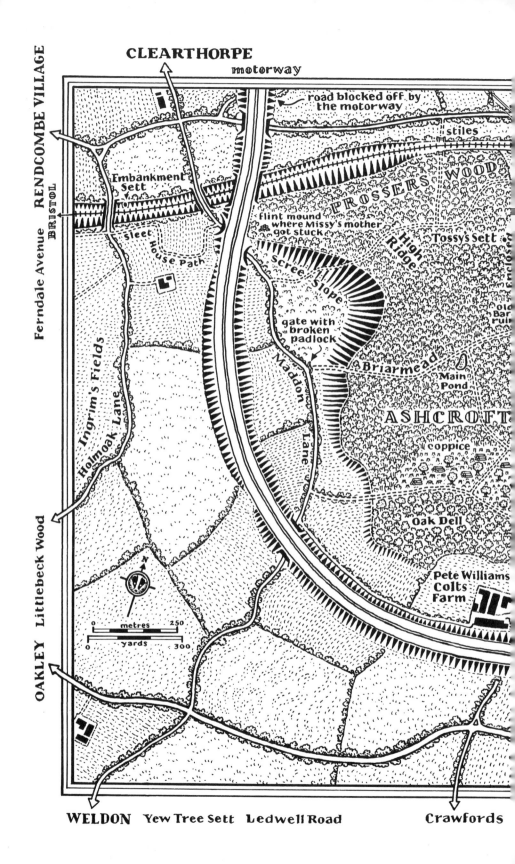